Y0-BCR-475

CONSTITUTIONAL ISSUES

THE DEATH PENALTY

CONSTITUTIONAL ISSUES

THE DEATH PENALTY

Mark Tushnet

A HAROLD STEINBERG BOOK

AN INFOBASE HOLDINGS COMPANY

The Death Penalty

Facts On File, Inc.
460 Park Avenue South
New York, NY 10016

Library of Congress Cataloging-in-Publication Data
Tushnet, Mark V., 1945–
The death penalty / Mark Tushnet
p. cm. — (Constitutional issues; v. 2)
"A Harold Steinberg book."
Includes bibliographical references and index.
ISBN 0-8160-2502-9 (acid-free paper)
1. Capital punishment—United States. I. Title. II. Series
KF9725.T87 1993
345.73'0773—dc20
[347.305773] 93-20643

A British CIP catalogue record for this book is available from the British Library.

Facts On File books are available at special discounts when purchased in bulk quantities for businesses, associations, institutions or sales promotions. Please call our Special Sales Department in New York at 212/683-2244 or 800/322-8755.

Composition by Facts On File, Inc.
Manufactured by the Maple-Vail Book Manufacturing Group
Printed in the United States of America

10 9 8 7 6 5 4 3 2 1

This book is printed on acid-free paper.

Contents

	Publisher's Preface	*vii*
	Author's Preface	*ix*
1	The Death Penalty in Constitutional Law	1
2	Challenging the Death Penalty, 1791–1972	19
3	The Modern Death Penalty	55
4	Death Stories	95
5	The Death Penalty in the Twenty-first Century	113
6	Chapter Notes	134
	Appendixes: Table of Contents	141
	Bibliography	229
	Index	231

Publisher's Preface

According to many political observers, the enduring legacy of the Reagan-Bush presidencies may not be any legislation enacted or other political initiatives effected. Rather, the long-lasting accomplishment of the Reagan-Bush presidencies may be that between the two presidents they appointed five Supreme Court justices: O'Connor, Scalia, Kennedy, Souter, and Thomas, who will significantly affect the course of constitutional law for the coming decades.

This observation is a reflection of the U.S. Supreme Court's influence in the political, social, and economic life of the country—an influence that has never been greater than during the past 50 years. The court's influence is evident in its ground-breaking *Brown v. Board of Education* decision, which ushered in the civil rights movement, the reapportionment cases that have restructured our political system, as well as the court's many rulings on such controversial issues as abortion, search and seizure, and prayer in the schools.

The debate over the death penalty once again thrusts the court into the role of national arbiter on a highly charged public issue. *The Death Penalty* by Professor Mark Tushnet, a recognized authority on the Supreme Court, examines the way the Court has dealt with the death penalty. Professor Tushnet considers his book an introduction to the main questions surrounding capital punishment in constitutional law. Along those lines, he has chosen to discuss those enduring issues—the role of juries in capital sentencing, race discrimination and others—that he feels "will play the most part in discussions of the death penalty and the Constitution over the next decade."

Professor Tushnet expresses the hope that his book will be useful to readers who are not lawyers and enlighten people about the many questions and issues raised by the constitutional debate over capital punishment.

Professor Mark Tushnet is associate dean of the Georgetown Law Center. He is a graduate of Yale Law School and served as a law clerk to Supreme Court Justice Thurgood Marshall.

The first book in the Constitutional Issues series is *Freedom of the Press,* by Professor Bernard Schwartz.

Harold Steinberg
Series Publisher

Author's Preface

My aim in this book is to offer readers an introduction to the main questions about the death penalty in constitutional law. The focus is on *the Constitution*—what the Constitution has to say about the death penalty—not on whether capital punishment is a wise or unwise policy (although understanding some aspects of what the Constitution has to say requires information about some of the policy arguments about capital punishment). And the introduction is *not* comprehensive. Each year the Supreme Court considers a number of death penalty cases; most of them involve technical matters or details of the death penalty statute in a particular case, and nonspecialists need not understand these technical matters to be in a position to think for themselves about the Constitution and capital punishment. Instead of seeking to be all-inclusive, I have chosen those enduring issues—the role of juries in capital sentencing, race discrimination, and others—that will play the most part in discussions of the death penalty and the Constitution over the next decade. Finally, I hope that this book will be useful to readers who are not lawyers. Lawyers might want to refine the arguments I describe, to define their contours more precisely, but I have presented the arguments as I have because the lawyers' distinctions would make the arguments more complicated without adding much to what nonlawyers need to understand about the constitutional issues surrounding the death penalty.

Capital punishment is a highly charged policy issue, and although I have tried to present information as neutrally as I can, I think it worthwhile to indicate my position at the outset so that readers can assess my presentation in light of my predispositions. On the most fundamental issue—is capital punishment justified?—I am quite ambivalent. The cases that trouble me the most are these: A man hires someone to kill his wife so he can marry someone else without losing insurance benefits or paying alimony; a man kidnaps, tortures, and murders a number of women. I find it difficult to believe that the death penalty is an inappropriate punishment here, and sometimes I think that it is an entirely appropriate punishment. Responding to this side of my ambivalence, I have included short descriptions of the crimes underlying most of the cases I discuss so readers can understand what the criminals in the cases really did.

Yet the experience with the death penalty in the United States, both before and after 1976, convinces me that it is impossible to devise a system of administering the death penalty in which those *and only those* who truly deserve the death penalty actually receive it. In addition, although I believe that retribution is a proper basis for punishment, real systems of capital punishment appear to mobilize vengeful sentiments that are quite troubling and unrelated to retribution. In short, I find unpersuasive the general arguments against the death penalty but am persuaded by more particularized arguments that, for a number of unrelated reasons, we cannot create a death penalty system consistent with the arguments supporting capital punishment.

I would like to thank Margaret O'Herron and L. Michael Seidman for their helpful comments on a draft of this book and Harold Steinberg for prodding me to get it written.

CONSTITUTIONAL ISSUES

THE DEATH PENALTY

1

The Death Penalty in Constitutional Law

The Death Penalty Today

In the 1990s, candidates for election from the presidency on down find it essential to declare their support for the death penalty—even, as with the presidency, where the position has almost nothing to do with enforcing laws against murder. Nearly every murder (and almost all murders that threaten the public generally) is a crime under *state* law; federal death penalty laws deal with a handful of murders associated with the drug traffic and with assassinations, an even smaller handful of murders. The last execution for violating a federal law occurred in 1963—nearly a decade before the Supreme Court temporarily held the death penalty unconstitutional.

Candidates' vocal support for the death penalty is a striking change from the situation a generation ago. From the late 1960s to 1972, public support for the death penalty gradually declined. In 1972 the Supreme Court held that capital punishment, as it then existed, was unconstitutional. Legislatures responded by reenacting new death penalty statutes, and the Supreme Court allowed them to reinstitute capital punishment in 1976. In January 1977, Gary Gilmore became the first person executed after the Court's temporary invalidation of capital punishment.

In the decade and a half since Gilmore's execution, over 2,500 people have been sentenced to death. In a typical recent year, about 270 new death sentences were imposed. However, only 157 criminals had actually been executed between 1976 and the end of 1991 because the Court's 1976 decision left many questions open. Resolving those questions, and the ordinary questions that arise in any criminal case, takes time. By 1990, though, the Court had rejected essentially all of the challenges to the death penalty that might have substantially reduced the number of people on death row: It allowed states to execute young offenders and mentally retarded offenders, and it rejected the claim that the new death penalty statutes discriminated against African-Americans. The number of executions per year continues to be small, but in the next few years, the rate at which executions are carried out is sure to increase: The Supreme Court and Congress have communicated their impatience at delays in executing condemned prisoners and have removed many of the legal obstacles that slowed the pace of executions in the 1980s.

Why is the death penalty a *constitutional* question? Of course whether we have capital punishment is something legislatures and the public can debate, but what does the Constitution have to do with our discussion?

Why the Death Penalty?

To understand how the Constitution deals with capital punishment, we have to understand why legislatures have the death penalty in the first place and to understand the purposes of punishing people for their crimes.

There is a traditional list of reasons for criminal punishment, though the details vary. One of the traditional reasons, rehabilitation—putting the criminal in a situation that results in his becoming a better person, no longer a threat to society—is obviously irrelevant to discussion of the death penalty: A person who has been executed cannot be rehabilitated.

(Sometimes people suggest that capital punishment is justified as a less costly punishment than imprisonment. It is not clear that that would be a good argument for taking someone's life. Also, it almost certainly is not true: The efforts devoted to capital cases are extraordinarily expensive when compared to the efforts in noncapital cases. When the costs of litigating over the death penalty are added in, the costs of maintaining people on death row for years are greater than the costs of ordinary imprisonment, so the total cost for death row prisoners—even taking into account the fact that they will eventually be executed—is probably greater than the total cost of life imprisonment for the same group.)

A second reason for punishment, incapacitation—preventing each criminal from continuing to commit crime—is almost as irrelevant. Prison sentences incapacitate and so do executions, in a sense: Just as a prisoner cannot commit crimes against the general public while in prison, so an executed criminal will never commit such crimes again.

But thinking about the death penalty as incapacitation is more complicated than that. We have to compare the incapacitative effect of a death sentence to the incapacitative effect of alternative sentences. In particular, we need to know whether a criminal imprisoned for life will commit crimes (which an executed criminal cannot).

And since we know that a criminal is not going to be executed the moment after the sentence is handed down, we have to know whether a life prisoner will commit crimes after the period of appeal has run out: Life prisoners and those with death sentences have a chance to appeal, and the death penalty incapacitates more only if a prisoner serving a life term commits a crime after the period for appealing has ended.

When prosecutors ask for the death sentence, they sometimes tell jurors to think about the possibility that a prisoner could escape or that a life sentence might be commuted. The Supreme Court upheld an instruction telling the jury that a life sentence without the possibility of parole might be commuted by the governor to a life sentence *with* the possibility of parole.[1] This instruction, the Court said, did not refer to an event that was so unlikely to occur as to distort the jury's deliberations; rather, it brought to the jury's attention a fact that had some bearing on the possibility that the defendant would pose a danger to society in the future. People can escape from death row too, and death sentences can be commuted.

Still, so long as a prisoner is alive, there is some risk that he will commit a new crime, either in prison or after an escape. In that sense, a death sentence incapacitates more than a life sentence does. Yet although there is some additional risk, by every indicator that additional risk is quite low. A number of studies—of prisoners whose death sentences were vacated when the Supreme Court first held the death penalty unconstitutional, for example—indicate that "prison homicides are not usually committed by persons serving sentences for capital murder and that such persons, whether in prison or on parole, pose no special threat to the safety of their fellow-men." Murders in prisons occur, of course, but not particularly by those convicted of capital murder; according to one study by sociologist Thorsten Sellin, "of the 91 known [prison] killers in 1964–65, only 15 were in prison for capital murder, compared with 28 robbers."[2] By the time appeals are over, criminals have aged, and violent crime is a young person's occupation. In short, we might prevent a small number of murders by executing *all* convicted murderers, and just about the same number if we executed any other group of felons. Few proponents of capital punishment defend either of those policies.

The two remaining purposes of punishment—retribution and deterrence—are far more important in thinking about the death penalty. The biblical phrase "an eye for an eye" captures the intuition underlying retribution. Pinning down that intuition, however, is harder than it initially seems.

The intuition has two forms. Retribution might mean vengeance, the discharge of hostile emotions against the criminal whose actions caused the harm that, in turn, produced those emotions. Or in a more complicated way, retribution might mean restoring moral order. The criminal's actions disrupted the world's moral order, and something must be done to restore that order.

Each form has its own difficulties. People can understand what we mean by vengeance. Capital punishment might be a "safety valve" for vengeance: Without it, our vengeful feelings might be discharged lawlessly through vigilante justice. Yet on reflection, we frequently think that it is not a good thing to be vengeful: The emotions we have cannot be denied, but we think that we ought to deal with them in some other way than striking back at the person who caused them. (Again in biblical terms, "vengeance is mine, saith the Lord" usually is taken to mean that vengeance is for the Lord, not for humans.) If capital punishment is a society's expression of its collective anger, anger can too easily get out of hand, and the death penalty will be imposed on people who—even on the society's own retributivist terms—do not deserve it.

Also, it is one thing to feel anger immediately after a murder; many people, though, would find it troubling to discover that they were still feeling that same degree of anger throughout the criminal trial and up to the point of execution. They certainly would have some feelings about the wrongfulness of the murder, but "anger," in the ordinary sense, is unlikely to be one of them.[3] These feelings may make it just and necessary to punish criminals, but it is not clear that they—or at least the ones society ought to respond to—support capital punishment.

The other explanation of retribution, restoring the moral order, may seem too metaphorical: How would we know that the moral order had indeed been restored? Why, for example, isn't a life sentence for murder enough to restore the moral order? Also, every proponent of the death penalty agrees that some mistakes will happen. If the justification for capital punishment is deterrence, mistakes can be accepted as the necessary cost of doing a greater good—capital punishment may reduce the number of deaths by murder even if it causes some "unnecessary" deaths itself. But when retribution is at stake, mistakes are really serious: If we execute the wrong person, not only have we not "repaired" the moral order that the original crime disrupted, but we have ourselves disrupted the moral order again.

In either version of retribution, the punishment we inflict has to fit the crime. That is why the death penalty appears particularly appropriate for murder: We take from the criminal just what the criminal took from the victim—life itself. Unfortunately, this notion of "fit" cannot be used throughout the punishment system. It is what underlies the idea that we ought to cut off the hands of a thief, a punishment that appears disproportionate to most people in the United States today. And consider how difficult it is to work out retributive punishments of imprisonment: How many years in prison restore the moral equilibrium disrupted by a bank robbery? Yet once we have decided to develop a scale that reconciles disruption of the moral world with terms of years in prison, it is not obvious why murder somehow cannot fit on that scale. If we compared the disruption of the moral world caused by a bank robbery to that caused by murder, for example, we might conclude that whatever it is that leads us to think that twenty years in prison is enough punishment for bank robbery ought to lead us to think that a life sentence is enough punishment for murder.

As political theorist Walter Berns puts it in his argument for capital punishment, "A country that does not punish its grave offenses severely thereby indicates that it does not regard them as grave offenses." Yet while that is certainly true, Berns's conclusion—"if [the United States] may rightly honor its heroes, it may rightly execute the worst of its criminals"—does not follow.[4] The moral order would be restored, the nation could punish grave offenses severely, by imposing the greatest punishment available for the most serious crime, but that does not tell what the greatest punishment should be.

(A similar problem comes up with retribution understood as vengeance. Some crime victims may have extremely strong vengeful attitudes, but if most of us think those attitudes out of proportion to the crime, we will decide that a smaller penalty, or a shorter term of imprisonment, is all that is needed. Proportionality is important under this approach to retribution, and the problem of determining what is proportional again occurs.)

Deterrence is the final reason for punishment. Imprisonment deprives people of liberty, which most people want. By threatening people with imprisonment if they rob or murder, we can keep some of them from robbing or murdering. The point, of course, is not that punishment is a perfect deterrent; some people will rob or murder no matter what we threaten them with. Rather, punishment reduces the number of crimes because some people, who would rob or murder if they thought they would get away with it untouched, decide that, all things considered, it is not worth the risk of going to prison.

To think about capital punishment as a deterrent, we have to carefully sort out a number of questions. It is silly, for example, to frame the question as, "Does the threat of capital punishment *ever* deter crime?" The answer to that has to be yes. We can be sure that there would be less overtime parking if it was punished with death, even occasionally.

A better way to ask the question is, "How much *more* does the threat of the death penalty deter crime—particularly murder—than the threat of long terms of imprisonment?" Again, there is a side issue to get out of the way. Many death penalty opponents point out, correctly, that a substantial number of murders are not committed by people who have carefully thought about the risk of punishment: A robbery goes wrong, and the victim is killed; or a man beating his wife "goes too far" and she dies. Others are committed by people who believe that they will not be caught or executed; particularly if the rate of execution is low, potential murderers may underestimate their chances of being caught and executed. Death penalty opponents say, also correctly, that a substantial portion of these murders cannot be deterred by the threat of the death penalty.

Still, the death penalty might be a good deterrent for some other set of murders, like murders-for-hire, where the criminal is likely to think about the risk of punishment. If we could devise a death penalty system that sorted out the robberies that go wrong, where fear of a death sentence is unlikely to affect the criminal's behavior, from the murders-for-hire, where that fear is much more likely to have some effect, we could defend the system as a deterrent. (Even in the cases where killing is not part of the plan, the risk of the death penalty might make some difference: Robbers who know that murder during the course of a robbery may lead to a death sentence may decide to take knives rather than guns on the job, and then the chance that a killing will occur when the robbery goes wrong is smaller.)

In other words, the threat that a murderer will be executed is likely to deter in only a subset of all murders. If we try to find out whether the death penalty is a deterrent by examining the relation between executions and the murder rate, we are likely to find a relatively small deterrent effect. That is reinforced by the fact that a relatively small number of murderers are actually executed; the effect of those executions on the homicide rate is likely to be dwarfed by other factors.

Whether the death penalty deters more than life imprisonment is, at bottom, a question of fact. Scholars have tried to find out what the deterrent effect of the death penalty is.[5] They have used three types of studies. The least satisfactory examines murder rates in states before and after they adopt (or abolish) the death penalty. The problem here is that there is likely to be some connection between whatever it was that led the state to change its death penalty rules and the state's murder rate. Still, these studies tend to show that changing the rules has no effect one way or the other on the murder rate, which suggests that the death penalty does not add much deterrence.

Death penalty opponents have more substantial evidence from the second type of study, which examines murder rates in neighboring states, one with the death penalty and the other without it. Again, these studies show rather dramatically that murder rates in neighboring states did not differ very much. For example, they show that states with the death penalty had somewhat *higher* rates of killings of police officers than states without the death penalty.[6] These studies all lead to the conclusion that the death penalty had no discernible deterrent effect. Yet they are unlikely to be fully persuasive, because states with the death penalty are likely to be more violent in general than states without it; that may be why they have the death penalty after all.

Until 1975 these studies were essentially the only empirical examinations of the deterrent effect of the death penalty. Using a variety of techniques, none had shown a deterrent effect. Then economist Isaac Ehrlich published what is known as an "econometric" study of the death penalty. This study is a more formal and more general version of the "neighboring states" kind of study. The idea behind those studies is that neighboring states are probably pretty similar in terms of demographics, racial composition of the population, culture regarding violence, and the like. Econometric studies try to measure the elements that a neighboring-states study assumes to be the same.

Ehrlich compared national murder rates with national execution rates and controlled his results for a large number of demographic characteristics. He concluded that each execution deterred seven or eight murders. The economic assumptions behind Erhlich's study can be tested only by comparing its predictions with the actual results in a large number of cases. Because of the small number of executions recently, his statistics involved executions in the period ending in the 1960s.

Other economists and sociologists challenged Ehrlich's study.[7] They had several criticisms:

- Ehrlich relied on *national* murder and execution rates. That, however, obscures the effects of death penalty statutes, which work only in individual states. Suppose, for example, that the execution rate increased in Alabama and the murder rate declined in California. Ehrlich's model would lead you to think that the death penalty acted as a deterrent because it lumped together the decrease in California and the increase in Alabama. That cannot be right (unless you have a complicated theory about how potential murderers in California take national execution rates into account).

- Ehrlich's results were extremely sensitive to the fact that he included the years 1963–67 in his data base and to other more technical aspects of the economic model he developed. In the early 1960s, the rate of executions declined sharply and the murder rate also went up dramatically, though probably for reasons—including social disintegration and the wider availability of guns—unrelated to the decline in executions. A dramatic decline in executions—unless offset by an extraordinary drop in the murder rate—would inevitably support the conclusion that the death penalty deterred. In fact, when Ehrlich's model was applied to the data up to 1963, it showed no deterrent effect.

- Ehrlich omitted some arguably relevant variables, such as the availability of guns and emergency treatment. For example, if states without the death penalty have bad emergency services, it is going to look like the higher death rates occur because potential murderers are not deterred, when in fact the higher death rates occur because people who die from assaults would have lived if the emergency services had been better.

- Ehrlich compared the deterrent effect of the death penalty with the deterrent effect of the number of years in prison *actually served,* which declined during the 1960s. Perhaps, though, the policy choice really is between the death penalty and a substantial increase in the number of years murderers serve. (A response might be that the threat that murderers will actually serve true life terms—or even thirty-year terms—is not credible because potential murderers will not believe the threat. The same difficulty, of course, affects the death penalty itself: The fact that *some* murderers are executed may not be much of a deterrent if, as is true in the United States today, *very few* are.)

- Figuring out whether capital punishment deters has been complicated, in ways not yet reflected in these studies, by the Supreme Court's new death penalty rules. Under those rules, discussed in more detail in chapter three, states cannot punish *all* murders with death; they must narrow the class of murderers "eligible" for capital punishment. We do not have, and probably never will get, accurate measures of the "death-penalty-eligible murder" rate. If imposing the death penalty only on people who commit such murders deters *only* such murders, measuring deterrence by seeing what happens to the overall murder rate may show very small deterrent effects (because the death penalty has no deterrent impact on the larger class of "noneligible" murderers).

All the evidence taken together makes it hard to be confident that capital punishment deters more than long prison terms do. Richard Lempert puts it even more strongly: "There is little reason to believe that the availability of capital punishment is—except possibly in certain rare circumstances—a substantial marginal deterrent. The empirical evidence is overwhelmingly to the contrary." For him, the evidence is "sufficiently strong and one-sided that we should approach the question of the morality of the death penalty with the assumption that capital punishment does not deter."[8]

Yet Ehrlich's study, for all its flaws, shifted the contours of the debate over the facts of deterrence. Even if his number of murders deterred was too high—and each execution deterred only two, one, or even less than one murder—Ehrlich provided some support for the commonsense judgment that the threat of the death penalty would have *some* deterrent effect.

If there is uncertainty about how much capital punishment deters, a pretty good argument supporting capital punishment becomes available. In the face of uncertainty, the question becomes, How do we allocate the risk? If the death penalty does not in fact deter, and we have the death penalty, we are going to execute some people needlessly—but, after all, they will have murdered someone else. And if the death penalty does deter but we abolish it, someone will murder another person who would not have died if there had been a death penalty (that is precisely what it means to say that the death penalty deters). The murder victim, killed because there is no death penalty, is entirely innocent; the executed murderer, killed because of the perhaps false belief that the death penalty deters, is not. That is a reason to say that, if we are uncertain about the death penalty's deterrent effect, we ought not abolish it.[9]

A similar argument introduces the constitutional dimensions of the death penalty debate. Suppose everyone agreed that mere vengeance was not a good reason for the death penalty and that no other retributive theory made sense. The case for the death penalty would then rest entirely on deterrence. And suppose further that many people, including legislators, believed that the death penalty was a deterrent. Finally, suppose that social scientists could show, with a high degree of confidence, that the death penalty did not deter. On these assumptions, it might make sense to allow courts to find the death penalty unconstitutional: It was not doing the only thing people agreed it should do—deter, and it was on the law books only because most people did not understand the facts. We could strengthen that argument by pointing out that judges are appointed for life and are therefore removed from the kinds of direct political influence to which legislators respond. A legislator might have to bend to her constituents' false beliefs about the deterrent effect of the death penalty if she wanted to be reelected, but judges could assess the evidence in a detached and nonpolitical way.

That argument for letting judges find the death penalty unconstitutional breaks down, though, either if there is a decent retributive justification for the death penalty or if the evidence about the death penalty's deterrent effect is more ambiguous (and more consistent with voters' commonsense assessments). Does the Constitution support any other challenge to capital punishment?

The Eighth Amendment: No "Cruel and Unusual Punishments"

The Eighth Amendment to the Constitution says that "cruel and unusual punishments [shall not be] inflicted." The Eighth Amendment is part of the Bill of Rights, which begins with the words, "Congress shall make no law. . . " Since 1972 the Supreme Court has decided many death penalty cases, but they all involve capital punishment statutes adopted by *state* legislatures. The first words of the Bill of Rights suggest, though, that what follows, including the Eighth Amendment, limits only the national government, not state governments. How did the Supreme Court end up invoking the Eighth Amendment against state governments?

Second, how could the Eighth Amendment possibly make capital punishment unconstitutional? The Fifth Amendment was adopted at the same time that the Eighth Amendment was, and it refers to capital punishment twice: "No person shall be held to answer for a *capital*. . .crime, unless on a presentment or indictment of a Grand Jury;. . .nor be deprived of *life,* liberty, or property, without due process of law. . ." (emphases added). How could the same people who indicated in the Fifth Amendment that they accepted capital punishment have made it unconstitutional a few lines later?

"Incorporation" The answer to the first part of the question is easier than the answer to the second. In 1833 a clever lawyer tried to persuade the Supreme Court that the Bill of Rights—except for the First Amendment—limited the power of state governments. After all, the argument went, the First Amendment referred specifically to Congress, while the rest of the Bill of Rights spoke in more general terms: "nor shall cruel and unusual punishments be inflicted." The Supreme Court would have none of this, saying that the question was "of great importance, but not of much difficulty."[10] When the Constitution was adopted, many opponents feared that the new national government would be too powerful. The Constitution's supporters tried to reassure them by promising to write restrictions on national power into the Constitution, which they did in the Bill of Rights. So the Eighth Amendment itself does not directly limit state governments.

The Constitution was amended again, though, after the Civil War. Abolitionists and supporters of Abraham Lincoln's Republican party understood that slavery resulted from excessive state power. They abolished slavery in the Thirteenth Amendment, but they remained concerned that state governments would be too powerful. In 1868 the Fourteenth Amendment was adopted to limit state power. It says that "no State shall make or enforce any law which shall abridge the privileges and immunities of citizens of the United States; nor shall any State deprive any person of life, liberty, or property, without due process of law. . ." When Jacob Howard of Michigan presented the proposed amendment to the Senate, he defined "privileges and immunities" as the list of protections in the Bill of Rights, including "the right to be secure. . .against cruel and unusual punishments."

Howard's interpretation of the Fourteenth Amendment came to be known as the *incorporation* theory: The Fourteenth Amendment incorporated—that is, made applicable against the states—the restrictions on government power contained in the Bill of Rights. The Supreme Court rejected the incorporation theory in 1908 and again in 1937, when the Court said that, although the states were not bound by the specific prohibitions in the Bill of Rights, the Fourteenth Amendment did mean that they had to respect rights that were "of the very essence of a scheme of ordered liberty."[11]

Justice Hugo Black, appointed to the Court in 1937, persisted in raising the question of incorporation. The Court rejected the theory again in 1947, but by then Black had started to gain some allies on the Court. The Court actually never fully adopted the incorporation theory. Instead it engaged in what is called *selective incorporation.* In one case after another, the Court decided that specific rights in the Bill of Rights were indeed "of the very essence of a scheme of ordered liberty."

In 1962 the Eighth Amendment's turn came. California made it a criminal offense simply to be a drug addict. The Court held, first, that state governments could not inflict cruel and unusual punishments and, second, that punishing someone for having what the Court considered to be a disease was cruel and unusual.[12] As the Court saw it, making it a crime to be an addict served neither of the traditional purposes of punishment—retribution for doing something wrong or deterring the defendant from doing something again—because being an addict was something over which the addict had no control.

From a technical standpoint the Court's selective incorporation approach was hard to defend, but the public found it easy to understand that the Bill of Rights ought to limit every government in the country. Some of the Court's interpretations of the Bill of Rights were intensely controversial, none less so than its death penalty decisions. But few criticized the Court for selective incorporation. The Court's critics would not have been much happier if the Court had said that the national government could not use capital punishment but that the states could. And of course, opponents of the death penalty found incorporation of the Eighth Amendment entirely compatible with their position.

Original Intent The second question—how people could seriously argue that the Eighth Amendment banned something the Fifth Amendment permitted—is harder to answer. Often, in thinking about what the Constitution means, it helps to examine a provision's history, although history is not the only basis for constitutional interpretation. The historical question has two parts: Did the drafters of the Eighth Amendment intend to bar only punishments that they themselves would have regarded as cruel and barbarous, or were they willing to let future generations decide for themselves that a punishment was cruel even if the drafters would not have? And if a punishment was used at the time when the amendment was adopted and the drafters did not believe that it was cruel and unusual, could a court in the future rely on the amendment to invalidate that punishment anyway? As with nearly all questions about original intent, these have no easy answers. Probably the best we can do is say that the drafters probably did not mean to prohibit only punishments they themselves believed to be cruel and unusual and—with even less assurance—that they probably did not mean to bar future courts from finding unconstitutional punishments that were in use in 1791 when the amendment came into effect.

A ban on cruel and unusual punishments first entered Anglo-American law in the English Bill of Rights of 1689. For about a century before 1689, some English courts had been using torture to extract confessions and to punish criminals. Religious strife divided English society, and the use of torture became part of the overall charge against the government. Near the end of the reign of the Stuart kings, Titus Oates, an opposition leader convicted of perjury, was dragged by a horse through London's streets, all the while being whipped. And after an uprising in 1685, Lord Chief Justice Jeffreys ordered the execution of hundreds of participants.

In 1688 the Glorious Revolution replaced James II with William of Orange as king. Parliament immediately began to consider a bill of rights. Drafts of the bill of rights referred to James II's use of "illegal and cruel punishments," and the final bill banned "cruel and unusual punishments." Although no one knows exactly what the drafters meant, the background suggests that they wanted to ban punishments, like some of Jeffreys's sentences, that were not authorized by statute. More important for the United States Constitution, the drafters may also have wanted to bar penalties that were grossly out of line with the severity of a criminal's offense, as Oates's had been. Seventeenth-century dictionaries, for example, said that cruel meant "severe" or "hard." The evidence taken as a whole supports the conclusion that the drafters of the 1689 Bill of Rights were concerned about proportional punishments, but the case here is not overwhelming.

When the states began to form governments, they wrote the language of the English Bill of Rights into their constitutions. The framers of the Constitution, in contrast, did not spend much time in defining the limits on government power. They believed that they were creating a national government whose power would be limited to specific topics, listed in Article I. Proponents of the new Constitution discovered that they had made a political mistake in failing to specify limits on government power. The failure gave fuel to their opponents, the Anti-Federalists, who argued against adopting the Constitution in part because it did not contain a bill of rights. Because the ban on cruel and unusual punishments was already part of the Anglo-American tradition, opponents referred in passing to the absence of such a ban in the new Constitution. Aside from saying that, without such a provision, Congress might adopt "racks and gibbets," or "tortures," the references did not give much content to its terms.

To assure that the Constitution would be adopted, its supporters promised to introduce amendments at the earliest opportunity. The first amendments, including the Eighth Amendment, were considered by the first Congress, but very little was said specifically about the "cruel and unusual punishments" clause. Two opponents of the clause discussed it in the House of Representatives. One said that it was "too indefinite." The other suggested that the clause might be interpreted in the future to bar punishments—hanging and whipping—that were common in 1789. Referring to other parts of the Eighth Amendment, he asked, "Who are to be the judges?," which suggests that already someone had in mind the possibility of judicial determinations of unconstitutionality. He thought that Congress ought not write into the Constitution a provision that would keep legislatures in the future from adopting punishments they thought most suitable.

This history is rather scanty, and not much can be drawn from it. Justice William Brennan suggested that the fact that Congress adopted the clause after being warned that it might be used in the future to rule out hanging and whipping showed that it "was prepared to run that risk."[13] And the obvious vagueness of the provision, which an opponent mentioned, suggests that Congress understood the possibility that courts sometime in the future might give it content—like a ban on capital punishment—that they themselves would not adopt. Finally, the framers must have had reasons for believing that "the rack" was a cruel and unusual punishment. Later generations—and, perhaps, courts—might conclude that capital punishment was inconsistent with the reasons the framers had for thinking that some specific punishments were cruel and unusual. (Circumstances might have changed—prisons might have become more effective punishments, so capital punishment might not be thought necessary any more—or the framers might have overlooked the fact that their reasons for banning the rack applied just as much to make capital punishment cruel and unusual.) But in the end, probably the most that can be made of the framers' original intent is that they did not clearly rule out the possibility that judges in the future would give the clause a rather expansive meaning.

Precedent Between 1791 and 1910, the Court took up a few Eighth Amendment cases, and state courts interpreted their local prohibitions on cruel and unusual punishments. The state courts generally said that their constitutions did not invalidate punishments that had been in use when the constitutions were adopted. The United States Supreme Court initially took the same position. In 1889 William Kemmler became the first person to be sentenced to die in the electric chair. He argued that using this new technique of execution violated the Constitution. Although the Supreme Court agreed that courts had the duty to determine whether a punishment was cruel and unusual, it rejected his claim. Although the courts would invalidate "manifestly cruel and unusual [punishments], as burning at the stake, crucifixion, [or] breaking on the wheel," only "inhuman and barbarous" methods of execution, not the death penalty itself, could be unconstitutional.[14]

In 1910, though, the Supreme Court changed course and abandoned the position that the Eighth Amendment permitted all punishments prevalent in 1791 and prohibited only those that would have been regarded as cruel and unusual then. *Weems v. United States* arose in the Philippine Islands.[15] After the United States seized the Philippines from Spain, the local administration continued to follow some aspects of Spanish law, although the Constitution did apply. Paul Weems was a cashier in the Coast Guard. He was convicted of falsifying a public document, as part of a scheme to embezzle public money. Weems was sentenced to fifteen years of *cadena temporal,* a punishment drawn from Spanish law under which criminals were "always [to] carry a chain at the ankle, hanging from the wrist" while working for the government at "hard and painful labor" with "no assistance from friend or relative."

Justice Joseph McKenna, writing the Court's opinion, could not contain his indignation at how Draconian this sentence was: "Such penalties for such offenses amaze those who have formed their conception of the relation of a state to even its offending citizens from the practice of American commonwealths." Here Justice McKenna introduced the idea that a penalty might be unconstitutional because it was, in his word, "disproportionate"—that is, grossly excessive in relation to the crime.[16]

Justice McKenna devoted his main effort to show that the Eighth Amendment should not be interpreted in a limited historical sense, to outlaw only those punishments that had been inflicted before the Glorious Revolution. Rather, he said, consider the Anti-Federalists, who pushed for the adoption of the Bill of Rights. As McKenna put it, they "would take no chances." They feared power, and "surely they intended more than to register a fear of forms of abuse that went out of practice with the Stuarts." McKenna said that "[t]ime works changes, brings into existence new conditions and purposes," which meant that "a principle, to be vital, must be capable of wider application than the mischief which gave it birth." That was particularly true of constitutional provisions. "[O]ur contemplation cannot be only of what has been, but of what may be." Otherwise, McKenna wrote, "Rights declared in words might be lost in reality." And, McKenna wrote, the Eighth Amendment "may therefore be progressive, and is not fastened to the obsolete, but may acquire meaning as public opinion becomes enlightened by a humane justice."

After reviewing what state courts had said, the Court returned to the cadena temporal. Discussing the question of proportionality, the opinion noted that "there are degrees of homicide that are not punished so severely" and that crimes far more serious than falsifying a public record received much less severe punishments. This made the sentence unconstitutional. Justice McKenna noted, though, that invalidating the sentence did not really harm the state: "The purpose of punishment is fulfilled, crime is repressed by penalties of just, not tormenting, severity, its repetition is prevented, and hope is given for the reformation of the criminal."

Weems is the source of the modern law of the Eighth Amendment. It rejected a narrowly historical approach to the amendment, although in doing so it simply restated, with unusual clarity, the

Court's earlier position that it was for the courts and not the legislature to say whether a punishment was cruel and unusual. It adopted the view that the amendment's interpretation was connected to the "enlightened" views of "humane justice" among the public. And, it held that, in determining whether a punishment was cruel and unusual, the Court would examine whether the punishment was disproportionate to the crime and whether other punishments would serve the goals of punishment—retribution, deterrence, rehabilitation—just as well.

The Supreme Court under Earl Warren simply reiterated the basic insight of *Weems* and its predecessors in its major consideration of the Eighth Amendment. *Trop v. Dulles* held unconstitutional a statute that punished soldiers who deserted in wartime by depriving them of their citizenship.[17] Chief Justice Warren took the history and precedents to show that "the words of the [clause] are not precise, and that their scope is not static." Instead, Warren wrote, the Eighth Amendment "must draw its meaning from the evolving standards of decency that mark the progress of a maturing society."

Warren's phrase, "evolving standards of decency," accurately describes both what examination of the framers' intention reveals and how the Supreme Court consistently dealt with the Eighth Amendment. Intention and precedent thus point in the same direction: The Eighth Amendment authorizes the justices of the Supreme Court to use their best judgment to decide whether a particular punishment is so inconsistent with contemporary standards of justice and with widely accepted theories of punishment as to be "cruel and unusual." Justices will of course disagree over what those standards and theories are, but original intent and precedent mean that there is nothing wrong in deciding that those standards and theories make some punishments unconstitutional. There is no need, in this field, to worry that the theory of "original intent" bars judges from determining what justice requires.

Still, what is the significance of the fact that the Constitution itself accepts capital punishment as part of the criminal justice system? Maybe the answer is that the Constitution may accept capital punishment as a fact about the system in 1791, when the Bill of Rights was adopted, but it does not endorse capital punishment as something that necessarily will be a feature of the system forever. Or maybe the answer is that the Constitution does not accept capital punishment unconditionally. It says that *if* there are capital crimes, there have to be indictments, and *if* the government takes someone's life, it has to be done with "due process." That does not rule out the arguments that no process is adequate to satisfy the demands of due process or that capital punishment might be cruel and unusual even if it is imposed with full process.

Finally, it is worth noting that the Eighth Amendment was adopted just when theories of punishment were changing. The framers were part of the intellectual movement known as the Enlightenment, which insisted that standards of rational judgment ought to replace reliance on tradition alone to justify public institutions like punishment. In 1764 the Italian thinker Cesare di Beccaria applied Enlightenment principles to punishment and sharply criticized what he regarded as the barbaric modes of punishment, including execution, prevalent at the end of the eighteenth century. Of course, alternatives to execution were few: Exile was a possibility, but prisons were rare. Yet the framers, as Enlightenment thinkers, may have believed that, as soon as alternatives to execution became available—when prisons became widespread, for example—capital punishment would have to be tested against ordinary standards of rational justification. It would be inconsistent with Enlightenment thought to rule out, from the very start, the possibility that capital punishment would not survive that scrutiny.

In any event, no justice during the period of challenges to the death penalty, or during the present era, believed that the Constitution's references to capital punishment provided a conclusive answer to those challenges. Original intent, precedent, and contemporary notions of justice have been what mattered.

But there is still a problem. *Weems* referred to the views of an enlightened public, and Chief Justice Warren spoke of the evolving standards of a maturing society. When the Supreme Court finds a practice unconstitutional, it sets itself against the judgment made by the legislature that adopted the practice. In a case like *Weems,* where the Court clearly found itself repulsed by what it regarded as the barbaric legacy of Spanish rule, there may be nothing special about doing that: The Court was not rejecting something that the people of the United States truly endorsed. In death penalty cases, though, the problem is serious. If the Court invalidates the death penalty, it must be saying that it knows better than legislatures what an enlightened public would believe and that it can say that the society is more mature than its legislation indicates.

Yet the Court cannot simply rubber-stamp whatever legislatures—or a fair number of them—do. The entire theory of judicial review rests on the idea that legislative decisions cannot be conclusive, in part because legislators face political pressures that do not bear as heavily on the courts and in part because judges, through their training and immersion in the law, may actually do a better job than legislators in discerning what justice demands. Intent and precedent indicate that the Supreme Court is not supposed to simply ratify the society's "evolving standards of decency." It can lead rather than follow the evolution of those standards. Yet how far out front should it get? The Court might "lead" by noting a substantial trend—laws in forty states going one way—and enforcing that trend against the laggards. Or it could lead more forcefully by asserting, against a substantial consensus, that standards had evolved yet were not acknowledged in existing statutes.

Working out what courts should do when the interpretation of the Eighth Amendment refers to an enlightened public is not easy. Public opinion, found through surveys and reflected in legislation, has to be relevant to the Court's decisions, but it cannot be the end of the inquiry.

Justice McKenna's point that punishments would be unconstitutional if they were severe and unnecessary—because the goals of punishment could be achieved equally well in other ways—might point the way to what the courts need. If they could show that the death penalty did not really serve acceptable purposes, despite what the public might think, they could say that an "enlightened" public would reject the death penalty. Unfortunately for opponents of the death penalty, although they can mount a substantial case that capital punishment is unnecessary, in the sense Justice McKenna meant, it is hard to say that legislators who take a contrary view and decide that only the death penalty will be sufficient punishment for some criminals are completely unreasonable and unenlightened.

During the 1960s and 1970s, death penalty opponents showed how traditional policy arguments against the death penalty could be converted into constitutional arguments. They emphasized evolving standards of decency and sought to show that the death penalty failed to serve any acceptable goals of punishment. For a brief period, they succeeded in their constitutional attack, but the Supreme Court changed course after only a few years.

2

Challenging the Death Penalty, 1791–1972

Capital punishment has been part of the American criminal justice system from its beginning. Statutes authorized death sentences for many offenses in England and its colonies, and executions were common: The Salem witch trials of 1692, for example, produced nineteen hangings.

From the middle of the eighteenth century on, though, capital punishment was under attack. Enlightenment thinkers demanded secular, nonreligious justifications for capital punishment, which they could not find. They also tended to have an optimistic view of human nature. Believing that everyone could reform, they argued that imprisonment in "reformatories" should replace capital punishment. These attacks, often in the form of arguments for the complete abolition of capital punishment, whittled away at the death penalty. The number of crimes for which it was authorized dropped dramatically, judges were given discretion on whether to impose it, and some states simply abolished it.

The Enlightenment Attack on Capital Punishment

Cesare di Beccaria's 1764 attack on capital punishment was enormously influential among the intellectual and political leaders of the Enlightenment. Beccaria argued, "Nothing in the social contract gives the state any right to take human life." Society was formed to protect people, and no one would agree to an arrangement that would "leave to other men the choice of killing him." Further, he argued, penalties more severe than necessary to deter were unjust. And, according to Beccaria, imprisonment was more effective than death as a way of leading criminals to atone for their crimes and as a deterrent. Imprisonment offered a "long and painful example of a man deprived of liberty, who, having become a beast of burden, recompenses with his labors the society he has offended." Even worse, "[t]he death penalty becomes for the majority a spectacle and for some others an object of compassion mixed with disdain," not the source of "the salutary fear which the laws pretend to inspire. . ." These arguments joined social contract theory with the Enlightenment's optimism about human nature: Criminals could atone and become better people, and the government should not abort those processes by executing them.

Beccaria's themes were taken up in the United States by Philadelphia physician Benjamin Rush, a signer of the Declaration of Independence. Like Beccaria, Rush argued that capital punishment "tends to multiply murders" by reducing the "horror of taking away human life." In addition, when life was at stake, "[h]umanity, revolting at the idea of the severity and certainty of a capital punishment, often steps in, and collects such evidence in favour of a murderer, as screens him from death altogether. . ." The death penalty, that is, actually led juries to acquit rather than accurately find a person guilty and condemn him to death. Rush also was the first abolitionist to rely on the fact that many murders resulted from "a sudden gust of passion"; although it was later taken up to show that the death penalty could not deter, Rush used this argument to show that not all murderers had a "malign" heart.

Beccaria was a thorough-going secularist who did not think it important to reconcile his opposition to the death penalty with the Bible. Rush, writing in the United States, spent much more time on biblical arguments. Inflicting the death penalty was, for Rush, "an usurpation of the prerogative of heaven." He offered an elaborate interpretation of biblical passages dealing with killing to support his conclusion that, "in the mature state of society," God had not "delegated his power over human life to his creatures." And, Rush pointed out, perhaps the Old Testament references to capital punishment were designed "to illustrate the perfection and mildness" of the New Testament, under which Christian America should be governed. Indeed, "[t]he conduct and discourses of our Saviour should outweigh every argument that has been or can be offered in favour of capital punishment. . ." Jesus "forgave the crime of murder, on his cross" and died "to reconcile men to each other."

These attacks became more effective as newly created penitentiaries made it possible to punish without execution and as the theory of rehabilitation took hold. Capital punishment eroded in stages:[1]

- The number of crimes for which death was the sentence was dramatically reduced. In the 1770s, death was the punishment, not only for murder, but for arson, rape, robbery, kidnapping, burglary, and several other offenses. The proliferation of statutes setting capital penalties was most dramatic in the South, where slaves were threatened with capital punishment for an extremely large number of offenses. After a few decades, most states reserved capital punishment for the most clearly serious crimes: murder, rape, and occasionally robbery. Slavery's abolition, too, eliminated one source of capital statutes.

- Before the 1790s, the death penalty was mandatory. When many crimes could be punished by death, juries often rebelled. They refused to convict even if the evidence was clear because they did not believe the defendant deserved to die.[2] Mandatory death penalties eroded in two ways.

  In 1794 Pennsylvania was the first state to adopt "degrees" of murder. First-degree or premeditated murder still would be punished by death, but a jury could now convict a defendant of second-degree homicide—everything that was not premeditated—which would not carry a mandatory death sentence. Courts struggled to explain how first-degree murder differed from second-degree; Justice Benjamin Cardozo wrote that "the distinction is much too vague to be continued in our law" and that it relied on "a defective and unreal psychology." Courts developed instructions telling juries what the differences were, but, as Cardozo put it, the differences were "so obscure that no jury hearing it for the first time can fairly be expected to assimilate and understand it." It did not really matter, though, that the differences between the degrees of murder were not clear to anyone: The point of creating degrees of murder was to let juries make a moral judgment whether the defendant deserved to die, and the instructions were simply a legalistic way of giving them that choice.

  Second, later in the nineteenth century, legislatures eliminated mandatory death sentences and explicitly gave juries discretion. Tennessee was the first, in 1838. Sometimes juries were told to impose a death sentence if they chose; sometimes they were told that they could recommend mercy, but if they did not, the defendant would be executed. Either way, juries now could make the moral judgment directly.

- States ended the practice of holding executions in public. Traditionally people argued that public executions were necessary for capital punishment to be an effective deterrent: If the public did not know exactly what it meant to be executed, they could not be deterred from crime by fear of death. In the first part of the nineteenth century, counterarguments took hold: Rather than deterring, public executions actually encouraged crime, as viewers were brutalized by the experience of watching executions and came to admire the "manliness" with which criminals faced the gallows.[3]

- Michigan, while still a territory, abolished capital punishment completely in 1846. Prodded by celebrated miscarriages of justices—improper convictions and acquittals against the evidence by juries reluctant to impose death sentences—Rhode Island and Wisconsin followed early in the next decade. Each succeeding decade saw another state abolish capital punishment, and from 1910 to 1919, eight more states either abolished capital punishment or experimented with abolition and then restored it. After that, the formal abolition of capital punishment ended until the 1960s, when a half-dozen states, including New York, ended capital punishment.
- By the middle of the twentieth century, the number of executions had dramatically declined. From a peak of 199 in 1935, the number drifted downward. Executions dropped substantially during the Second World War. The last year in which more than 100 executions occurred was 1951. By 1961 that had been cut in half. Notably, this decline occurred even though the number of murders was slowly increasing. And because most executions took place in the South, the decline occurred in large part because southern states started to execute fewer and fewer people. (Texas and California are exceptions to the overall patterns.)

These changes occurred slowly, but their direction has been clear. Constant pressure from death penalty opponents and a lack of concerted resistance by death penalty supporters meant that capital punishment has been in a slow decline since the late eighteenth century.

The Supreme Court and the Death Penalty Before the 1960s

The Supreme Court's 1890 *Kemmler* decision, upholding execution using the electric chair, temporarily ended the Court's direct involvement with the death penalty as a constitutional matter. Death penalty cases, though, continued to come to the Court, and the justices were particularly sensitive to constitutional claims in cases where life was at stake. As Justice Robert Jackson put it, "When the penalty is death, we. . .are tempted to strain the evidence and even, in close cases, the law in order to give a doubtfully condemned man another chance."[4]

Straining the law, though, was not always necessary; developing it was. For example, the Court began its transformation of criminal procedure in two death penalty cases. *Powell v. Alabama* was one of the famous Scottsboro cases.[5] In 1931, nine African-Americans were accused of raping two white women who joined them as hoboes on a train. *Powell* involved the constitutional right to assistance of counsel.[6] The defendants had almost been lynched, a mob was surrounding the courthouse, the defendants were—as the Supreme Court put it—under "close surveillance" by "military forces," and the judge was under strong pressure to get the case over with. To preserve the forms of law, he appointed all seven lawyers in town to represent the defendants, but one by one, they found themselves with conflicts of interest. In the end, only one lawyer was available to represent the defendants. He had a week to prepare for a trial that everyone knew was going to be a sham anyway. An out-of-town lawyer showed up on the day of trial and offered to help the appointed lawyer, who wanted to get through the case as quickly as possible. When the case got to the Supreme Court, Justice George Sutherland, one of its most conservative members, wrote the opinion reversing the convictions. The Court found that the judge had not really appointed *anyone* to represent the defendants for the trial. No one, Sutherland said, had "been given that clear appreciation of responsibility or impressed with that individual sense of duty which should and naturally would accompany" an appointment for trial purposes. The so-called appointments were, in Sutherland's view, "little more than an expansive gesture."

Powell said that states had to provide attorneys for defendants. A decade later the Court confirmed that death penalty cases were different, when it interpreted *Powell* to apply only to capital cases, not to all felony cases. (It overturned *that* limit in *Gideon v. Wainwright.*)[7]

Another death penalty case from the deep South produced another important expansion of defendants' rights. *Brown v. Mississippi* was the first case in which the Court reversed a state criminal conviction because the police had beaten a confession out of the defendant.[8] Ed Brown, Henry Shields, and Yank Ellington were accused of a murder that had been discovered on the afternoon of March 30, 1934. That night a deputy sheriff took Ellington to the victim's house, where a mob was waiting. They strung him up twice, then beat him, but he would not confess. The next day they arrested him again and, while taking an out-of-the-way route to jail, beat him again. This time he signed a confession the deputies dictated. Brown himself was arrested on Sunday, April 1, and taken to the same jail. He was beaten with a leather strap with buckles until he confessed, adjusting his confession to details supplied by the deputies. On Monday, having been warned not to repudiate the confessions, the defendants repeated them in court. The men were indicted on Tuesday and tried and convicted on Thursday. Chief Justice Hughes, acknowledging the state's power to regulate its own procedures, said that, although the state did not have to give anyone a jury trial, "it does not follow that it may substitute trial by ordeal." He found it "difficult to conceive of methods more revolting to the sense of justice than those taken to procure [these] confessions. . . "

Powell and *Brown* were typical of cases in which the fact that the defendant had been sentenced to death made the Supreme Court sensitive to more pervasive problems with criminal procedure that affected a much larger group of defendants and citizens.

The Extraordinary Case of Willie Francis

The justices came closer to the death penalty itself in the extraordinary case of Willie Francis.[9] Francis, a fifteen-year-old African-American, had been convicted of murdering Andrew Thomas, a white druggist in St. Martinville, Louisiana in 1945. As he was putting his car away, Thomas was shot five times from the bushes. The local sheriff could not find the killer. Several months later, though, Willie Francis was arrested in Texas on an unrelated charge. He had Thomas's wallet, and he confessed to the killing. Francis repeated his confession later; some of the details he added that indicated his guilt were confirmed and some with which he sought to diminish his responsibility were not confirmed. After a three-day trial at which his lawyers put on no defense witnesses, Francis was convicted and sentenced to death.

On May 3, 1946, Francis was to be executed. Louisiana's electric chair was brought to the St. Martinville jail, where it was reassembled. The portable electric generator that came with the chair was started. At noon Francis was brought to the chair for his execution. When the executioner pulled the switch, Francis strained and groaned as electricity went through his body. Something was wrong, though. Francis squeezed out, "Let me breathe." The executioner asked for "more juice," but the electrical system just was not working. After two minutes, the electricity was turned off, and Francis was taken from the chair.

The state planned to try to execute Francis again six days later. His case, though, had caught the public's attention, and frantic maneuvers started to delay the execution. Even if electrocution was not cruel and unusual punishment, Francis's new lawyer said, surely it was cruel to try to put someone to death twice. Although it did delay Francis's execution, the Louisiana Supreme Court ultimately refused to consider the claim, and Francis's lawyer tried to get the state pardon board to recommend that the governor stop the execution. Meanwhile another lawyer, J. Skelly Wright—later to become one of the country's most famous liberal federal judges—prepared an appeal to the Supreme Court. The state pardon board refused to recommend clemency, and Wright filed his papers in the Supreme Court. Justice Hugo Black ordered that the execution be delayed until the Court announced whether it would hear the case.

On June 10 the Supreme Court issued its decision. The Court's clerk notified Wright that the Court would not hear the case, and Francis's Louisiana lawyer told him the outcome. The next day, the clerk discovered that he had made a terrible mistake: The Court had actually decided to *hear* the case. The stay of execution was extended.

A majority of the Court had not yet decided to "incorporate" the Bill of Rights and apply its provisions to the states. They were, however, deeply divided, with Justice Black leading a strong minority in favor of incorporation. Francis's case posed hard questions of constitutional theory: Was it contrary to deeply rooted traditions of fairness to try to execute him again? Would it violate the ban on putting someone "twice in jeopardy" for the same offense? Would it be cruel and unusual punishment? At first, the justices found the case fairly easy. Six voted to affirm the state supreme court and allow the second attempt; only Justices Frank Murphy, Harold Burton, and Wiley Rutledge initially thought the attempt was unconstitutional.

Justice Stanley Reed, a moderate conservative on most constitutional issues, drafted an opinion rejecting "incorporation" arguments based on double jeopardy and cruel and unusual punishments and finding that the second attempt would not deny Francis his right to fundamentally fair treatment. The three dissenters quickly circulated individual opinions, then decided to have Burton take the lead. In addition, Justice William Douglas changed his vote.

Meanwhile, Justice Felix Frankfurter dithered. A strong advocate of what he called judicial restraint, Frankfurter wanted to assure himself and his admirers that he was a decent and humane person even if, on occasion, his judicial philosophy led him to seem hard-hearted. His difficulty in the Francis case was straightforward: He told his colleagues when they discussed the case that his standard for deciding whether due process was violated was, "Does it make me puke?" But he found it hard to explain why the second attempt at execution did not make him puke. His judicial philosophy demanded some external, community standard of fairness, but he could not close the gap between his subjective, "make me puke" standard and the external sources that were available to him.

Burton tried to persuade Frankfurter to join the dissenters and thereby to make a new majority, but in the end, Frankfurter could not bring himself to do that. Instead, he wrote a separate opinion urging the governor of Louisiana to grant clemency to Francis. Frankfurter's opinion explained why his philosophy of restraint led him to conclude that Louisiana's second try at executing Francis did not violate the traditions embedded in the Due Process Clause. Frankfurter's opinion set Justice Black off. Black, an incorporationist, was upset at Frankfurter's suggestion that only the judicial restraint philosophy kept him from voting to uphold the state court. After all, Black, who did not share that philosophy, was voting the same way. All this maneuvering left Justice Reed in an awkward position. Justice Robert Jackson had also circulated a proposed concurring opinion. With all these opinions, it seemed as if the "majority" opinion would have the support of only two justices—Reed and Chief Justice Fred Vinson. Reed appealed personally to Jackson to withdraw his opinion. He also inserted language in his own draft that "assum[ed], without. . .deciding" Black's incorporation point of view. After further negotiations, Black withdrew his opinion.

In the end, there were five votes to affirm the Louisiana court: Reed's opinion with four votes and Frankfurter's separate opinion. Reed wrote that the "unforeseeable accident" that aborted Francis's execution did not make the second attempt cruel, because "[t]here is no purpose to inflict unnecessary pain. . ." It was as if, Reed wrote, Francis had barely managed to escape "a fire in the cell block" before his scheduled execution date: There too he would have suffered "mental anguish and physical pain." Justice Burton's dissent said that capital punishment would be cruel and unusual punishment if it involved more than the infliction of "death itself." And, he asked, "How many deliberate and intentional reapplications of electric current does it take" to make the method of execution unconstitutional? If the state's officials had deliberately put Francis in the electric chair four times and each time deliberately used too little power to kill him, surely that would be unconstitutional; what they actually did was not different enough to satisfy Burton.

After the Court's opinion was released on January 13, 1947, Frankfurter tried to get Louisiana's governor to commute Francis's sentence. Not surprisingly, the effort failed. Francis died in the electric chair on May 9. He had lived one year and six days after the first attempt to execute him.

Justice Goldberg Reopens the Question

After *Francis,* the Court avoided direct confrontation with the death penalty, although it continued to give special attention to death penalty cases. The cases of Julius and Ethel Rosenberg, executed for their involvement with atomic espionage, and Caryl Chessman, executed for rape after a long, public controversy, kept the death penalty issue near the surface. Not until 1963, though, was the Court faced with a direct challenge. And, surprisingly, this time it came from within the Court.

President John Kennedy appointed Arthur Goldberg, his secretary of labor, to the Court in 1962. A year later Goldberg, working with his law clerk Alan Dershowitz, picked out six cases where defendants were trying to get the Supreme Court to review their convictions. As Justice Brennan said, this was "highly unusual."[10] Justices rarely write memoranda on cases that have not been accepted for review and even more rarely use those cases as vehicles for discussion of issues that the parties have not raised. Goldberg, though, was not deterred by tradition.

Goldberg's memorandum dealt with two cases where defendants had been sentenced to death for rape and four involving murders. It asked "whether, and under what circumstances, the imposition of the death penalty is proscribed" by the Constitution. After reviewing the Court's decisions, the memorandum said that Goldberg was "convinced" that evolving standards of decency "now condemn as barbaric and inhuman the deliberate institutionalized taking of human life by the state." He noted that "[m]any, if not most, of the civilized nations of the western world have abolished the death penalty" and that "the worldwide trend is unmistakenly in the direction of abolition." He cited recent surveys indicating declining public support for the death penalty and said that, even where opinion was divided, in criminal procedure cases "this Court traditionally has guided rather than followed public opinion in the process of articulating and establishing progressively civilized standards of decency." He also expressed concern that the death penalty was particularly unfair when people were executed after trials that, although lawful at the time, came to appear unconstitutional as the Court continued to develop constitutional law.

Beyond evolving standards of decency, Goldberg continued, was the question of "unnecessary and excessive punishment." For him, "vengeance" was not "an acceptable goal of punishment." The death penalty had to rest on deterrence, where, for Goldberg, the evidence was uncertain. In such a situation, "the State must. . .show an overriding necessity before it can take human life." After noting that his broad attack on the death penalty might not be persuasive, Goldberg argued that the death penalty "at least for certain types of crimes and on certain types of offenders" was unconstitutional. His first example was rape. Sexual crimes, he suggested, were unlikely candidates for deterrence by the threat of execution. And although the "value" protected by statutes punishing rape was "important," Goldberg suggested that "the general consensus is that the value is less than life." Here he noted that abolition of the death penalty for rape "would also eliminate the well-recognized disparity in the imposition of the death penalty for sexual crimes committed by whites and nonwhites."

Goldberg's broad attack on the death penalty failed. Four votes are needed to get the Supreme Court to consider a case fully. Only Justices Douglas and Brennan joined Goldberg in a scaled-down version of his challenge.[11] They dissented from the denial of review in the two rape cases, saying that "[t]he following questions. . .seem relevant and worthy of argument": "In light of the trend both in this country and throughout the world against punishing rape by death," does the death penalty for rape violate evolving standards of decency? "Is the taking of human life to protect a value other than human life consistent with the constitutional proscription" against disproportionate sentences? And "can the permissible aims of punishment (e.g., deterrence, isolation, rehabilitation) be achieved as effectively by punishing rape less severely than by death. . . ?"

The NAACP Legal Defense Fund Challenges the Death Penalty

Goldberg's memorandum catalyzed action by one of the nation's most important public interest law groups, the NAACP Legal Defense and Education Fund, Inc. (LDF or Inc. Fund).[12] The course of the death penalty in the Supreme Court was determined by the complex interactions between the LDF's legal strategy and the views of a changing set of justices on the Supreme Court.

The NAACP itself was founded in 1909, and throughout its life, it had challenged the nation's system of apartheid. Almost from the beginning, too, its members had been concerned with lynch law—mob killing of African-Americans accused of crimes—and kangaroo courts—trials, conducted in the full glare of intense white outrage, that lasted only a few hours—in the South. Their lawyers challenged exclusions of African-Americans from juries and admission of coerced confessions. In 1939, for tax purposes, the NAACP set up a separate litigating arm, the Inc. Fund. From 1939 to 1961, the Inc. Fund was headed by Thurgood Marshall, and after Marshall was appointed a federal judge, it was headed by Jack Greenberg.

The Inc. Fund's lawyers sporadically handled criminal cases, but for many years, the organization could not take such cases in any systematic way. The Fund's headquarters were in New York, and its lawyers too often learned of serious criminal cases well after the most blatant constitutional violations had already occurred. They had to perform salvage operations rather than structure cases to challenge fundamental aspects of the criminal justice system. In addition, during the 1940s and early 1950s, nearly all of the group's resources were devoted to attacking segregation in the schools and on buses and trains. Then, in the aftermath of *Brown v. Board of Education,* the South attacked the NAACP and its lawyers, and they had to spend time fending off those challenges to their very existence.

By the early 1960s, though, the situation had stabilized. In addition, some internal politics came to the fore. Again for tax reasons, the NAACP and the Inc. Fund separated even further in 1956. Robert Carter, formerly Marshall's chief assistant, became general counsel to the NAACP. When Marshall named Greenberg as his successor instead of Carter, Carter was alienated from the Inc. Fund even more. The NAACP's moral base was in the South, and the NAACP took charge of Southern desegregation. The Inc. Fund lawyers needed their own specialty. Eventually they developed cases challenging school segregation in the North and, after the Civil Rights Act of 1964 came into force, took up large-scale employment discrimination cases. But in 1963, the opportunity to focus on the death penalty was attractive.

Shortly after Goldberg's dissent was published, the Inc. Fund's lawyers held one of their usual discussion sessions and decided to investigate the possibility of challenging the death penalty in rape cases, where racial discrimination was, for them, self-evident. Gradually, as the lawyers' investigations proceeded, the scope of the challenge broadened. In 1963 Anthony Amsterdam, a dynamic law professor at the University of Pennsylvania, joined the Inc. Fund team. Amsterdam had been a brilliant law student, deeply committed to civil rights. He became an equally brilliant strategist and advocate, able to develop ingenious arguments that others would have dismissed without the legal backing and rhetorical power Amsterdam brought with them. He became the lead advocate in the death penalty challenge.

The campaign expanded mostly because the lawyers in charge of the campaign believed that capital punishment was unjustified and immoral. Other influences, though, deserve note. One was professional pride—it would be more invigorating to eliminate the death penalty entirely than to eliminate it for a few crimes or merely to get states to develop better procedures for deciding who should die. Another was a tension between limited arguments and the lawyers' abolitionist views—each argument against a particular form of capital sentencing carried the implication, which the lawyers wanted to reject, that everything would be satisfactory if only that one difficulty were cleared up. And perhaps as important as the lawyers' abolitionist views, a third reason for broadening the challenge was professional ethics—these lawyers had clients facing execution, and they had a professional duty to make every argument that could possibly serve their clients' interest.

Expanding the challenge, though, had its own drawbacks. The attack on the death penalty for rape had a clear racial connection. As two scholars put it, "From the 1880s on, almost all executions for rape in this country took place in the South, and the overwhelming majority of those executed—85 percent—were black."[13] As the attack broadened, the link to race weakened. Even more, the lawyers became saddled with increasingly unattractive clients; if their argument was that the death penalty was unconstitutional no matter what, they had to be prepared to say that the most vicious murderers could not be executed. And, perhaps even more unfortunate, when the expanded campaign was tied to a civil rights organization, the racist association of African-Americans with violent crime could be reinforced.

The campaign's expansion had two facets: a moratorium on executions and the strategy against capital punishment.

The Moratorium on Executions The lawyers managed to create a moratorium on executions. Their primary motive was to increase the stakes of the challenge: As they saw it, judges who might be willing to allow one person to be executed might be reluctant to let loose a "bloodbath," as it was described, by authorizing the execution of several hundred people whose executions had been delayed until all questions about the death penalty's constitutionality had been resolved.

Putting the moratorium in place called for a combination of legal creativity and substantial resources. Death sentences were handed down all over the country. The Inc. Fund lawyers in New York could take only a few defendants on as clients themselves. Instead, they developed a standard-form complaint and brief that lawyers could use to raise the challenges to the death penalty. Once these challenges were raised, the lawyers had to persuade a judge to stay—that is, delay—an execution until the legal challenge had been resolved. Few government officials were happy about putting off an execution. Many judges would not even consider applications to delay executions until they were actually scheduled. They hoped that governors would themselves delay the execution. Governors, in turn, delayed, trying to pass the buck back to the courts. That meant that the lawyers often faced extremely short—and quite literal—deadlines. In the end, some judge somewhere was certain to stay any execution, but the process of obtaining stays was harrowing. Dramatically, in November 1967, the California Supreme Court, acting on its own, stayed *all* executions in the state.

When death penalty cases eventually got to the Supreme Court, the lawyers could take advantage of the Court's practice of holding cases: When the Court has decided to consider one case in detail, it holds—takes no action on—all other cases raising the same issue. With stays of execution in place, cases would pile up in the Supreme Court.

A lawyer in Florida was even more ingenious. Tobias Simon persuaded a federal judge to treat death penalty cases as a class action. In a class action, a small number of plaintiffs stand in for everyone who would be affected by a court decision: In death penalty cases, the few named plaintiffs would raise the challenges, and everyone sentenced to death would benefit from a favorable ruling. The argument for a class action in death penalty cases turned on the fact that many defendants did not have lawyers at the final stages of their cases. Class actions were designed for similar situations: The named plaintiff, who did have a lawyer, would represent all the others who did not. Of course, if the state could not execute the named plaintiffs while the challenge was before the courts, it could not execute anyone else in the class.

This was, to say the least, an innovative use of class actions, and no other judge went along with it. Their objections were simple: True, everyone else sentenced to death would benefit if the plaintiffs won, but they would all suffer if the plaintiffs lost. And it was desperately unfair to let a person go to his death because the lawyer for someone else had not been persuasive enough. The Florida class action contributed to the moratorium, though, because Florida was one of the states with the largest numbers of people of Death Row.

The Strategy Against Capital Punishment At the outset, the Inc. Fund's lawyers believed they could nibble away at the death penalty. Goldberg's dissent pointed the way to one challenge: that the death penalty ought not be imposed for crimes other than murder. It might be excessive—beyond the retributive "eye for an eye" principle—for robbery. And as Goldberg's memorandum had said (although not his published dissent), everyone knew that the death penalty for rape was a penalty reserved for African-Americans who raped white women. It was, that is, another expression of race discrimination in the United States. From the viewpoint of complete abolitionists, though, this line of attack had one drawback: In arguing that death could not be imposed for anything besides murder, they might convince the courts that of course it could be imposed there.

The second line of attack was procedural: challenge the methods by which the death penalty was imposed, to make it more difficult for prosecutors to obtain death sentences. In some states, death penalty trials were bifurcated: A jury first decided whether a defendant was guilty or innocent and then heard additional evidence before deciding whether to impose a death sentence. Most defense attorneys believe that bifurcated trials reduce the risk that the jury will impose a death sentence. In a unified trial, lawyers would hesitate to put on some evidence that might decrease the likelihood of a death sentence—the defendant's own testimony, for example, or evidence about his background—but that might increase the chance that the jury would convict—because, for example, when the defendant testified, the prosecutor would ask about whether the defendant committed the crime. And everywhere, the decision to impose a death sentence was standardless: Juries were given essentially no guidance, through instructions or otherwise, about which murderers ought to be punished by death. The procedural attack was that death penalty systems had to have bifurcated trials and provide standards for the death sentence. Again, though, for abolitionists this attack had an underside: It might suggest that the death penalty was acceptable when these procedural problems were overcome.

Developing a strategic and organized attack on the death penalty proved impossible. The substantive issues about capital punishment itself could not easily be separated from the procedural ones. And as lawyers with clients facing execution, the Inc. Fund lawyers found themselves under an ethical obligation to raise every issue whenever they could. They could not, that is, move one step at a time. Then, once they had raised all the issues, they were at the Court's mercy: Although the lawyers might prefer to nibble away at the death penalty, the Court could set the agenda by structuring its decisions to be broad or narrow.

In the end, the Court took one step down the road to abolition—it restricted "death-qualified" juries, screened to ensure that no one opposed to capital punishment was a jury member. Then it almost took two more steps, coming close to requiring separate trials on guilt and sentence and to requiring standards for imposing the death penalty. It ducked the question of whether death could be imposed for rape and robbery. Although the Court had accepted only one of the opponents' constitutional arguments against the death penalty, the strategy of nibbling away seemed to be working.

Then, facing the questions of separate trials and standards, the Court appeared to change direction, refusing to require either. The death penalty appeared to be entrenched in constitutional law. The Supreme Court still had the capacity to surprise even the closest

Court-watchers, though. The next step was the biggest. With no further ado, the Court found the death penalty unconstitutional. The reaction led the Court to withdraw and to allow states to reinstitute the death penalty. If the lawyers had been able to exert more control over the process, they might have had a more long-lasting success.

"Death-Qualified" Juries

In April 1959, a woman broke free from a struggle with William Witherspoon and ran to some nearby police officers. She told them Witherspoon had a gun. Witherspoon ran into a parking lot and hid in a trailer. When one of the police officers entered the trailer, Witherspoon shot and killed him. In criminal trials, jury selection has two parts. Jurors are first asked some questions, and on the basis of their answers, both the prosecution and the defense can challenge them "for cause." For example, a juror who says that she had read so much about a case that she could not possibly change her mind on hearing evidence in court can be removed for cause. Then, both sides can remove a limited number of jurors without giving any reason. When Witherspoon was prosecuted for murder, an Illinois law said that jurors with "conscientious scruples against capital punishment" could be removed for cause. During the jurors' examination, the prosecutor said, "Let's get these conscientious objectors out of the way, without wasting any time on them." Forty-seven people were then removed for cause; only five said that they would never vote for the death penalty, and the remainder were excluded without any attempt to determine if they could set aside their scruples and vote to impose it.

Witherspoon was represented in the Supreme Court by Albert Jenner, a prominent Chicago lawyer.[14] Jenner relied on two unpublished opinion surveys to argue that the Illinois statute was unconstitutional because "death-qualified" jurors were biased in favor of conviction. Anthony Amsterdam, leading the Inc. Fund's campaign against the death penalty, was concerned that that claim was so far-reaching—it would invalidate not just Witherspoon's death sentence but his conviction as well—and was based on so little evidence that it would scare the justices off. Amsterdam prepared an extensive amicus, or "friend of the court," brief on behalf of other death row inmates arguing that the Court should put off ruling on the claim of "prosecution-bias." It pointed out that the Inc. Fund had commissioned a large-scale survey of attitudes that would provide better evidence on that question. Amsterdam argued that the Court should vacate Witherspoon's conviction because his jury was not a fair "cross-section" of the community: So many people were opposed to capital punishment that excluding them from juries, whatever its effect on the jury's inclination to assess the evidence, meant that the jury decision would not represent the full community.

The Court took an even narrower view of the case. Justice Stewart's opinion said that the survey evidence was "too tentative and fragmentary" to establish pro-prosecution bias.[15] But, Stewart said, it was "self-evident" that the jury was not impartial on the question of sentence. Imposing a death sentence was within the discretion of the jury, and, Stewart said, "a juror's general views about capital punishment play an inevitable role in any such decision." The jury "can do little more—and must do nothing less—than express the conscience of the community on the ultimate question of life or death." But, a jury "[c]ulled of all who harbor doubts about the wisdom of capital punishment" can "speak only for a distinct and dwindling minority." The Illinois approach "produced a jury uncommonly willing to condemn a man to die."

Justice Stewart ended his opinion by calling Witherspoon's jury a "hanging jury" and by saying that the state "has stacked the deck" against Witherspoon. Justice Black's dissent found that description unfair and said that if the Court "is to hold capital punishment unconstitutional. . .it should do so forthrightly, not by making it impossible for States to get juries that will enforce the death penalty." Prosecutors reacted similarly, declaring that *Witherspoon* effectively ended the death penalty.

Actually, a crucial footnote in Justice Stewart's opinion indicated that the holding was not so sweeping. The footnote said that the state *could* exclude jurors who "made unmistakably clear. . .that they would *automatically* vote against the imposition of capital punishment without regard to any evidence that might be developed at the trial" and that the state could ask whether a juror was "willing to *consider* all of the penalties provided by state law." As the Court later put it, the state had a "legitimate interest in obtaining jurors who could follow their instructions and obey their oaths."[16] Prosecutors would have to examine prospective jurors in more detail, but they could still persuade a judge that a juror's reservations about capital punishment were so strong that the juror would not fairly consider the possibility of a death sentence.

In the 1985 case of *Wainwright v. Witt,* the Court gave prosecutors even more room.[17] The Court said that it was proper to exclude a juror who said that she had "personal" objections to the death penalty, was "afraid" that those objections would "interfere" with her sitting in the case, and "thought" they would interfere with judging the defendant's guilt or innocence. Chief Justice Rehnquist said that trial courts had to find jurors "who will conscientiously apply the law and find the facts." A strict standard, requiring jurors' objections to the death penalty to be "unambiguous" and "unmistakable," was, he said, a "standard that allows jurors to be seated who quite likely will be biased" in the defendant's favor. Many jurors "simply cannot be asked enough questions to reach the point where their bias" is unmistakable; they "may not know how they will react when faced with imposing the death sentence, or may be unable to articulate, or may wish to hide their true feelings." Further, the Court said, appellate courts should rely heavily on a trial judge's determination that a juror's misgivings were so great as to give cause for exclusion. They should not read transcripts with exquisite care to determine whether the juror was "unambiguously" opposed to the death penalty under all circumstances.

But no matter how the law *developed,* when *Witherspoon* was announced, it seemed to be a step in the direction of abolishing the death penalty. The tone of Justice Stewart's opinion was itself unmistakable. It called supporters of the death penalty a "dwindling" minority, and the opinion included a footnote quoting death penalty opponent Arthur Koestler calling the "division" between abolitionists and supporters a division "between those who have charity and those who have not." And although the prosecution could still exclude people who said they would never vote to impose a death sentence, juries would now include many more people whose misgivings about capital punishment might make them reluctant to impose it.

The Death Penalty for Rape

Because the Inc. Fund was at its core a civil rights organization, the obvious racial aspect of the death penalty for rape made it probably the most attractive target for the Inc. Fund's initial attack. They came across a long-pending rape case from Arkansas and used it as the vehicle for this challenge.[18] In 1962 William Maxwell, a 22-year-old African-American, was convicted of raping a 35-year-old white woman a year earlier. The rapist was interrupted as he tried to rob the woman's house, and in a struggle, the telephone was knocked to the floor. The operator heard the woman's screams and called the police. Before they arrived, however, the intruder dragged the woman two blocks away and raped her. At the trial, the victim identified Maxwell as the rapist, and the jury voted against mercy. Maxwell's lawyer included a modest statistical challenge to the death penalty for rape in his appeal to the state supreme court but got nowhere with it.

Maxwell then moved to the federal courts, which can hear constitutional challenges to criminal convictions through a procedure known as habeas corpus (for more detail on this procedure, see chapter three). Again he presented the death penalty challenge, and again it was rejected. His execution was scheduled for September 1966. In July, Inc. Fund lawyers filed a second habeas corpus petition for Maxwell. As the law stood in 1966, they could do that, but they had to do something to indicate that there were new facts they could present or some new law since the first habeas decision.

The lawyers suggested in the second habeas case that recent Supreme Court decisions implied that death penalty trials had to be bifurcated and that juries had to have standards for imposing the death penalty. The core of their case, though, was factual. During the summer of 1965, the Inc. Fund coordinated a study by law students under the direction of sociologist Marvin Wolfgang, examining sentences for rape in the South. The study took a wide range of factors into account: the defendant's age, family background, prior criminal record; the victim's age, status, reputation; whether the defendant and the victim had a prior relationship; whether the rape occurred in a house or outside; and many more. Wolfgang used factors that someone might think would make a particular rape more serious, so that he could find out whether something other than race alone explained why African-Americans, and essentially only African-Americans, were sentenced to die for raping white, and essentially only white, women. The conclusion was simple: Race alone was the explanation. African-Americans convicted of rape were seven times more likely to be sentenced to death than white men; African-Americans convicted of raping white women were *eighteen* times more likely to be sentenced to death than any other combination.

Wolfgang presented the results of his study to the federal court in August 1966. J. Smith Henley, the trial judge, denied Maxwell's claim. Henley was skeptical about whether Wolfgang's study had in fact been comprehensive enough to show that race alone mattered. But perhaps more important, he was skeptical that statistical evidence could ever show race discrimination in criminal justice. Maxwell's execution was imminent. His lawyers tried to get a court of appeals judge to postpone the execution, but he refused. They flew to Washington and persuaded Supreme Court Justice Byron White to postpone the execution until the full court could consider—not Maxwell's fundamental claim—but whether the court of appeals judge should have postponed the execution so that *that* court could take up his case. In January 1967, the Supreme Court said that the court of appeals should indeed consider the merits.

Over a year later, the court of appeals affirmed the lower court's decision. In an opinion written by Judge Harry Blackmun, the court concluded that Wolfgang's study was insufficient to show race discrimination: "We are not certain that, for Maxwell, statistics will ever be his redemption." Maxwell's lawyers had not tried to get the Supreme Court to review his conviction in 1963, but now the Inc. Fund lawyers were ready. Under the Court's rules, the full Court will hear a case if four of the nine Justices want it to. In Maxwell's case, six Justices—Warren, Brennan, Stewart, White, Fortas, and Marshall—agreed to hear his appeal.

Maxwell in the Supreme Court

When the case got to the Supreme Court, things fell apart. The justices were entirely uninterested in the centerpiece of the lower court litigation, the race discrimination claim. Their questions at oral argument focused instead on the issues of standards and unitary trials. The justices were concerned that it would be impossible to draft standards guiding juries. Amsterdam tried to alleviate their concern by suggesting that Maxwell would win if the Court simply said that *some* standards were needed, leaving it to state legislatures to develop them. That, however, was not what a Court trying to "solve" the problem of capital punishment wanted to hear. The oral argument dramatically brought out an additional point: The state's attorney conceded that the trial transcript, which was not included in the materials presented to the Supreme Court, showed a clear violation of *Witherspoon.* (Because the second habeas petition was filed before *Witherspoon* was decided, neither it nor the Inc. Fund's appeal to the Supreme Court actually included that claim.)

When the justices discussed the case in what is known as their conference, a solid majority agreed that Maxwell's death sentence could not stand; only Justice Black voted to uphold the sentence.[19] The other justices disagreed sharply, though, on why the sentence had to be vacated. The fundamental problem occurred because some justices thought the questions of standards and bifurcation could be separated and others thought they were completely intertwined. Perhaps, for example, a state could *not* have a unitary trial if it did not have standards but *could* have a unitary trial if it did. But of what use was a separate trial for penalty if the defendant did not know what sort of evidence to produce—that is, if the state did not provide standards for the jury to apply in sentencing?

After two rounds of discussion, a majority did emerge. Chief Justice Warren and Justices Douglas, Brennan, Fortas, and Marshall agreed that *both* bifurcation and standards were constitutionally required. Justice Harlan was firmly set against requiring standards: "Where do we stop?" he asked his colleagues. He was unsure about the unitary trial. He was concerned about rules of evidence: A defendant who simply wanted to plead for mercy in his testimony would nonetheless be questioned about the crime itself; Harlan thought that the risk of questioning about the crime might make it too difficult for a defendant to decide to testify and ask for mercy.

Chief Justice Warren asked Douglas to draft an opinion. A quick worker, Douglas got a draft to his colleagues within four weeks. He may also have been prodded by the fact that Warren, who supported his position, had already announced his intention to retire at the end of the Court's term in July 1969. The draft stressed the importance of a defendant's own testimony in persuading the jury to be merciful and argued that the unitary trial impermissibly made it too difficult for defendants to present their pleas for mercy: "[T]hough he uses his [testimony]. . . to obtain mercy rather than complete exoneration, his efforts to obtain a lesser punishment may only worsen his position on the issue of guilt." Then Douglas turned to the question of standards. His draft pointed out that "[t]he law normally gives a jury guidelines" about what "fault" means in car accident cases, or about what "premeditation" means in murder cases. Without guidelines, juries were exercising "arbitrary" power. Here Douglas mentioned the risk of race discrimination—"one jury may decide that one defendant is not 'fit to live' because he is a black who raped a white woman, while another defendant is 'fit to live' because he is a white who raped a black"—and problems of poverty—"the death penalty is seldom suffered by the affluent member of society; it is reserved, in practice, for the indigent and those otherwise inferior or somehow incapacitated." In the disjointed manner not rare in Douglas's later opinions, the draft then raised some questions about what the guidelines should be, quoting from the American Law Institute's proposals. But, Douglas wrote, defining the guidelines presented "profound questions," which were for "local legislatures" to resolve.

A few days later Justice Stewart sent around a draft relying on *Witherspoon* to vacate the death sentence, and Justice Black circulated a brief dissent, opening with the line, "If this Court is determined to abolish the death penalty, I think it should do so forthrightly, and not by nibbles." These were expected. The majority began to unravel, though, when Justice Fortas indicated that he could not go along with Douglas's treatment of the standards issue. How, he asked, could legislatures "prescribe different punishments for the kaleidoscope of crime and the infinite variety of persons who commit them"? He noted his concern that specific standards would *increase* the number of death sentences handed down. (In a letter, Douglas wondered why, as the Court had already held, states had to come up with standards when the Court allowed juries to require *acquitted* defendants to pay the costs of prosecution, but could not come up with standards for the death sentence.) Without Fortas's vote—and without Harlan's—there was no majority on the "standards" question, and Douglas withdrew the section of the opinion dealing with standards. There were still six votes requiring bifurcated trials, though.

Now Warren and Brennan jumped ship. They refused to let the case go forward without at least some discussion of standards. On May 14, Brennan prepared a draft addressing Fortas's concerns. He suggested a number of "sets of criteria" that a legislature might use in deciding "who among those convicted of rape should be put to death"; it could create degrees of rape, or specify "factors relating to the personal status of each defendant." Instead, Brennan wrote, the legislature "chose to abdicate its decision-making role, leaving questions of general social policy to be answered by individual juries, indeed by individual jurors . . . " Without some guidelines, defendants could not know "which arguments will hurt him and which might save him."

The day before Brennan sent his draft around, Fortas resigned from the Court over questionable financial arrangements he had made. Harlan's vote now became crucial. It still seemed possible that Harlan would go along with requiring bifurcated trials; he prepared an opinion saying that defendants in capital cases had a constitutional right to present mitigating evidence, including personal testimony. Harlan called this a concurrence, meaning that he voted to vacate the death sentence, but his opinion did not actually say that the defendant's right to testify and ask for mercy implied that there had to be bifurcated trials. And, within a week, Harlan appears to have realized that his argument did not get him to his conclusion. He said that he needed more time to work on his opinion. Without Harlan's vote, there was no majority position. The justices decided to have the case reargued the following year.

By the time of reargument, Chief Justice Warren and Justice Fortas, two resolute liberals, were gone. Warren's replacement, Warren Burger, had a very different position on law-and-order. (Because he had written the court of appeals decision in *Maxwell,* Fortas's replacement Harry Blackmun did not participate in the reargument.) Burger saw no way to define standards; jury decisions rested on "the sum total of the life experience of the jurors." By this time, Harlan seemed firmly in favor of bifurcation. His vote, though, was no longer enough: The Court was evenly divided on the question, with Burger, Black, Stewart, and White rejecting it. And, the standards issue was already gone: Only Douglas, Brennan, and Marshall would have required guidelines for juries.

Maxwell survived because the Court went along with Stewart's view that the case had to be sent back to the lower courts to consider the *Witherspoon* issue.[20] No advance had been made in the campaign against the death penalty. Indeed, from within the Court, it would have seemed that the campaign had lost ground: The Court simply ignored the race discrimination attack on the death sentence for rape, and a majority now rejected the standards argument. The Court immediately selected two cases to deal with the standards and bifurcation issues.

The Court Rejects the Main Attacks on Capital Sentencing

On the same day it sent *Maxwell* back to the lower court, the Supreme Court announced that it would hear cases from Ohio and California raising the issues of bifurcation and standards.

Crampton v. Ohio The Ohio case involved James Crampton, who murdered his wife and pleaded insanity. Ohio had a unitary trial in capital cases. The evidence at trial showed that, about two months before the murder, Crampton got permission to leave the mental hospital where he was being treated for alcoholism and drug addiction so he could attend the funeral of his father-in-law. While attending the funeral, he stole a knife and ran off. Later he called his wife, who pleaded with him to return to the hospital. When she said she would call the police, Crampton threatened to kill her. She called them anyway, and they picked him up. Shortly before the murder Crampton left the hospital again. Three days before the murder Crampton met a man he had met while in prison. The two men spent the next few days drifting in Michigan, stealing petty cash and amphetamines. The day before the murder Crampton called his wife and then told his companion that he had to get back to Ohio as fast as possible because, he later said, he found out his wife was having an affair. When they got to Ohio, they broke into the home of Crampton's mother-in-law and stole a rifle and some handguns. On the evening of the murder, Crampton had his companion drop him off at his wife's house, where Crampton shot his wife in the face at close range while she was using the toilet.

That was the evidence the jury heard about the murder itself. The defense had Crampton's mother testify about Crampton's background, his several marriages, and his drug addiction. It also introduced hospital reports showing, among other things, Crampton's long criminal record, his court-martial conviction, and his claim that the gun he used to kill his wife had discharged accidentally. The jury convicted Crampton and did not recommend mercy.

McGautha v. California California tried capital cases in two stages. Dennis McGautha and codefendant William Wilkinson robbed two neighborhood grocery stores on February 14, 1967. Both men had guns during the robbery. Benjamin Smetana, who was helping his wife run the second store, was killed there. Later, Wilkinson's former girlfriend testified that McGautha told her he had killed a man. The jury convicted both men of murder, and the case went on to the penalty stage before the same jury.

Wilkinson testified on his own behalf, describing his unhappy childhood, his honorable discharge from the army because of low intelligence, his church attendance, and the difficulties he had getting jobs after he was shot in the back in an unprovoked street assault. Then, he said, he fell in with a bad crowd, including McGautha. The two robberies were the first crimes he had ever committed. He testified that McGautha shot Mr. Smetana. To support that, he called a witness who testified that they had seen McGautha practicing a quick draw. Other witnesses testified to Wilkinson's "horror at what had happened."

McGautha testified as well. He said that he and Wilkinson had traded guns and that Wilkinson had shot Smetana. He described his background and acknowledged what he described as minor participation in several felonies, including robbery and manslaughter. The jury sentenced Wilkinson to life imprisonment and McGautha to death.

Both cases presented the standards issue. The Court's deliberations during *Maxwell* showed that only a minority would require standards. By the time *Crampton* was decided, the majority included the new chief justice and Justice Blackmun. Blackmun came to the Court after a bitter political struggle that saw the Senate reject two nominees—Clement Haynsworth and G. Harrold Carswell—to take Fortas's seat. Although personally opposed to capital punishment, Blackmun's opinion as a court of appeals judge in *Maxwell* showed that he did not find it unconstitutional. With Burger's and Blackmun's votes, a majority was prepared to reject the claim that the Constitution required separate trials for guilt and penalty; Harlan's position no longer mattered. But as he considered the question further, Harlan too changed his mind. Apparently he concluded that, although defendants in capital cases had a right to testify, forcing them to choose between testifying at a unitary trial—opening themselves up to questions about guilt if they tried to present evidence to persuade the jury not to sentence them to death—and not testifying at all did not violate their right against self-incrimination.

After hearing oral arguments, the justices decide who writes the Court's opinion. If the chief justice is a member of the majority, he assigns the opinion. It is often a good idea to assign the opinion to the justice with the *least* strongly held views; that way, as the judge works on the opinion, he or she may become increasingly committed to a result that the judge had been less certain about at the start, and the other justices in the majority will certainly go along. Burger may have had that in mind when he assigned the opinions in *McGautha and Crampton* to Justice Harlan; in addition, of course, Harlan's memorandum in *Maxwell* indicated that he was the one justice in the majority who had begun to work out an opinion on the bifurcation issue.

Harlan's forceful opinion basically asked whether the procedures in Ohio and California were fair.[21] In answering that, he focused mainly on policy questions; if those questions were difficult, their answers should come from legislatures, not courts. After saying that the standards issue had an "undeniable surface appeal," the opinion surveyed the history of capital punishment to show that there was a long and largely unsuccessful history of efforts "to identify before the fact those homicides for which the slayer should die"—that is, to provide standards for capital punishment. The more rigid systems, with death as the penalty for all crimes within a category, led to jury nullification. Legislatures responded by "forthrightly" giving juries discretion in sentencing. For Harlan, this history showed that "[t]o identify before the fact those characteristics of criminal homicides and their perpetrators which call for the death penalty, and to express these characteristics in language which can be fairly understood. . .appear to be tasks which are beyond present human capacity." A prestigious legal study group, the American Law Institute, had developed a list of aggravating and mitigating circumstances, but, said Harlan, it did not "purport to provide more than the most minimal control" of sentencing discretion and gave "no protection against the jury determined to decide on whimsy or caprice." All they did, he said, was "suggest some subjects for the jury to consider during its deliberations." If the courts tried to develop standards, "[t]he infinite variety of cases. . .would make general standards either meaningless 'boiler-plate' or a statement of the obvious that no jury would need."

Harlan's opinion then turned to the bifurcation issue. Its focus was self-incrimination, and its tone was set by the observation that "[t]he criminal process. . .is replete with situations requiring 'the making of difficult judgments' as to which course to follow." The

Constitution, it said, did not bar the government from forcing a defendant to choose between two paths, each one of which was constitutionally protected. Harlan acknowledged that it was "hard" to force a capital defendant who wanted to testify only on punishment "to make nice calculations of the effect of his testimony on the jury's determination of guilt." But, he said, the Court had permitted the government to force defendants to make quite similar choices: A defendant cannot take the stand and then stop cross-examination; when a defendant takes the stand, the prosecution has a chance to introduce evidence of prior crimes that it might not have been allowed to bring in if the defendant did not testify. The "peculiar poignancy" of the capital defendant's situation did not distinguish those cases from the unitary trial. At the sentencing stage, a personal plea from the defendant for mercy might be especially forceful but at the guilt stage so too might personal testimony denying that he had committed the crime for which he was standing trial; the government could force the defendant to choose between saying nothing on guilt or testifying and having evidence of prior crimes come in; and for Harlan, the capital sentencing claim really was not that different.

Harlan concluded his opinion with a "broader observation." Perhaps standards and bifurcated trials were best, but, he said, the Constitution required only that trials be fairly conducted. The facts of the cases—including the fact that the California jury sentenced McGautha to death but Wilkinson to life—showed that juries, without guidelines, could do a decent job of sorting out those who did not deserve to die from those who did.

Justice Douglas's disjointed dissent focused on the bifurcation issue. Defendants had a right to plead for mercy, but, Douglas said, for that right to be "meaningful," it had to be available before sentencing. A unitary trial, though, effectively denied defendants that right because exercising it forced the defendant to "surrender" the right against self-incrimination on the question of guilt. Echoing *Witherspoon,* Douglas said that the procedure "stacked" the trial in favor of death, placing "the weights on the side of man's sadistic drive."

Justice Brennan wrote a long, impassioned dissent. Although part was devoted to strengthening Douglas's legal argument on bifurcation, most dealt with the standards issue. Brennan criticized the majority for treating the question as if McGautha was demanding "predetermined standards so precise as to be capable of purely mechanical application," when the true issue, according to Brennan, was whether the legislature had abdicated its duty in designing capital sentencing procedures that "allow the maximum possible variation from one case to the next." The absence of standards was, Brennan said, the absence of the "rule of law." Brennan refused to believe that legislatures were "so devoid of wisdom and the power of rational thought" that they could not devise *some* standards. There were, Brennan thought, many ways to solve the problem of guiding sentencing: guidelines, specifying factors whose presence or absence mattered; lists of factors that could be "illustrative or exhaustive." But California and Ohio "have sought no solution at all. . .We are faced with nothing more than stark legislative abdication."

Treating capital sentencing as a method by which legislatures delegated to juries selection of those who would die—or, as Justice Brennan repeatedly put it, selection of those the state chose to kill—he insisted that delegation had to be guided by standards precise enough to eliminate the risk that the selection would be arbitrary. And unlike Justice Harlan, Brennan saw "no reason whatever to believe that the nature of capital sentencing is such that it cannot be surrounded with the protections ordinarily available to check arbitrary and lawless action." At the least, the legislature had to explain to juries what its purposes were in authorizing capital punishment for some but not all murderers.

Justice Douglas indicated his sympathy for the piecemeal attack on capital punishment, calling the Court's decision "a dam. . . placed across the stream of the law on procedural due process, a stream which has grown larger with the passing years." And it indicated Douglas's ultimate judgment: Capital punishment was a "barbaric" procedure that served "man's deep-seated sadistic instincts." Notably, though, these comments came in a dissent; the abolitionist sympathies that worked their way into the majority opinion in *Witherspoon* had disappeared.

The Court Faces the Issue

Justice Black wrote a separate opinion in *McGautha.* In part, it simply expressed some long-standing disagreements he had with Harlan's approach to constitutional law. Partly, though, it announced his understanding of the Inc. Fund's campaign against the death penalty. For the first time since the campaign began, a Supreme Court justice said that in his view capital punishment did not violate the "cruel and unusual punishments" clause. For Black, it was enough that capital punishment "was in common use and authorized by law. . . at the time the [Eighth] Amendment was adopted." Black found it "inconceivable" that the framers "intended to end capital punishment."

Oddly enough, Justice Black was joined in that view, at least temporarily and within the Court's confines, by Justices Douglas,

Brennan, and Marshall. After *McGautha* was announced on May 3, 1971, the justices met to decide what to do about the numerous death penalty cases that the Court had held off deciding until *McGautha*. Justice Stewart pointed out that the Inc. Fund's basic challenge had not been addressed. He proposed that the Court take up the Eighth Amendment issue.[22]

Douglas objected. He relied on the Court's action in a 1969 case, *Boykin v. Alabama*.[23] As a participant in the Inc. Fund's campaign put it, Edward Boykin was "one of the few men on death row for a crime other than murder or rape."[24] He had pleaded guilty to five armed robberies, in one of which a shot he fired ricocheted and injured a young woman. Nothing in the record indicated that Boykin understood that, by pleading guilty, he opened himself up to a death sentence. The jury recommended a death sentence on each robbery.

Boykin's lawyers appealed the death sentences. They argued that Boykin would never have pleaded guilty if he had known of the risk of capital punishment; it was unconstitutional, they said, to accept a guilty plea under those circumstances. And for the first time in the attack on the death penalty, they raised the Eighth Amendment issue. The argument was simple: Death for robbery was disproportionate—"an eye for an eye, a life for a life" was one thing, but a life for $1,500 was another.

Amsterdam prepared a brief supporting Boykin's lawyers that put before the justices the first broad-scale attack on the death penalty. The brief reviewed the death penalty's history and its use in contemporary criminal justice systems. Amsterdam's main innovation, though, was to emphasize the discrepancy between the legislative support for capital punishment and the actual willingness of the public itself to impose the death penalty. There was a difference, the brief said, "between what public conscience will allow the law to *say* and what it will allow the law to *do*." Many states had death penalty statutes, but juries actually ordered it "sparsely, and spottily to unhappy minorities." That occurred because the public knew, deep down, that capital punishment was indeed inconsistent with the evolving standards of morality that the Court said were the Eighth Amendment standard.

When a person was actually executed, then, it was essentially a random event. Amsterdam made the point in connection with robbery—out of the hundreds of thousands of armed robberies each year, only a tiny handful led to death sentences—but, consistent with his broad goals, he argued that it applied to the death penalty for murder as well.

In a way, Amsterdam's strategy may have backfired. When the justices discussed Boykin's case, only Justice Douglas and Marshall voted to overturn the death penalty for robbery. And, at least as Douglas later reconstructed his views, he was willing to do so only because death was disproportionate to the offense; in thinking about *Boykin,* Douglas later said, he assumed that the death penalty was obviously appropriate for murder.

The Court avoided a decision on the "death for robbery" issue. Douglas wrote an opinion saying that the procedures for Boykin's guilty plea were unconstitutional. Now when Stewart proposed to postpone executions while the Court considered the basic Eighth Amendment challenge, Douglas balked. Only two years before, only two justices found a much narrower claim persuasive; it was "frivolous" to continue dealing with challenges to the death penalty. Far from nibbling away at the death penalty, the Court had repeatedly let it stand; Douglas thought the time had come to stop encouraging challenges. Brennan also wanted to deny review but said that he would write an opinion explaining his view that capital punishment was prohibited by the Eighth Amendment under all circumstances.

Their colleagues disagreed, though. Justice Black thought it essential to address—and, for himself, reject—the Eighth Amendment challenge. Law clerks for Justices Stewart and Brennan went through the cases held for the *McGautha* decision. The Court voted to hear four cases:

- *Furman v. Georgia* William Furman, who suffered from psychotic episodes, broke into William Micke's house late at night. When Micke came downstairs to see what was making noise, Furman ran from the house. On the back porch, he tripped over an electric cord, and the gun he was carrying went off. The shot went through the closed door and killed Micke.

- *Jackson v. Georgia* Lucious Jackson raped a woman after he escaped from a prison work gang. After the woman discovered him hiding in her baby's closet, Jackson held a pair of scissors to her throat and demanded money. When she got a five-dollar bill, Jackson put the scissors down. The woman grabbed the scissors and, after a struggle, Jackson raped her.

- *Branch v. Texas* Elmer Branch, with a below-normal IQ, raped a 65-year-old woman, surprising her in her bed.

- *Aikens v. California* Earnest Aikens raped and murdered three women. In 1962, before his eighteenth birthday, Aikens broke into a house, stole about $60, forced the woman in the house to a railway embankment, and raped her. When she escaped, Aikens chased her and stabbed her to death. Aikens did not receive a death sentence for this murder because California law allowed capital punishment only for crimes committed by people older than eighteen. Aikens spent most of the next three years in prison for other crimes. On April 26, 1965, Aikens raped and murdered another woman, this time in the middle of the day. He knew the woman's family and probably got into the house with her permission. Although the evidence of Aikens's guilt was not as clear as in the first case, Aikens did have two of the victim's rings on the evening of April 26, and he made statements suggesting his guilt.

From the point of view of death penalty opponents, Aikens's case was one of the worst possible vehicles for taking up the Eighth Amendment issue. Branch and Jackson had not murdered anyone, and Furman had killed entirely by accident. Aikens, though, was what one Inc. Fund lawyer called a "monster," and the Supreme Court's procedures meant that his name would head the announcement of the Court's decision. For the justices to focus their thinking on the facts of Aikens's case would make winning the argument that much more difficult. And even if the Eighth Amendment challenge succeeded, the public relations effect of allowing Aikens to escape execution was likely to be disastrous.

The California Supreme Court came to the rescue. In 1968 that court had rejected a constitutional challenge to the death penalty in a case involving Robert Anderson. It sent his case back for a new trial, though, finding a violation of the *Witherspoon* rule. Anderson was convicted and again sentenced to death. The California Supreme Court decided to reconsider its earlier decision. This time, relying solely on the state constitution, it found the death penalty unconstitutional. That meant that Aikens no longer faced a death sentence, and the U.S. Supreme Court dismissed his case. (California's voters later amended the state constitution to permit capital punishment; the state's first execution under the new provision took place in 1992.)

When the Court decided to take up the Eighth Amendment challenge, only Justice Brennan had clearly taken the position that capital punishment was "cruel and unusual." By the time the cases were argued in January 1972, though, several other justices had suggested to Brennan that they might agree: White said that he was "not sure how he would come out," Douglas indicated that he "had not yet made up his mind," and Marshall showed Brennan a draft opinion finding that the death penalty "served no legitimate purpose and was repugnant to contemporary standards of decency."[25] And when the vote was taken, to Brennan's surprise there were five Justices who found the death penalty unconstitutional. The vote, though, was tentative, and the justices agreed that each would work on an opinion explaining his position.

The opinions issued on June 29, 1972, occupied 233 pages of the official reports. Each justice who found the death penalty unconstitutional wrote a separate opinion; the four dissenters joined each other's opinions. Justices Brennan and Marshall found the death penalty unconstitutional without qualification. Justice Douglas was particularly troubled by selective and discriminatory uses of capital punishment. Justices Stewart and White relied on the infrequency with which the penalty was imposed to justify, in different ways, their conclusion that capital punishment, as practiced in 1972, was unconstitutional.

Justice Brennan's opinion reviewed the background of the Eighth Amendment and the Court's treatment of capital punishment. He endorsed the position taken in *Weems v. United States* that the amendment did not fix in stone any particular list of prohibited punishments and the view in *Trop v. Dulles* that the key was whether a punishment violated "evolving standards of decency." "At bottom," he wrote, the Eighth Amendment "prohibits the infliction of uncivilized and inhuman punishments." Such punishments did not "comport with human dignity." This requirement had several aspects:

- Punishments could not be "degrading." Torture was condemned not simply because it was painful but because it "treat[s] members of the human raced as nonhumans, as objects to be toyed with and discarded."
- Punishments could not be arbitrary.
- "[A] severe punishment must not be unacceptable to contemporary society." This judgment had to be "as objective as possible."
- Punishment "must not be excessive," by which he meant "unnecessary": "If there is a significantly less severe punishment adequate to achieve the purposes for which punishment is inflicted," the punishment was unnecessary and excessive. And for Brennan, these principles were "cumulative" rather than absolute: The Constitution would be violated if the degree to which the punishment was degrading, the randomness with which it was inflicted, the amount of social disapproval, and the amount it promoted the goals of punishment, taken together, were insufficient.

  Applying these principles to the death penalty, Brennan found it "today" a cruel and unusual punishment.

- It was a uniquely severe punishment, "the only punishment that may involve the conscious infliction of physical pain." It was "irrevocable," and it was, "by its very nature, a denial of the executed person's humanity."

- "The outstanding characteristic of our present practice. . .is the infrequency with which we resort to" capital punishment. With only 50 executions a year, "the inference is strong that the punishment is not being regularly and fairly applied. . .Indeed, it smacks of little more than a lottery system." The states claimed that executions were rare because they reserved death sentences for extreme cases. But, Brennan said, if Furman's crime was extreme, nearly all murders were just as extreme.
- History showed that "this punishment has been almost totally rejected by contemporary society." As Brennan put it, "the likelihood is great that the punishment is tolerated only because of its disuse. . .Rejection could hardly be more complete without becoming absolute." Brennan stressed the "acute public controversy" associated with capital punishment "[f]rom the beginning of our Nation," a "battle. . .waged on moral grounds." The reduction in capital crimes, the elimination of public executions, jury decisions, all showed that "[w]hat was once a common punishment has become, in the context of a continuing moral debate, increasingly rare" and that "our society seriously questions the appropriateness" of capital punishment today.
- Capital punishment did not incapacitate any better than long-term imprisonment. So few executions could hardly deter a significant number of potential criminals: "The risk of death is remote and improbable; in contrast, the risk of long-term imprisonment is near and great." And the "popular demand for grievous condemnation of abhorrent crimes" could be satisfied by imprisonment too: "There is no evidence whatever" that eliminating the death penalty would "encourage[] private blood feuds and other disorders"—consider, Brennan suggested, the enormous number of murders that were not punished by death. Finally, Brennan cast "retribution" as a demand for justice as defined by "certain public beliefs." That allowed him to refer to what he had already said about the infrequency of the death penalty: "The asserted public belief that murderers and rapists deserve to die is flatly inconsistent with the execution of a random few."

Justice Marshall began by noting that the moratorium on executions meant that the Court's decision was "truly a matter of life and death" for over 600 people on death row. After his own review of history and precedent, Marshall too discussed the purposes of punishment. He was more forthright in ruling out "[r]etaliation, vengeance, and retribution" as an acceptable "aspiration for a government in a free society," at least as a justification for a particular punishment; otherwise, he said, "all penalties selected by the legislature would by definition be acceptable means for designating society's moral approbation of a particular act." And against the claim that "morality requires vengeance to evidence society's abhorrence of the act," Marshall set the Eighth Amendment, "our insulation from our baser selves." After reviewing the evidence on deterrence, Marshall concluded that opponents of the death penalty had shown "all that they must"—they had "clear and convincing evidence" that capital punishment was unnecessary.

More starkly than Brennan, Marshall relied on public opinion to explain why capital punishment was "unacceptable to the people of the United States at this time in their history." Public opinion polls, though, were not helpful, because what mattered were the views of "fully informed" people who knew "all information presently available." Marshall believed that the evidence—particularly about deterrence—"would almost surely convince the average citizen that the death penalty was unwise." The desire for retribution, Marshall said, posed a "problem." The "solution," though, was that "no one has ever seriously advanced retribution as a legitimate goal in our society." Rather, defenses of capital punishment "are always mounted on deterrent" theories. Nor, he said, was this surprising. The American people had "injected a sense of purpose in our penology." He could not believe "that at this stage in our history, the American people would ever knowingly support purposeless vengeance." If that were not enough, Marshall continued, surely evidence about the discriminatory infliction of the death penalty—on African-Americans and "the poor, the ignorant, and the underprivileged"—and about the execution of innocent people would make a difference. Finally, Marshall said, when people appreciated how the death penalty "wreaks havoc" on the criminal justice system, they would "find it shocking to [the] conscience and sense of justice."

Marshall ended his opinion by sounding a patriotic theme:

> No nation in the recorded history of man has a greater tradition of revering justice and fair treatment for all its citizens in times of turmoil, confusion, and tension than ours. This is a country which stands tallest in troubled times, a country that clings to fundamental principles, cherishes its constitutional heritage, and rejects simple solutions that compromise the values that lie at the roots of our democratic system.

Ruling against the death penalty, he concluded, "does not malign our system of government." Rather, the Court "pays homage to it," for "[o]nly in a free society could right triumph in difficult times."

Brennan and Marshall found that "standards of decency" had "evolved" to the point where capital punishment was always unconstitutional. Douglas's position was somewhat different. For him the difficulty arose from *McGautha,* which held that states did not have to provide standards for administering capital punishment. As long as that holding stood, death sentences were "imposed under a procedure that gives room for the play of. . .prejudices." As a result, death sentences were handed down "selectively to minorities. . .who are unpopular, but whom society is willing to see suffer though it would not countenance general application of the same penalty across the board." The cases before the Court illustrated the risks: All three defendants were African-American, two were moderately mentally disabled. The Eighth Amendment, Douglas believed, "require[d] legislatures to write penal laws that are even-handed, nonselective[], and nonarbitrary" and required judges to assure that such laws were administered even-handedly. Douglas suggested that mandatory death penalty statutes might be constitutional; he did not consider whether his objections would be satisfied if a state legislature actually tried to write the guidelines that *McGautha* said were not required.

Justices Stewart and White also emphasized, in their own ways, the equality theme. Although he thought that Brennan and Marshall stated a "strong" case against capital punishment, Stewart thought it unnecessary to go that far. Mandatory death penalty statutes posed the problem. They could be defended on retributive grounds. And, Stewart said, the "instinct for retribution" was so deep-seated that legislatures could try to "channel" it: "When people begin to believe that organized society is unwilling or unable to impose upon criminal offenders the punishment they 'deserve,' then there are sown the seeds of anarchy—of self-help, vigilante justice, and lynch law."

But, Stewart continued, "death sentences are cruel and unusual in the same way that being struck by lightning is cruel and unusual." Only a "capriciously random handful" of those who commit equally heinous crimes received death sentences. Stewart said that the Constitution "cannot tolerate the infliction of a sentence of death under legal systems that permit this unique penalty to be so wantonly and freakishly imposed."

Justice White's opinion turned on how infrequently death sentences actually were handed down. When they were so rare, he suggested, no "existing general need for retribution would be measurably satisfied" nor would "community values" be "measurably reinforced by authorizing a penalty so rarely invoked." And deterrence was unlikely "where the penalty is so seldom invoked that it ceases to be a credible threat essential to influence the conduct of others." Because a rarely imposed penalty did nothing to promote the purposes of punishment, it led to the "pointless and needless extinction of life." His experience as a judge led him to conclude that "the death penalty is exacted with great infrequency even for the most atrocious crimes and that there is no meaningful basis for distinguishing the few cases in which it is imposed from the many cases in which it is not." For White, then, the problem was that not enough people received death sentences. If the numbers increased or if a legislature identified a specific group that deserved death and juries imposed it on a large proportion of people in that group, his objections to the death penalty would disappear.

Justice Blackmun's dissent opened by saying that the death penalty cases "provide for me an excruciating agony of the spirit." He "abhorre[d]" the death penalty, he wrote, "with all its aspects of physical distress and fear and of moral judgment exercised by finite minds." As he saw it, it "serves no useful purpose that can be demonstrated" and "violates childhood's training and life's experiences." It was "antagonistic to any sense of 'reverence for life,'" and, "[w]ere I a legislator, I would vote against the death penalty. . ." But, he said, he was not; he was a judge, and as a judge he could not "allow [his] personal preferences as to the wisdom of legislative and congressional action. . .guide our judicial decision in cases such as these." He chided his colleagues in the majority for "suddenly"—in the year that had passed since *McGautha*—perceiving that "the passage of time has taken us to a place of greater maturity and outlook." And if Justices Stewart and White were suggesting that mandatory death penalty statutes would be acceptable, surely, Blackmun said, that "encourages legislation that is regressive and of an antique mold."

Chief Justice Burger sounded similar themes, saying that as a legislator he might vote to abolish the death penalty or restrict it "to a small category of the most heinous crimes." Like Blackmun, though, he thought it essential to avoid "enact[ing] our personal predilections into law." For him, "[t]here are no obvious indications that capital punishment offends the conscience of society to such a degree that our traditional deference to the legislative judgment must be abandoned." Legislatures had recently adopted death penalty laws, and public opinion polls did not show anything "approximating the universal condemnation. . .that might lead us to suspect that the legislatures in general have lost touch with current social values." That juries rarely imposed death sentences simply showed that they were "increasingly meticulous." At several places, Burger used the opinions of Justices Stewart and White to provide a road map for legislatures to follow in attempting to reinstitute capital punishment: They could provide standards or narrowly define capital offenses, which, Burger noted, "cannot be detrimental"; or they could use mandatory death sentences, an alternative he found distasteful.

Justice Rehnquist's dissent dealt almost exclusively with the question of judicial deference to legislative judgments. He criticized the majority for being "beguile[d]. . .into imposing their own views of goodness, truth, and justice upon others." That was, he argued, inconsistent with the democratic premises of the Constitution. Invalidating statutes "impose[s] upon the Nation the judicial fiat of a majority of a court of judges whose connection with the popular will is remote at best." The decision to invalidate the death penalty was "not an act of judgment, but rather an act of will."

Justice Powell's dissent was the most elaborate. Still in his first year on the Court, he regarded it as the most important opinion he had yet worked on, and for a long time, he held on to the hope that his opinion might persuade someone to switch his vote. Acknowledging that he should consider "evolving standards of decency," Justice Powell objected that the majority, relying on its "personal preference[s]," was "saying, in effect. . .that the evolutionary process has come suddenly to an end. . ." He thought that the "objective" grounds for determining evolving standards of decency were not nearly enough to invalidate capital punishment: States continued to enact death penalty laws, voters approved capital punishment in referenda, juries returned death sentences at a "relatively constant" rate. Turning to the basis of punishment, Justice Powell found retribution a permissible, although somewhat "unworthy," justification and concluded that the evidence on deterrence, "a more appealing justification," was insufficient to allow courts to override legislatures that thought capital punishment did deter.

Justice Powell found the argument that death sentences were imposed on the poor and underprivileged "more troubling" but ultimately rejected it because of the "quicksands" it involved. After all, he said, the "have-nots" were, as "a tragic byproduct of social and economic deprivation," more likely to commit crimes, and "[t]he same discriminatory impact argument could be made with equal force and logic with respect to those sentenced to prison terms."

Finally, Justice Powell took up the question of allowing the death penalty for rape. He said that the death penalty was not "*grossly* excessive, [or] *greatly* disproportionate" to the crime: Rape was "widely viewed as the most atrocious of intrusions upon the privacy and dignity of the victim; never is the crime committed accidentally; rarely can it be said to be unpremeditated; often the victim suffers serious physical injury; [and] the psychological impact can often be as great as the physical consequences." Nor did he believe that courts could allow death sentences only in rapes where "the victim's life is endangered": The risk of serious injury was ever-present, as Jackson's use of a scissors and Branch's rape of a vulnerable older woman showed. He conceded that, in "specific" cases, a death sentence might be imposed "for a crime technically falling within the legislatively defined class but factually falling outside the likely legislative intent in creating the category." But that approach could not justify the invalidation of the death penalty across-the-board.

With *Furman,* the Inc. Fund's campaign against the death penalty appeared to have reached a successful—and, in the light of the Court's decisions in *Maxwell* and *McGautha,* surprising—conclusion. True, Justices Stewart and White appeared to suggest that some new death penalty statutes might be upheld. Their opinions, though, focused on statutes that would require juries to impose the death sentence. Death penalty opponents could reasonably believe that the public would indeed reject mandatory death penalties as incompatible with its values. The Court, it might have seemed, had abolished the death penalty.

3

The Modern Death Penalty

Perhaps the five justices in the *Furman* majority believed that they had effectively ended capital punishment. Public opinion surveys indicated that their decision might be in tune with what a majority of the country in 1972 believed. And though they had not outlawed capital punishment directly, they might have thought that states would find it impossible to eliminate the arbitrariness that infected capital punishment. Chief Justice Burger reportedly agreed, saying, "There will never be another execution in this country."[1]

Dissenting in the McGautha case involving standards, Justice Brennan had said that the majority's position appeared to "rest[] upon nothing more solid than its inability to imagine any regime of capital sentencing other than that which presently exists." In rejecting existing systems, the *Furman* majority may have suffered from a similar failure of imagination—leading not to Harlan's pessimism that nothing could be done to salvage capital punishment but to an abolitionist's optimism that only abolition could eliminate the problems the *Furman* majority identified.

If that is what the majority believed in 1972, they turned out to be wrong. *Furman* put the issue of capital punishment on the political agenda—and not in the concrete form of asking whether this particular murderer should be executed (a form that invites ambivalent answers) but in the abstract form of asking whether someone, sometime could be executed for some as-yet-unknown crime (a form that invites unqualified answers). The American people, according to the legislators they elected, wanted the death penalty.

Then the membership of the Supreme Court changed. Justice Douglas suffered a severe stroke in 1975 and retired. President Gerald Ford appointed John Paul Stevens, an antitrust lawyer and court of appeals judge, to replace Douglas. When Potter Stewart retired in 1981, President Ronald Reagan appointed Sandra Day O'Connor, the first woman to serve on the Supreme Court. The transformation of the Supreme Court continued with the appointments of Justices Antonin Scalia (1986), Anthony Kennedy (1988), David Souter (1990), and Clarence Thomas (1991). Each new justice was less sympathetic to challenges to the death penalty than the justice he or she replaced. As early as 1976, only four years after

Furman, the reconstituted Supreme Court was willing to revalidate the death penalty. The path it chose, however, has meant that the Court continues to have death penalty cases on its agenda.

Reestablishing the Death Penalty

Furman itself provided the reasons why the death penalty might be reestablished. Although two justices would have banned it completely, the other three Justices who invalidated it argued that it was unconstitutional only because it was administered "freakishly," as Justice Stewart put it. Supporters of capital punishment began to work on death penalty statutes that might eliminate this objection.

A statute might eliminate arbitrariness in two ways. The legislature might require that a death sentence be imposed on everyone convicted of murder, or of murder under some circumstances. By the time *Furman* was decided, only one state had a mandatory death penalty statute (Rhode Island, for murder by a prisoner serving a life term). American society apparently regarded such sentences as unjustified. Yet put to the choice between no death sentences and mandatory death sentences, some states chose the latter. Or following the path the Court rejected in *McGautha,* it might try to give juries and judges clear guidance about when they could impose a death sentence.

In 1976, according to Bob Woodward and Scott Armstrong, the justices carefully selected five cases to deal with the new death penalty statutes.[2] Two involved mandatory death penalty statutes: North Carolina's, which required the death sentence for all premeditated murders or murders committed during another felony (like robbery), and Louisiana's, which required the death sentence for first-degree murder but allowed jurors to authorize a life sentence by finding the defendant guilty of second-degree murder. The other three offered variants on systems aimed at reducing the randomness in imposing death penalties that had led Justice Stewart to find capital punishment unconstitutional in 1972. Each statute listed specific "aggravating circumstances" that a jury had to find before it authorized a death sentence. The statutes appeared to allow juries to take various "mitigating circumstances" into account as well, although they differed in how clear they were about that. Florida's statute was the most explicit, and Texas's statute simply asked the jury to consider whether the defendant might commit future violent crimes.

How would the Court respond to the new statutes? Before the Court heard the cases, Justice Powell believed that the Court would strike down the death penalty completely, but Justice Brennan was convinced that Justice White would uphold mandatory death penalty statutes and that Justice Stevens would also find the new statutes constitutional.

Justice Brennan was right. At the Court's initial vote, only Justices Brennan and Marshall said that the death penalty was always unconstitutional. The other justices, though, divided on what to do with the new statutes. Chief Justice Burger and Justices White and Rehnquist would have upheld them all. Justice White's position was the most interesting, because he had voted in *Furman* to invalidate the death penalty. There, though, he said that the death penalty was applied so infrequently as to belie the claim that society wanted to impose it. When states adopted mandatory death penalty statutes, Justice White believed, it showed their determination to carry through on their commitment. Yale law professor Professor Robert Burt says that "White's position in these cases is reminiscent of the attitude expressed in some quarters about American military policy during the Vietnam War—that if we were truly engaged in war then we should be prepared to use every weapon at our disposal, but if we had no real taste for warfare then we should abandon the enterprise."[3]

Justices Stewart and Powell were most troubled by the mandatory death penalty statutes, but they wanted to uphold the statutes with guidelines for jurors to decide when to impose a death sentence. Initially Justices Powell and Blackmun voted to uphold the Louisiana mandatory death penalty but were unsure about North Carolina's, where Justice Blackmun was troubled by the five-fold increase in the number of capital sentences under the mandatory system. Justice Stevens thought that mandatory death sentences were "lawless" and "monstr[ous]."

After this initial vote, Chief Justice Burger, who believed that a majority had voted to uphold all the statutes, told Justice White to write opinions in all five cases. Justices Powell and Stevens, though, were puzzled: They thought that five justices had voted to strike down North Carolina's statute. After a meeting with Justice Stewart, Justices Powell, Stevens, and Stewart—who, Woodward and Armstrong say, came to be called the "troika"—decided to work out an opinion that might deal with all five statutes. Justice White reacted to this development by turning his opinions into plurality opinions (opinions stating the Court's result but expressing the views of less than a majority of the Court), for him, Justice Rehnquist, and Chief Justice Burger. The Court met to reassign the cases, but there still was no majority for a unified approach to all five cases.

By this time, the Court was running out of time. Opinions had to be prepared in time to let the Court adjourn for the summer.

The troika met to divide up the work on their new, as-yet-unspecified approach. They had the most difficulty with the mandatory death penalty statutes, which had precipitated the division from Justice White. The difficulty was that the troika accepted the proposition, crucial to Justice Stewart's position in 1972, that the real problem with death penalty statutes was that death sentences were imposed randomly. A mandatory statute, though, was certainly not susceptible to that charge. Justice Stewart persuaded his colleagues in the troika that a mandatory death penalty was arbitrary because it treated different cases the same: Not all murders were equally heinous, and not all murderers deserved death sentences, and yet mandatory statutes lumped everyone together.

That still left a problem with the other statutes. By emphasizing that each murder might be unique, the troika might be reopening the way to arbitrary decisions. They found the solution in emphasizing that, as they understood the statutes before them, juries were allowed to consider aggravating and mitigating circumstances in a way that "structured" or "guided" their actions. Here the difficulty was precedent: *McGautha* had held that guidelines for imposing the death sentence were not constitutionally required, and yet saying that the "guided discretion" statutes were constitutional only because of the guidance appeared to mean that guidelines *were* required in any constitutional death penalty system.

Mandatory Death Sentences

The Court rejected mandatory death sentences, in its opinion dealing with North Carolina's statute, which covered every first-degree (that is, premeditated) murder. Justices Stewart, Powell, and Stevens found that mandatory death sentences were inconsistent with the evolving standards of decency that the Court enforced under the Eighth Amendment.[4] Reviewing history, the troika found that mandatory death sentences often led juries to acquit guilty defendants and that gradually the nation had come to prefer sentencing systems giving juries and judges discretion about the sentence to impose. And, they added, any constitutionally acceptable death penalty system had to allow "particularized consideration" of the character and record of every defendant. The circumstances of crimes and the characters of criminals varied so much that it would be inhumane, the Court concluded, to execute everyone convicted of first-degree murder.

Louisiana's statute was somewhat narrower than North Carolina's—it required death sentences, not in all murder cases, but only in five categories of murders (like murder during the commission of a felony such as armed robbery) where the killer had a specific intent to kill—but the same justices found it unacceptable.[5] As they viewed history, attempts to define narrow categories of cases where a death penalty was required had failed the test of time. And of course, no mandatory death penalty statute could allow individualized consideration of the killer's character.

The Court's emphasis on individual character suggested that, although it might not reject retribution outright as a reason for punishment, retribution alone could not justify a death sentence; scholars usually say that retribution focuses on the crime, not on the character of the criminal. What about deterrence? The troika noted in the North Carolina case that the case did not involve a mandatory death penalty for "an extremely narrow category of homicide, such as murder by a prisoner serving a life sentence." The deterrence argument in such cases is much stronger than it is in the run of murder cases: After all, what threat other than capital punishment can the state hold over the head of prisoners already facing life imprisonment?

The Court faced this issue in *Sumner v. Shuman*.[6] From 1973 to 1977, Nevada had a mandatory death sentence statute applicable to murders committed by prisoners under life sentence.[7] The Court said that, even in these circumstances, a death sentence was not always an "appropriate sanction." Justice Blackmun, who wrote the Court's opinion, said that "the level of involvement of an inmate in a violent prison incident" could vary and he might kill someone in circumstances where a jury or judge might believe it wrong to impose a death sentence. And again, the killer's character ought to be relevant: Justice Blackmun pointed out that Shuman, serving a life sentence for murder, had not been the triggerman in *that* crime and might have had a good record during the fifteen years he had already served. Finally, Justice Blackmun said that mandatory death sentences were not necessary for deterrence because Nevada still could get a death sentence under its nonmandatory death penalty statute: "Those who deserve to die. . .will be condemned to death under such a statute."

(After the troika had been reduced to Justice Stevens by the retirements of Justices Stewart and Powell, the awkwardness of their argument against mandatory death penalties came home. Justice Stewart had argued against mandatory death penalties that not all aggravated homicides were equally aggravated. Pennsylvania's death penalty statute put that argument to the test in 1990. Scott Blystone was driving with his girlfriend and another couple when he saw Dalton Smithburger trying to hitch a ride.[8] Blystone announced that he was going to pick Smithburger up and rob him. After

Smithburger got in the car, Blystone pulled out a revolver and ordered Smithburger to go into a nearby field. Once there, Blystone took Smithburger's money and told him to lie face down without moving. Blystone went back to the car, where he told his friends that he was going to kill Smithburger. Blystone returned to the field, where Smithburger had remained, "paralyzed by fear." When Smithburger responded to a question by accurately describing Blystone's car, Blystone shot him six times in the head.

Blystone's jury found one aggravating circumstance, that the murder had been committed during a robbery, and no mitigating ones. The Pennsylvania death penalty statute says that, under these circumstances, "the verdict must be a sentence of death." Blystone argued that this was simply a mandatory death penalty statute, restricted not by the definition of the crime, as in *Shuman*, but by the automatic weight it gave to the aggravating circumstance. Chief Justice Rehnquist, for the Court, disagreed. The problem with mandatory death penalty statutes, he wrote, was that they barred juries from considering mitigating circumstances. Pennsylvania juries could have considered such evidence, and it was simply a matter of chance that Blystone did not present any; his death sentence was therefore not infected by the vice of mandatory death penalty statutes.

Justice Stevens joined Justice Brennan's dissent, which pointed out that the troika's argument against mandatory death penalty statutes was that not all aggravated murders were alike and that mandatory death penalty statutes did not allow juries to give varying weight to *aggravating* circumstances. In a case like Blystone's, where there was no mitigating evidence, Pennsylvania's statute did suffer from *that* vice—the jury could not refuse to impose the death penalty even if it believed that the aggravating circumstances it found were not serious enough to justify the penalty.)

"Guided Discretion" Statutes

With mandatory death penalties—at least of a certain type—ruled out, the states were left with their efforts to guide the discretion of judges and juries in death penalty cases. The Court upheld such statutes. *Gregg v. Georgia* was the lead case. Capital trials in Georgia had two steps. First the jury would consider whether the defendant committed murder. Then the same jury moved to the penalty phase, where it had to find that the murder was accompanied by one of ten listed aggravating circumstances, and then considered whether there were mitigating circumstances.

In voting to uphold the Georgia statute, Justice Blackmun simply cited his dissenting opinions in the 1972 cases. Justice White wrote for himself, Chief Justice Burger, and Justice Rehnquist. For them, by identifying aggravating circumstances, the Georgia legislature had substantially reduced the risk that the death penalty would be imposed freakishly:

> As the types of murders for which the death penalty may be imposed become more narrowly defined and are limited to those which are particularly serious. . .it becomes reasonable to expect that juries—even given discretion *not* to impose the death penalty—will impose the death penalty in a substantial portion of the cases so defined.

If so, Justice White concluded, the penalty would *not* be imposed wantonly or freakishly. But, he continued, the Georgia legislature went further to insure that the system would not operate arbitrarily by requiring appellate review of death sentences to see if the sentence in a particular case was consistent with the penalties imposed in similar cases.

The analysis of the troika (Justices Powell, Stevens, and Stewart) was more complicated. Justice White's opinion appeared to say that the Constitution would be satisfied if a death penalty statute insured that quite a few defendants would receive a death sentence, as his endorsement of mandatory death penalty statutes showed. The troika, in contrast, emphasized the role of mitigating circumstances in *reducing* the possibility of arbitrary jury decisions.

The troika's opinion began by conclusively rejecting a position nominally left open in 1972: whether capital punishment was itself unconstitutional under all circumstances. Invoking the idea of majority rule, it placed "a heavy burden on those who would attack the judgment of the representatives of the people." That was especially true because the Court's Eighth Amendment cases showed that "contemporary standards" played a central role, and "legislative judgment weighs heavily in ascertaining such standards." In 1972 the Court had been asked to find that "standards of decency had evolved to the point where capital punishment could no longer be tolerated," and it had refused to do so. "Developments" since then, particularly the renewed public desire for capital punishment reflected in legislative action in thirty-five states, had "undercut substantially" that argument.

Of course, the troika's opinion continued, the Eighth Amendment required "more than that a challenged punishment be acceptable to contemporary society." It also had to "comport. . .with the basic concept of human dignity at the core of the [Eighth] Amendment." The death penalty, the troika continued, might serve retributive and deterrent purposes. "[M]oral outrage at particularly offensive conduct"—as the troika described retribution—"may be unappealing to many," but it was a permissible basis for punishment. Quoting Justice Stewart's opinion in the 1972 cases, the troika said that "the instinct for retribution is part of the nature of man, and channeling that instinct. . .serves an important purpose in promoting the stability of a society governed by law." And for the troika, the fact that the evidence about deterrence was "inconclusive" showed only that it was "a complex factual issue the resolution of which properly rests with the legislatures, which can evaluate the results of statistical studies in terms of their own local conditions and with a flexibility of approach that is not available to the courts." Finally, when imposed for murder, the death penalty was not "invariably disproportionate to the crime."

The next section of the troika's opinion found that Georgia's "guided discretion" statute met the objections that had led to the 1972 decisions: Under it, "discretion [was] suitably directed and limited so as to minimize the risk of wholly arbitrary and capricious action." By dividing the trial into a guilt and a penalty phase, Georgia ensured that the jury would have all relevant information. And by enumerating aggravating circumstances, the statute helped guide the jury's decision and "thereby reduce[d] the likelihood that it will impose a sentence that fairly can be called capricious or arbitrary." The opinion clearly endorsed bifurcated trials and standards guiding jury decisions, although it noted that other systems might be acceptable. The tension with the *McGautha* decision was apparent. *McGautha* refused to require standards in large part because specifying the circumstances under which death was an appropriate penalty was impossible; the troika now thought that standards were *necessary* to make the death penalty acceptable.

Georgia's statute being considered in *Gregg* satisfied the troika's requirements. "No longer can a Georgia jury. . .reach a finding of the defendant's guilt and then, without guidance or direction, decide whether he should live or die." Rather, its "attention is directed to the specific circumstances of the crime"—was it committed for money? was the victim a police officer?—and to "the characteristics of the person who committed the crime"—did he have a prior record? are there "any special facts such as the defendant's youth" or "emotional state at the time of the crime" that mitigate against a death sentence?

The troika then rejected the argument that these changes were "only cosmetic" because arbitrary decisions could still occur. The main challenge was that the statute guided only the discretion of the jury. It said nothing about prosecutors, who could decide who to charge with capital crimes and who to make plea bargains with. And the governor might pardon people too, making it arbitrary who among those sentenced to death actually would be executed. The troika described this as an objection to the possibility that various other actors would exercise mercy and gave it no weight. Like Justice White, the troika also thought appellate review important in "substantially eliminating the possibility that a person will be sentenced to die by the action of an aberrant jury."

Although Justice Brennan dissented, restating the objections to capital punishment he had made in 1972, Justice Marshall's dissent was more focused on the troika's analysis of guided discretion. "I would be less than candid," Marshall wrote, "if I did not acknowledge that these developments [since 1972] have a significant bearing on a realistic assessment of the moral acceptability of the death penalty to the American people." But, he said, he believed that what mattered were "informed" views. In addition, he argued, the reenactment of death penalty statutes had no bearing on the separate question of whether the death penalty was excessive. For him, there was nothing that undermined his earlier conclusion that the opponents of the death penalty had provided enough evidence to show that it was not a distinctively effective deterrent.

He also dismissed the troika's discussion of retribution, calling it "the most disturbing aspect" of the 1976 decisions. Marshall called the argument that the death penalty was needed to avoid lynch law and vigilante justice "wholly inadequate to justify the death penalty," whatever its merits as an argument for the existence of some system of criminal punishment, because "it simply defies belief to suggest that the death penalty is necessary to prevent the American people from taking the law into their own hands." Nor was it necessary to impose the death penalty to signal society's retributive disapproval of the underlying crimes. Finally, there was the purely retributive argument, "that the death penalty is appropriate, not because of its beneficial effect on society, but because the taking of the murderer's life is itself morally good." The purely retributive argument, though, was "fundamentally at odds with the Eighth Amendment. . .[T]he taking of life 'because the wrongdoer deserves it' surely must fail, for such a punishment has as its very basis the total denial of the wrongdoer's dignity and worth." The opinion hinted at another argument as well, that the very fact that none of the justices accepting the constitutionality of the death penalty openly offered the purely retributive argument suggested that no one actually believed it.

The Court also had to deal with revised capital punishment statutes from Florida and Texas. The Florida statute was easy, because it was not significantly different from Georgia's. Capital cases had bifurcated trials, and the statute listed aggravating circumstances. In addition, the Florida statue listed mitigating circumstances, which caused difficulties later but which did not seem important in 1976.

Texas's statute appeared to be different in important ways. Although it too listed aggravating circumstances, it dealt with mitigating circumstances in an apparently more restricted way than either Georgia or Florida. In Georgia the jury clearly could consider any mitigating evidence, and in Florida the statute listed seven mitigating circumstances that appeared to cover a fairly broad range of possibilities. In Texas, though, after a jury found a defendant guilty of a capital offense, it was asked three questions. The first was whether the defendant committed the crime deliberately and with the reasonable expectation that death would result, and the third was whether the defendant's action in killing the victim was an unreasonable response to provocation by the victim. The third question arose in few cases; the first question simply asked whether the murder was deliberate and would be answered yes in almost any case where the jury found the defendant guilty. Texas's second question was "whether there is a probability that the defendant would commit criminal acts of violence that would constitute a continuing threat to society." On its face, that question is forward-looking and might not allow a jury to consider factors like the defendant's mental capacity when he killed or the circumstances of his upbringing that might explain and perhaps mitigate the killing. The troika upheld the Texas system, though, after concluding that the Texas courts had interpreted the second question to allow jurors to rely on "whatever evidence of mitigating circumstances the defense can bring before it."[9] On that assumption, the troika found that the Texas statute was just like the Georgia one.

Who Decides? Juries and Judges in Capital Cases

The Court rested its revalidation of the death penalty in part on the ground that the new death penalty statutes reflected society's willingness to impose the death penalty. Another aspect of that willingness, of course, was the fact that some states wanted to impose the death penalty in *particular* cases. Not just the statutes but also the sentences imposed reflected social desires.

In criminal cases, the jury usually is taken to represent society as a whole. When juries impose death sentences, then, the

Court could be as confident as it needed to be in finding that the sentence reflected a particularized social judgment that death was an appropriate penalty for the crime. The Court repeatedly has confronted cases where defendants claimed that the Court should not be so confident.

The problem has arisen in several settings. First, after juries find aggravating circumstances, they have to weigh whatever mitigating circumstances there are to decide whether to impose or recommend a death sentence. Suppose, though, that some jurors believe that the defendant's youth weighs *against* the death penalty but others believe that it is irrelevant or even counts *in favor* of a death sentence (perhaps because they believe that the defendant is likely to commit more crimes before he matures). Do the jurors have to agree on what counts as a mitigating circumstance before they can get into the weighing process? Second, every conviction can be appealed, and the judges who hear the appeals can inject their own perspectives on appropriate punishment. What is the significance of the judicial role in appeals? Third, in some states, juries only recommend punishment, and sometimes judges reject a jury recommendation of a life sentence in favor of their own determination that a death penalty is appropriate. Should that be allowed?

Juries *Mills v. Maryland* (1988) raised the first question, whether jurors have to agree on the same mitigating circumstances.[10] Mills killed his cell mate and was convicted of murder with the aggravating circumstance that he was confined in prison when he committed murder. Mills's attorney used Mills's youth, mental infirmity, and lack of future threat as reasons to weigh against the death penalty. The jury received a form that had a checklist of mitigating circumstances, and they were told to mark yes or no next to each item. According to the Supreme Court, though, the instructions about the checklist were confusing. As the Court read the instructions, they told jurors that they could mark yes only if they *all* agreed that the circumstance was present. The Court held that the state could not require juries to be unanimous as to each mitigating circumstance before they could weigh it. Justice Blackmun pointed out that requiring unanimity as to particular circumstances might mean that *all twelve* jurors might believe that there were mitigating circumstances—two each finding a different one—and *all twelve* might believe that the circumstance each found was enough to rule out the death penalty, and yet—because the jurors could not unanimously agree that any *one* circumstance existed—they would have to check no beside each item on the checklist, and the defendant would get a death sentence that *no* juror believed appropriate.

No one on the Court disagreed with that argument, but the Court was divided five-to-four nonetheless for reasons that have a broader significance. The dissenters argued that the instructions really did not tell the jurors that they had to be unanimous about particular mitigating circumstances. It is clear that a juror *could* have taken the instructions to require that sort of unanimity, and it is equally clear that a juror did not have to take them that way. The question that divided the Court was how courts should determine whether jurors understood the instructions. A lot of what the Court has had to say about this turns on verbal hair-splitting. The dissenters said that a reviewing court should ask: Could a reasonable juror have understood that the instructions did not require unanimity? The majority said that it should ask a different question: Was there a substantial probability that a reasonable juror might have thought that it did? The very fact that the standards differ far more in tone than in substance means that judges reviewing death sentences have a fair amount of discretion to affirm or reject the sentences. That at least makes it possible that the arbitrariness the Court worried about in 1972 can return through the back door.

Appeals courts The second problem is a more general version of the difficulty with appellate review of jury instructions; it is tied to the role of judges in the death penalty process. When judges get into the process, several problems arise. Sometimes prosecutors are more confident that a judge will go along with a death sentence that a jury recommends than they are confident that the jury will recommend the death penalty in the first place. They are then tempted to try to get the jury to think that its role is not all that important. They will tell the jury that its decision is not final, that anything they do will be reviewed by several judges, and the like. In one case that reached the Supreme Court, the prosecutor responded to a defense argument that the defendant "has a life that rests in your hands" by saying that "the decision you render is automatically reviewable by the Supreme Court."[11] As the Court said, these arguments are designed to reduce the jury's sense of responsibility for the death recommendation. The Court told prosecutors that death sentences obtained after they make these "reduction in responsibility" arguments will be vacated, because they mislead the jury about the significance of their decision. Even so, prosecutors often walk close to the line.[12]

Appeals courts do have a role in capital sentencing, though. The Court has struggled with what to do but now appears to have settled on a rather elaborate scheme. Recall that a typical problem in death penalty cases is that juries are told that they can find an aggravating circumstance if they conclude that the murder was particularly "heinous." That term, though, is vague and does not channel the jury's discretion. Suppose a jury finds two aggravating circumstances. For example, consider *Maynard v. Cartwright.*[13] Cartwright had been fired by Hugh Riddle. One evening Cartwright broke into the Riddle home and shot Mrs. Riddle twice. He then killed her husband. Mrs. Riddle crawled to her bedroom and tried to use the phone, but Cartwright came in, slit her throat and stabbed her twice. Mrs. Riddle survived and identified Cartwright as her husband's killer. The jury found that the crime was "especially heinous" and that Cartwright had "knowingly created a great risk of death to more than one person." The problem was that the "heinousness" aggravating circumstance was unconstitutionally vague. What, though, should the Court do with the "risk to several people" circumstance?

There are two possibilities. First, the Court could say that the jury weighed the mitigating circumstances against the aggravating ones. With one aggravating circumstance knocked out, we cannot tell how the jury would have done the weighing. So the death sentence has to be vacated and a new jury given a chance to decide whether the mitigating circumstances outweigh the single aggravating circumstance that remains. Second, the Court could say, as it did in the Blystone case, that all that matters is that the jury found one permissible aggravating circumstance. After that, the only question is whether the appeals court reweighed the mitigating and aggravating circumstances and decided that, even if one aggravating circumstance was knocked out, the death penalty was appropriate.

The Court has said that states can choose between these two methods.[14] (In *Maynard* the Court found that the state had chosen the first method, and sent the case back for a new jury to decide the punishment.) If they want to rely heavily on juries to do the weighing, they may get a more accurate sense of what the state's citizens believe appropriate in particular cases. If juries get mistaken instructions, though, states that rely on juries run the risk that death penalties will have to be vacated. They can protect against that by saying that a jury simply has to find one permissible aggravating circumstance; after the jury does that, the aggravating circumstances simply drop out of the jury's consideration, and all it does is decide whether death is an appropriate penalty in light of whatever mitigating information it has received. (Or, the question of balancing aggravating and mitigating circumstances is left to the judges.) But in protecting capital sentences in that way, states run two risks: Juries, without guidance about what to do with mitigating circumstances, may become arbitrary again (although the Court did find that the risk of arbitrariness was not great enough to make such systems unconstitutional), and judges might get out of line with what the state's citizens really believe.

Justice Marshall pointed out the first problem when the Court upheld Georgia's system in which, once a jury finds a single aggravating circumstance, it is left to decide what to do. Marshall said that this left the jury with no guidance whatever. "[T]he jurors can be left completely at large, with nothing to guide them but their whims and prejudices." That, he argued, "makes an absolute mockery" of the requirement of "guided discretion."

Trial Judges Florida's unusual death penalty system runs the second risk. In most states—30 out of 37 with a death penalty—juries impose the penalties. Four states—Arizona, Idaho, Montana, and Nebraska—leave sentencing entirely to the judge. In Florida, Alabama, and Indiana, juries make an initial recommendation, but even if a jury recommends a life sentence, the judge can override that recommendation and sentence the defendant to death. The state supreme court has said, though, that a judge can reject a life sentence recommendation only if the judge believes that "no reasonable person could impose" anything less than death.

The defendant in *Spaziano v. Florida* was convicted of murdering two women whose bodies he left in a garbage dump.[15] Aside from the bodies, the main evidence against Spaziano was testimony from a drug user who told the jury that Spaziano had taken him to the dump and showed him the bodies. The case gave the jury a lot of trouble; after deliberating for over six hours, it reported a deadlock. The judge told them to try again, and the jury then found Spaziano guilty. Apparently reflecting uncertainty about his guilt, though, the jury recommended a life sentence. The judge overrode that recommendation, relying on a confidential report showing that Spaziano had a substantial criminal record. After further proceedings, the Florida supreme court affirmed the death sentence.

Spaziano argued that, because of the special role of community judgment in death cases, only juries could impose the death penalty. Justices Stevens, Brennan, and Marshall agreed, noting the substantial consensus against Florida's procedure in states that had the death penalty. The statutes reflected, they said, "a strong community feeling that it is only decent and fair to leave the life-or-death decision to the authentic voice of the community—the jury." A majority of the Court disagreed. Referring to the nearly universal practice in which judges sentence defendants in non-capital cases, Justice Blackmun said that the differences between capital and noncapital sentences "are not so clear." There was no reason, he thought, to bar a state from deciding that, in particular cases, a judge would do a better job of assessing retribution and deterrence than the jury.

Justice Stevens's dissent in *Spaziano* argued that juries should sentence because they were "more representative institutions than is the judiciary; they reflect more accurately the composition and experiences of the community as a whole, and inevitably make decisions based on community values more reliably." *Barclay v. Florida* illustrates Justice Stevens's point.[16] Barclay and some friends, calling themselves the "Black Revolutionary Army," drove around Jacksonville until they found a hitchhiker, who they drove to a trash dump and killed. One of Barclay's companions wrote an elaborate and disjointed note, setting out the purportedly political reasons for the murder. The jury convicted Barclay and this companion of murder; it recommended the death penalty for the companion and a life sentence for Barclay. The trial judge overrode the jury's recommendation about Barclay. In doing so, the judge committed a number of errors of state law, but a majority of the Supreme Court held that these errors did not violate the federal Constitution.

Justice Marshall, in dissent, called the trial judge's actions "lawless" and his performance "abysmal." Marshall examined the judge's comments when he overrode the recommendation. The judge said that he relied on his experience as a trial judge to show when a crime deserved the death penalty. But, the trial judge continued,

> my experience with the sordid, tragic and violent side of life has not been confined to the Courtroom. I, like so many American Combat Infantry Soldiers, walked the battlefields of Europe and saw the thousands of dead American and German soldiers and I witnessed the concentration camps where innocent civilians and children were murdered in a war of racial and religious extermination.

He followed that recitation by referring to the "race war" that Barclay and his companions attempted to initiate. He concluded by saying that, "having set forth my personal experiences above, it is understandable that I am not easily shocked or moved by tragedy—but this present murder and call for racial war is especially shocking. . ." This might appear a commendable attempt to explain the basis for the judge's reaction to the facts of the case before him—except that, as Marshall showed, much of the language was, in Marshall's terms, "boilerplate." Whenever this judge imposed a death penalty, he recited his wartime experiences and said that he was not easily shocked. For Marshall, the case "illustrates the capital sentencing process gone awry," and he criticized the state supreme court for "fail[ing] to conduct any meaningful review and instead shower[ing] the trial judge with praise for his performance."

Judicial overrides of jury recommendations of mercy raise special questions because in most states judges have to stand for reelection. Often it may make sense for judges concerned with reelection to show that they are tough on crime by overriding a jury recommendation. For a majority of the Supreme Court, though, neither the risk of jury arbitrariness nor the risk that judges will be politically motivated is enough to invalidate these forms of capital sentencing.

"Guided Discretion" at Work

Over the years following *Gregg* (1976), the Court gradually clarified what it meant by guided discretion. Its definition has two parts. First, the statute must significantly narrow the class of people "eligible," as the Court puts it, for a death sentence. Typically, statutes define murder and then list a number of aggravating or "special circumstances," as they are known in some states, that make a defendant "eligible" for a death sentence. But, as *Shuman*—the case involving a mandatory death penalty for prison murder—shows, it is not enough to narrow the class of death-eligible defendants. The second element in the Court's definition of guided discretion requires that every defendant be allowed to present the jury or judge everything that might mitigate the offense. Mitigating evidence is anything that might indicate that a death penalty would not be justified in this particular defendant's case.

Sometimes it is easy to explain what makes a defendant eligible for a death sentence. For example, in many states, juries are instructed that a defendant is eligible for a death sentence if he commits a murder for hire. Other special circumstances are harder to explain. Most people have images of "ordinary" murders and of "really horrible" murders in their minds, and the Court's emphasis on narrowing the class of defendants eligible for capital punishment strongly suggests that it too wants states to distinguish between ordinary and horrible murders. Yet spelling out the difference is not easy.

In *Godfrey v. Georgia,* after Godfrey's wife left him because he had threatened her with a knife, he killed her and her mother.[17] He had argued with her over reconciliation, and when he was rebuffed, he fired a shotgun through a trailer window at his wife, instantly killing her. He then entered the trailer and deliberately shot his wife's mother, killing her instantly. The Georgia death penalty statute, which had been upheld in *Gregg,* made defendants eligible for capital punishment if they committed murders that were "outrageously or wantonly vile, horrible or inhuman in that [they] involved torture, depravity of mind, or an aggravated battery to a victim." The prosecutor argued that Godfrey's actions showed that he fit into the "depravity of mind" category. The jury was instructed that Godfrey was eligible for a death sentence if the offense was "outrageously or wantonly vile, horrible and inhuman." The Supreme Court held that this instruction was too vague. It did not sufficiently narrow the class of death-eligible defendants. "There is nothing" in the instructions, Justice Stewart wrote, "that implies any inherent restraint on the arbitrary and capricious infliction of the death sentence. A person of ordinary sensibility could fairly characterize almost every murder as 'outrageously or wantonly vile, horrible and inhuman.'"

After *Godfrey,* the Court struggled with the problem it raised. The Court was committed to the view that death-penalty statutes had to narrow the class of death-eligible defendants. So legislatures had to spell out in advance what made a subclass of murders bad enough to warrant a death sentence. Doing that is easy in some cases: torture-murders or murders-for-hire. But, many murders are "bad" crimes yet do not have anything about them that a legislature could identify in advance. That is what Georgia was trying to get at with its category of "outrageous" cases. The Court repeatedly insisted that, although legislatures could use such general terms, state courts had to spell out more precisely what an "outrageous" murder was if a death sentence was to be upheld.[18]

The "guided discretion" decisions have transformed the death penalty process. Under the statutes invalidated in *Furman,* jurors were given essentially no guidance about how to exercise their discretion. They were sometimes puzzled about what to do, but at least they sometimes found it possible to invoke the full range of humanitarian and merciful sentiments they had. Old-fashioned appeals to fear and to the risk that the defendant will kill prison guards persist,[19] but the "guided discretion" statutes make the death penalty process more legalistic. They allow prosecutors to treat the list of mitigating circumstances as a checklist. The instructions will tell the jury that they can consider the full range of mitigating circumstances, but prosecutors present "the case for death in the most lawyerly, legalistic, dispassionate form," which, together with the list in the instructions, may overwhelm the unguided instructions.[20]

In the Blystone case, the prosecutor emphasized that, under Pennsylvania's death penalty statute, the jury had a "duty to impose the death penalty":

> Our law doesn't permit the jury to impose the death penalty or impose a life sentence as they feel it should be, but rather there are certain specific times when the death

> penalty should be imposed and there are certain specific times when it should not be imposed.

Law professor Robert Weisberg provides additional examples from prosecutors' arguments in California: "Ladies and gentlemen, it's not with any great passion that I will argue to you this morning. It's not my purpose or intent to arouse you or cause you to make a decision based on anything other than what is reasonable and what is required under the law and the evidence." The prosecutor reads a list of eleven factors and then "go[es] through them one by one." In arguments that skate near the line drawn by the "reduction in responsibility" decision, prosecutors may say, "It's never easy for someone to ask for another man's life. But your burden is lightened in this case because of the law." As Weisberg puts it, this sort of presentation helps jurors "escape from the anxiety of moral choice."

"Mitigating Circumstances"

Guided discretion statutes aim at making capital punishment less arbitrary, first by narrowing the class of people eligible for death sentences and then by providing guidance to jurors as they consider whether to impose a death sentence on a person who the statutes made eligible for one. Obviously, if mandatory death sentences were impossible, jurors had to be told what they might consider in deciding not to impose a death sentence. Were there limits on what the Court called "mitigating factors"?

In the 1976 cases, the troika indicated that juries had to be able to consider the entire range of mitigating circumstances. In *Lockett v. Ohio,* a majority of the Court accepted that proposition, which has now become settled law.[21] The Ohio death penalty statute resembled Texas's. The sentencing judge was allowed to consider whether the victim induced the murder, whether the defendant was "under duress, coercion, or strong provocation," and whether the murder was "primarily the product of the offender's psychosis or mental deficiency." Chief Justice Burger wrote that this statute, unlike the Texas one, "narrowly limits the sentencer's discretion to consider" the entire range of mitigating factors, such as the full circumstances of the crime and the defendant's record and character.

The Court's approach to mitigating circumstances introduced a number of new difficulties into death penalty law. The first became apparent as the Court continued to wrestle with Texas's death penalty system. The Court had held that the Texas statute, as interpreted by the state courts, allowed the defendant to introduce any mitigating evidence. Yet suppose the judge simply read the three questions to the jurors. Would they understand that the second question—whether there was "a probability" that the defendant would be a continuing threat to society—really allowed them to take all that evidence into account, rather than focusing them on the forward-looking question of future harm? Similarly, the Florida statute listed seven mitigating circumstances. Suppose, though, a defendant asked a jury to consider something that was not on the list. Did Florida allow jurors to consider these nonstatutory mitigating circumstances? Over time the Texas and Florida courts worked out instructions that tried to tell jurors that the second question really did give them a large range in which to exercise their judgment. The Supreme Court, though, sometimes found those instructions inadequate because, no matter how a lawyer or judge might interpret them, they were too likely to let a nonlawyer on the jury think that his or her judgment was quite constrained.[22]

The second difficulty was more fundamental. By allowing juries to consider the full range of mitigating circumstances, the Court reintroduced the possibility that death sentences would again be imposed arbitrarily. Some juries might respond to mitigating circumstances with "sympathy," others would not. The Court struck down the death penalty in 1972 because sentencing judgments were unconstrained and therefore arbitrary, but when juries consider mitigating circumstances, they always exercise judgment. And, in doing so, they might become arbitrary again.

Narrowing the Death Penalty

The Court did not give the states a free hand in defining the situations in which a defendant was eligible for death. After *Gregg,* the Court considered a number of "categorical" challenges to death penalty statutes. In these challenges, defendants argued that under no circumstances could people like them be executed.

Crimes Other than Murder The first categorical challenge came to the Court in 1977 when a defendant convicted of rape and sentenced to death argued that the death penalty was unconstitutionally "excessive" as a punishment for rape (*Coker v. Georgia*).[23] The historical background of capital punishment surely made a difference; African-Americans in the South were sentenced to death for raping white women, but whites were not sentenced to death for raping African-American women. Justice White wrote for a plurality of the Court that the defendant was right. His opinion pointed out that only a minority of states had ever authorized capital punishment for rape and that, when states reviewed their death penalty statutes after *Furman,* only Georgia ended up authorizing capital punishment for rape. Without "discount[ing] the seriousness of rape as a crime," the justices concluded that, "in terms of moral depravity and of the injury to the person and to the public, it does not compare with murder. . .Life is over for the victim of the murderer; for the rape victim, life may not be nearly so happy as it was, but it is not over and normally is not beyond repair."

Since 1977 it has been generally accepted that capital punishment is reserved for people who commit murder; if death is an excessive punishment for rape, it appears hard to come up with a crime other than murder for which it would not be excessive. Treason is a candidate, but the number of treason prosecutions is minuscule. Recently there have been suggestions that "drug kingpins" should be eligible for death sentences; the chances of finding a drug kingpin whose crimes were so heinous, and yet who was not implicated in murder, are so small that this proposal does not really add to the list of crimes for which the death penalty is possible.

Felony Murders People can be involved in murders in many ways. Like Godfrey, they can pull the trigger. Or they can hire others to kill their victims. In these cases, the defendants are involved in a rather direct way, and their responsibility for the deaths is clear. There are, however, another important group of murders where the issue of responsibility is not as clear. These are known as *felony murders.* Suppose two people drive to a convenience store, planning to rob it. One goes into the store with a gun; the other stays in the car, ready to get away as soon as his companion runs out of the store. Inside the store, the robber shoots the clerk. Under the felony murder doctrine, the person in the car can be convicted of murder: He helped plan and carry out an armed robbery—a felony—he knew that his companion had a gun, he knew that there was a high risk that the gun would be used, and a murder occurred during the commission of the felony. Nothing in the Supreme Court's death penalty jurisprudence casts doubt on traditional felony murder rules. So the car driver can be convicted of murder. But can he receive a death sentence?

The Court first addressed this question in *Enmund v. Florida.*[24] Earl Enmund was convicted of felony murder in connection with the killings of two elderly people, Thomas and Eunice Kersey, early on April 1, 1975. He and two friends planned to rob the victims, and Enmund drove to the victims' farmhouse. He parked about 200 yards from the house. His friends went to the farmhouse back door and asked Thomas for some water to cool their overheated car. When Thomas came out, the robbers grabbed him and, pointing a gun at him, demanded his money. He cried for help, and his wife came out of the house with a shotgun. She shot and injured one of the robbers, and the other responded by shooting both Thomas and Eunice. The robbers dragged both bodies back into the house, took their money, and went back to the car in which Enmund was waiting. He drove the group off.

Enmund was convicted of murder because he "actively aid[ed] and abett[ed]" the robbery, during which the murders occurred. This was a standard application of the felony murder rule. But, Enmund argued, nothing in the evidence showed that he "intended to take life," and therefore the death penalty could not be imposed on him. The Supreme Court, in an opinion by Justice White, agreed. As it has done in all the cases involving categorical challenges to the death penalty, the Court surveyed the states authorizing death penalties. Unlike *Coker* and *Shuman,* though, the state here was not the only one authorizing a death sentence for felony murder. The majority opinion examined the statistics closely and concluded that "only a small minority" of states allowed death penalties "solely because the defendant somehow participated in a robbery in the course of which a murder was committed." Instead, most states required that the defendant have some "culpable mental state." The Court also examined practice by juries and prosecutors, which it concluded showed that most considered death "a disproportionate penalty for those who fall within [Enmund's] category."

The Court also said that in deciding whether the death penalty was disproportionate, "the focus must be on [Enmund's] culpability, not on that of those who committed the robbery and shot the victims." Justice White said that it was "impermissible" for the state to treat "the robbers who killed" and Enmund alike by "attribut[ing to him] the culpability of those who killed the Kerseys." And, because the death penalty could deter only those who acted deliberately, "the possibility that the death penalty will be imposed for vicarious felony murder will not 'enter into the cold calculus that precedes the decision to act.'"

Enmund ruled out capital punishment where the defendant had no intent to kill. But, Justice White said, "[I]t would be very different if the likelihood of a killing. . .were so substantial that one should share the blame for the killing if he somehow participated in the felony." That was not true of felony murder in connection with armed robbery, but it might be true in other cases.

Tison v. Arizona showed what the Court meant.[25] Gary Tison was serving a life sentence in an Arizona prison; he had been convicted of murdering a prison guard in escaping from prison. His wife and three sons planned to help him escape again and got a large number of guns ready. Gary insisted that his cell mate Randy Greenawalt be included in the prison break. At the end of July 1978,

Gary's sons came to the prison with an ice chest filled with guns. They gave the guns to their father and Greenawalt, and after locking guards and visitors in a closet, Gary and Greenawalt escaped. The group spent two nights in an isolated house and then started to drive to Flagstaff, Arizona. Their car blew its tire on the desert roads, and they did not have a spare. They decided to steal a car from a passing motorist. When John Lyons stopped his car, the five Tisons and Greenawalt took the car and forced Lyons and the three people in his family traveling with him to go along with them. They drove both the stolen car and the disabled one into the desert. Gary, the father, was clearly in charge of the operation. He told one of his sons to get some water for the Lyons group, but while that was happening, Gary and Greenawalt shot their four victims. The escape continued. A few days later the Tisons and Greenawalt were in a shootout at a police roadblock. One son died; Gary escaped into the desert, where he died of exposure. The police caught the two remaining Tison brothers and Greenawalt and prosecuted them for murder.

According to Justice Brennan, the escape and murders raised a huge cry for justice in Arizona. Obviously Greenawalt, who had shot the victims, could be sentenced to death. The central figure in the case, Gary Tison, though, had died in the desert. Could the state satisfy the demand for justice and retribution by executing the Tison *brothers?* The state courts agreed that they had not specifically intended that killings occur and that they had not "plot[ted] in advance" that killing would take place. But, according to the Arizona Supreme Court, they did "play an active role" in the entire sequence of events, knew that their father was a violent man, and "could anticipate the use of lethal force" during the escape.

Justice O'Connor, who had dissented in *Enmund,* wrote the Supreme Court's opinion.[26] The Court rejected the Arizona court's theory that a death sentence could be imposed if the defendant could have foreseen that a murder would occur; that, according to Justice O'Connor, was a mere "restatement of the felony-murder rule itself." But, she continued, the Tison brothers' involvement in the murder was far greater than Enmund's had been—they were not merely the drivers of the getaway car; "their degree of participation in the crimes was major rather than minor." The Court concluded that people who did not actually kill could receive a death sentence if they were major participants in the felony and had "the culpable mental state of reckless indifference to human life." Although Justice O'Connor observed that the evidence in the case would support such findings, the lower courts had not applied the correct standards, and she sent the case back for them to reconsider their judgment.[27]

Youth and Mental Retardation Cases like *Coker* and *Enmund* exclude categories of people from capital punishment because, according to the Supreme Court's review of society's judgments, what they did—commit rape or drive a getaway car—does not deserve the ultimate penalty. Other categorical challenges aim at excluding categories of people because of who they are—for example, a defendant argues that no one as young as he was when he murdered his victim can be executed. The Supreme Court struggled with these claims, in cases involving youth and mental retardation, ending up rather unsympathetic to them. The difficulty with categorical exclusions was clear: Youth and mental retardation were obviously important as mitigating circumstances, and juries had to be told to consider them as such; but a categorical exclusion meant that juries could never decide that the crime was so horrible that the defendant deserved to die notwithstanding his youth or mental retardation. So except in an extremely narrow set of cases, the Court would not rule out capital punishment for young or retarded offenders.

The Court first tried to solve the problem in *Thompson v. Oklahoma,* where William Wayne Thompson, a fifteen-year-old boy, cooperated with three older friends to beat and murder his former brother-in-law, who had abused Thompson's sister.[28] Justice Stevens wrote for four Justices that "contemporary standards of decency," as revealed in statutes and jury determinations, showed that the society believed that "such a young person is not capable of acting with the degree of culpability that can justify the ultimate penalty." He noted that, of the states with capital punishment that specified a minimum age, all required that the defendant be at least sixteen at the time of the offense. He also pointed out that "other nations that share our Anglo-American heritage" and "the leading members of the Western European community" barred the execution of minors. Then, turning to jury behavior, Justice Stevens said that only 5 of 1,393 people sentenced to death between 1982 and 1986 were under sixteen at the time of their crimes. Young people, according to Justice Stevens, were "less able to evaluate the consequences of [their] conduct while at the same time [they are] much more apt to be motivated by mere emotion or peer pressure than is an adult." And concerning deterrence, he concluded, "The likelihood that the teenage offender has made the kind of cost-benefit analysis that attaches any weight to the possibility of execution is so remote as to be virtually nonexistent."

Justice O'Connor had misgivings about that analysis and agreed to vacate Thompson's sentence only because the Oklahoma legislature had not made a specific decision on the question of whether it was appropriate to execute people who committed their crimes at age fifteen. Three dissenters regarded it as enough that

Oklahoma juries were told to take youth into account as a mitigating circumstance.

Justice O'Connor's analysis signaled the outcome of the obvious next cases, involving people who killed when they were sixteen and seventeen. In an opinion by Justice Scalia, the Court concluded that there was no national consensus that it was inappropriate to execute such offenders.[29] Justice Scalia's opinion rejected as largely irrelevant the evidence that capital punishment for young offenders violated standards common in other countries because "it is *American* conceptions of decency that are dispositive."[30] The Court relied on what it called "objective indicia" of national standards, primarily statutes showing that about half of the states with capital punishment authorized it for sixteen or seventeen year-old offenders. That, according to the Court, was far from the sort of consensus that existed in *Coker* and *Enmund,* where only one or at most a handful of states would have allowed executions. Justice Scalia indicated some skepticism about statistics indicating that only a few young people had been sentenced to death, pointing out that relatively few young people committed crimes that would have made them eligible for death sentences in the first place. But even assuming that juries were somewhat reluctant to sentence young offenders to death, that was not enough to show that death sentences were "categorically unacceptable to prosecutors and juries." Rather, the statistics suggested to the Court that juries were quite careful in imposing death sentences on young people, confining them to those cases in which capital punishment was clearly appropriate.

Mental illness and retardation presented questions similar to the ones raised in the youth cases. *Ford v. Wainwright* held that a state could not execute a prisoner who was insane.[31] Justice Marshall, in one of his few death penalty opinions written for a majority, relied on the nation's "common law heritage" as the basis for constitutional protection against execution. The framers' generation believed that executing the insane was "savage and inhumane." Marshall's opinion indicated that, though the rule against executing the insane was clear, the reasons for the rule were not. It argued that "we may seriously question the retributive value of executing a person who has no comprehension of why he has been singled out and stripped of his fundamental right to life" and that "the intuition that such an execution simply offends humanity is evidently shared across this Nation." [32]

Yet although the state could not execute people who had gone crazy after the convictions, the Court refused to extend that protection beyond the insane to the mentally retarded. On the same day that it decided the juvenile death penalty cases, the Court held that executing mentally retarded murderers would not violate the Constitution.[33] James Penry, later found to have a mental age of about seven and described by a psychologist as having an IQ "in the borderline range," raped Pamela Carpenter in her home. He stabbed her with a pair of scissors, but before Carpenter died, she described her assailant. He was sentenced to death. The Supreme Court found that his sentence had to be vacated because the jury had not been told clearly enough that they could consider his mental retardation a mitigating circumstance, but it rejected his claim that a retarded person could not be executed at all.

Reviewing the treatment retarded people received in criminal law, Justice O'Connor concluded that the Constitution might bar imposing a death sentence on a profoundly retarded person, although she noted that it was unlikely that such a person would be found competent to stand trial in the first place. The juvenile death penalty cases indicated that the Court would examine how many states excluded a category of defendants from eligibility for the death penalty; here only one state specifically barred imposing the death sentence on retarded people. Public opinion polls indicating substantial discomfort with such sentences were not enough, either. Finally, Justice O'Connor asked whether executing mentally retarded offenders like Penry was inevitably disproportionate to their culpability. Penry argued that his retardation reduced his ability to control his impulses and to "think in long-range terms." For Justice O'Connor, retardation certainly might reduce culpability, which is why it was a mitigating factor. But, she said, people had different degrees of retardation, and she could not conclude that every retarded person "inevitably" fell short of the culpability that would make execution a disproportionate punishment. She was unwilling even to define some "mental age" below which execution would be barred, because, she indicated, the concept of "mental age" was too undefined for courts to use as a reason for barring legislatures from adopting the death penalty.

Race Discrimination in the Modern Death Penalty System

Opponents of capital punishment have always been concerned that the death penalty was simply another facet of race discrimination in the United States. The new death penalty statutes, though, attempted to eliminate race discrimination by insisting on guided discretion in capital sentencing. If opponents of the death penalty could show that racial discrimination persisted nonetheless, they might succeed in doing away with capital punishment, not because it violated the Eighth Amendment but because it inevitably led to race discrimination.

Ordinarily—in cases involving job discrimination, for example—someone who claims that she was denied a job because of race can prove the claim in two ways. First, she might be able to come up with evidence like a memorandum in which the employer says that he decided not to give the claimant the job because of her race. This is *direct* evidence of discrimination. Or she might be able to use statistical evidence to show that this employer regularly refused jobs to qualified African-American applicants at a much higher rate than to white applicants. This is *indirect* evidence of discrimination. It is not conclusive, though, and in job discrimination cases, the Supreme Court has said that once an applicant introduces substantial indirect evidence of discrimination, the employer can try to show that the statistics can be explained by something other than a racial motive.

Death penalty cases rarely provide direct evidence of discrimination. If discrimination occurs, it is because prosecutors decide to seek the death penalty more often in cases involving African-Americans or because juries impose it in cases involving African-Americans when they would impose a life sentence on a white defendant. And there is a further complication if juries are the reason for discrimination. A prosecutor brings a lot of cases, and it's fairly easy to understand how statistics about prosecutors' decisions might indirectly reveal a desire to discriminate against African-Americans. But juries are one-time-only decision-makers. It is much more difficult to understand how information—statistics—about how some *other* people—other juries—behaved tells us anything about how a jury in *this particular case* behaved. So even if the statistics show something, it is not clear why they should cast doubt on the death sentence imposed in any particular case.

Statistical evidence has some other peculiarities. Remember that under guided discretion statutes, a person is eligible for a death sentence only if a jury already has found one or more aggravating circumstances. So people who are sentenced to death "deserve" it. Suppose the statistical evidence shows that African-Americans—who are eligible under the guided discretion statutes and who therefore fit one or more of the aggravating circumstances—are being sentenced to death in circumstances where whites would not be. It is not obvious why the remedy for this discrimination ought to be vacating this death sentence rather than figuring out ways to insure that white defendants who equally deserve capital punishment receive it. In many ways that is Justice White's position: Only if society takes capital punishment seriously enough to impose it broadly can it be constitutional.

And finally, opponents can compile statistics only if a death penalty system is in place long enough to generate enough cases for analysis. Statistics tell us something only if we can be confident that the differences they reveal result from race alone; as statisticians say, they have to control for all sorts of other variables, including the viciousness of the crime, the defendant's age, and many more. If only a few defendants are sentenced to death, the statistical analysis will be unable to control for enough variables other than race, and it will not inform us whether discrimination affects the system's operation.

This peculiarity has two facets. Suppose Georgia imposes a lot of death sentences and Tennessee relatively few. We might be able to develop a statistical analysis showing discrimination in Georgia but could not do the same for Tennessee. So for no obvious reason other than the fact that someone committed murder in Tennessee rather than Georgia, the Tennessee defendant might be executed and a similar Georgia defendant would not be. Second, suppose the Supreme Court did find Georgia's death penalty system unconstitutionally discriminatory, based simply on statistics. Can Georgia vacate all existing death sentences, the ones that gave rise to the statistics, and simply start over? If so, how long do we have to wait until there are enough new statistics to revisit the question of discrimination?

For all these reasons and an additional one dealing specifically with juries in death penalty cases, it would have been quite difficult for the Supreme Court to rely on statistical evidence to show race discrimination in the death penalty system. And it did not. In *McCleskey v. Kemp,* opponents of the death penalty developed the best possible statistical case supporting the claim of race discrimination; once the Court rejected that claim, all that opponents could do was litigate case-by-case challenges, claiming that race discrimination had affected the decision in a particular case.[34]

Warren McCleskey and three accomplices robbed a furniture store in Fulton County, Georgia. McCleskey, an African-American, entered through the front door while his accomplices went in the back. The four men forced the store's employees to the floor and tied them up. Someone sounded a silent alarm, and a police officer came in the front door. As he walked through the store, he was killed by two shots from a revolver. After his arrest, McCleskey admitted taking part in the robbery but denied that he had shot the officer. The ballistics evidence supported the prosecution's claim that he had, but it was not conclusive. In addition, two jailhouse witnesses testified that McCleskey had said that he had indeed shot the officer, but as with all jailhouse witnesses, their testimonies might not have carried that much weight.

Challenging his death sentence, McCleskey's lawyers introduced a large-scale statistical study conducted by Professor David Baldus and his colleagues at the University of Iowa. The Baldus study used information drawn from over 2,000 death penalty cases under Georgia's guided discretion sentencing system. Because he had so many cases to deal with, Baldus was able to control for a number of variables that was extremely large for most statistical studies; he was able to deal with 230 variables that might explain disparity in sentencing on nonracial grounds.

Baldus's basic conclusions are straightforward. He found that there were roughly three types of death penalty cases. In some—cases in which the defendant killed several victims who were strangers to him, for example—juries would impose the death penalty no matter what. In others—a woman who deliberately stabbed her abusive husband—juries would almost never impose it. McCleskey's case fell into the midrange: The killing was not particularly vicious, and the evidence that McCleskey himself was the killer was not ironclad. Baldus found race discrimination in the midrange cases. But his finding introduced the final peculiarity into the statistical discussion. Most of the time, someone looking for race discrimination in criminal justice is going to be most troubled by evidence that African-American defendants are treated worse than whites who commit equivalent crimes: They get longer sentences or are convicted of felonies rather than misdemeanors, for example. Baldus did not find much evidence of that sort of discrimination. The 1991 statistics show this in a simplified form. Of the 14 men executed, seven were African-American, one Hispanic, and six white—not dramatically different from the different rates at which people in the different racial categories commit and are convicted of murder. More generally, for any category of murder, a white defendant was just as likely to receive a death sentence as an African-American defendant.

Baldus did find a different kind of discrimination. It was discrimination based on the race of the victim: Anyone, white or African-American, who killed a white victim was much likelier to get a death sentence than someone, white or African-American, who killed an African-American victim. According to the Supreme Court's summary of this point, "defendants charged with killing white persons received the death penalty in 11% of the cases, but defendants charged with killing blacks received the death penalty in only 1% of the cases." Or, as Justice Brennan put it in dissent, "almost 6 in 10 defendants comparable to McCleskey would not have received the death penalty if their victims had been black." Dramatically, in

Fulton County between 1973 and 1979, seventeen defendants were charged with killing a police officer; only McCleskey received a death sentence; the only other defendant whose case proceeded to the penalty phase received a life sentence for killing an African-American police officer. In the 1991 executions, only three victims were African-American; indeed, 1991 was the first year since 1944 in which a white was executed for killing an African-American (Donald Gaskins, executed for murder-for-hire, who had already been convicted of nine other murders of white victims). The conclusion of the Baldus study has been reproduced by every examination of capital sentencing; no other conclusion from social science studies of criminal justice has stood up so well.

The reason for this victim-based disparity is apparent: Jurors have to be so repelled by the defendant's behavior to choose to sentence him to death; they are more likely to be repelled by the defendant when they can see themselves as potential victims of his violence; and they are more likely to do that when the victims are pretty much like them. The point is driven home by a study of death sentences imposed during the brief period from 1972 to 1976 when some states tried to use mandatory death penalty statutes: The victim-based disparity was substantially reduced because jurors could not rely on their empathy with the victim to recommend death only in cases involving white victims.[35]

Opponents of the death penalty could say that, like the more traditional forms of race discrimination, this one too showed that the death penalty system valued African-American lives less than white ones. And they tried to argue that, even if the study did not establish discrimination, it showed that capital sentencing too often turned on an irrelevant factor—the victim's race—and was therefore arbitrary within the framework the Court had established in *Furman* and *Gregg*. But Baldus's study could not readily support the highly charged emotions that arise when more traditional forms of discrimination are shown. And of course, the question of remedy here has two solutions: The way to show that the system values white and African-American lives equally might well be to insist that those who kill African-Americans be executed just as often as those who kill whites. That, though, introduces another peculiarity: The "remedy" would mean executing more African-Americans, because they disproportionately kill other African-Americans. Opponents of the death penalty are unlikely to find that remedy attractive, even though it fully responds to the concern about avoiding discrimination.

The lower courts were skeptical about Baldus's study, noting that Baldus was sometimes forced to omit information about particular cases from his analysis and that he relied on information that was not always available to jurors. This skepticism, though, was almost entirely unjustified. Baldus's study satisfied the most rigorous standards ordinarily used by social scientists to determine what is the most likely explanation for disparities in outcomes. This is particularly true where, as in most cases involving indirect evidence of discrimination, the aim of the analysis is to shift the burden of proof, to require the government to explain how—race discrimination aside—the outcomes came about.

The Supreme Court accepted the statistical validity of the Baldus study but held that it did not establish that McCleskey's constitutional rights had been violated. For the Court, the Constitution prohibits "intentional discrimination," which meant that McCleskey had to "prove that decisionmakers in his case acted with discriminatory purpose." Jurors do not tell us why they decide as they do, so it is unlikely that a defendant would ever be able to do that through direct evidence. What about the statistical evidence? Justice Powell, writing for the Court, agreed that courts accepted statistical evidence in employment discrimination cases. But, he said, capital sentencing was "fundamentally different." Unlike employment decisions, where at some point one particular person decides who to hire, death penalty decisions arise from a more complicated process. Noting that even prosecutors varied from county to county, Justice Powell thought the most important difference was that one-time-only juries, "unique in [their] composition," made the decision after considering "innumerable factors that vary according to the characteristics of the individual defendant and the facts of the particular capital offense."

Of course, the point of a statistical analysis is to show that the factors that explain actual outcomes are not so innumerable after all. This, and passing comments elsewhere in the Court's opinion, suggest that the Court actually was uneasy with the statistical analysis itself, perhaps not believing that the study showed what the Court assumed it showed. Rather, as the Court said later in the opinion, the question for it was whether the Baldus study showed that the new death penalty statutes posed an "unacceptable risk of racial prejudice influencing capital sentencing decisions." The answer was no. Any jury sentencing system posed some risk, but it was important, Justice Powell wrote, to allow jurors to make a particularized moral judgment about this defendant and this crime. Eliminating this discretion might reduce the risk of racial discrimination, but at an unacceptable cost.

Further, after the statistics are presented in employment cases, the employer could try to explain the outcomes by referring to nonracial reasons not to hire each particular applicant. What, though, could the state do in the face of the Baldus study? To talk about "shifting the burden" in this setting, Justice Powell thought, was completely unrealistic: For all practical purposes, the statistics, if given their usual weight, would be conclusive.

Justice Brennan dissented, along with Justices Marshall, Blackmun, and Stevens. They suggested that disparities might arise in part because Georgia's prosecutors made their decisions to seek the death penalty with no guidance and that, just as the Court upheld statutes that guided the discretion of juries, so Georgia might eliminate the racial disparities by setting guidelines for prosecutors as well.

Justice Brennan's dissent opened with this powerful statement of the issue:

> At some point in this case, Warren McCleskey doubtless asked his lawyer whether a jury was likely to sentence him to die. A candid reply to this question would have been disturbing. . .The story could be told in a variety of ways, but McCleskey could not fail to grasp its essential narrative line: there was a significant chance that race would play a prominent role in determining if he lived or died.

At its core, the majority did not disagree with this analysis, although it quarreled with some of Justice Brennan's supporting points. Justice Powell concluded his opinion with a candid discussion of the Court's reluctance to accept the implications of the Baldus study. McCleskey's claim "challenges decisions at the heart of the State's criminal justice system." To accept it would "throw[] into serious question the principles that underlie our entire criminal justice system" because similar statistical cases could be made about every penalty and every stage of the criminal justice process. Justice Brennan responded pungently that "such a statement seems to suggest a fear of too much justice." Or as Professors Samuel Gross and Robert Mauro put it, "It's not broken because it can't be fixed."[36]

Victim-Impact Evidence

The Court itself exacerbated the problem. Under the Court's rules, defendants could present evidence to get sympathy. But to many that seemed unfair unless the victims' families and friends could present evidence showing how they had suffered as a result of the murder. Responding to this desire for symmetry and to the overall movement to allow victims to present their positions in court, some states began to allow "victim impact" testimony. At first, the Court rejected such testimony.[37]

Justice Lewis Powell's opinion said that victim-impact evidence was irrelevant to capital sentencing and would make sentencing decisions random. The impact a victim's death had on his or her family was, he wrote, "wholly unrelated to the blameworthiness of a particular defendant." The defendant might not even know the victim, and victim-impact evidence therefore dealt with facts "that were irrelevant to the decision to kill." And sometimes "the victim will not leave behind a family," or "the family members may be less articulate in describing their feelings even though their sense of loss is equally severe." Justice Powell also was "troubled" by the possibility that defendants "whose victims were assets to their community" would be thought "more deserving of punishment than those whose victims are perceived to be less worthy," which would be a form of discrimination among victims.

The Court divided five-to-four in this 1987 decision, and the dissents were quite bitter. Shortly after the decision, Justice Powell retired. His replacement, Justice Anthony Kennedy, was expected to be more conservative on law-and-order issues, and states tried to get the Court to overrule the victim-impact decision. Their first try failed, when Justice White, one of the initial dissenters, said that, although he was prepared to overrule the decision, his colleagues in dissent had not yet faced up to the need to overrule it.[38] A year later the situation was different. Justice Brennan had retired, and by 1991 six Justices held that states could introduce victim-impact evidence.[39] Chief Justice Rehnquist's opinion rejected the Court's earlier view, saying that traditionally the criminal law did say that people might be more or less blameworthy depending solely on the amount of harm they caused. Victim-impact evidence, to the Court, was not irrelevant to the purposes of capital punishment. And responding to Justice Powell's concern that victim-impact evidence might introduce arbitrary discrimination, Chief Justice Rehnquist said that, to the contrary, such evidence was "designed to show. . .each victim's 'uniqueness as an individual human being.'" Victim-impact evidence, for example, might show that the victim was "out of work [and] mentally handicapped, perhaps not, in the eyes of most, a significant contributor to society, but nonetheless a murdered human being." Without such evidence, the prosecution was at a disadvantage: The defendant could introduce all sorts of evidence designed to humanize the defendant, but without victim-impact evidence, the jury might not be able to consider "the full moral force" of the events.

Victim-impact testimony tries to offset sympathy for the defendant. California's courts began to use an "antisympathy" instruction telling jurors that, although they could consider all mitigating evidence, they should "not be swayed by mere sentiment, conjecture, sympathy, passion, prejudice, public opinion or public feeling." As Justice O'Connor noted, the case presented the Court with the tension that had pervaded its new death penalty jurisprudence.[40] Discretion had to be controlled to avoid arbitrary decisions, but sentencers had to consider all mitigating evidence, which allowed discretion back into the system. To Justice O'Connor, the antisympathy instruction was "designed to satisfy the principle that capital sentencing decisions must not be made on mere whim, but instead on clear and objective standards." A majority of her colleagues agreed, finding that jurors who were told to ignore "mere" sympathy would nonetheless understand that they could rely on all the mitigating evidence the defendant introduced and should ignore only "extraneous emotional factors."

In his dissent in the antisympathy case, Justice Brennan argued that the majority overlooked the way in which cases are actually presented to jurors. The Court paid careful attention to the words of the instruction. The Court's emphasis on ruling out only "mere" sympathy did not take into account what prosecutors say in their closing arguments. Instructions are standardized, and judges can often take them from books. Closing arguments, in contrast, are typically much more informal.

Prosecutors and defense attorneys use everyday language and are less careful to make distinctions that judges and instructions do. In the antisympathy case, for example, the defendant had introduced evidence of his background. The prosecutor called this "a blatant attempt to inject personal feelings in the case" and told the jurors that they "must steel yourselves against those kinds of feelings," a statement that he immediately followed by saying that the judge would instruct them not to be swayed by sympathy. In another case, the prosecutor described mitigating evidence as "simply a sympathy ploy. . . going outside the evidence and asking you to have sympathy, compassion." More accurately than the Supreme Court's interpretation of the instruction, the prosecutor's arguments capture how most jurors are likely to respond to an antisympathy instruction.

The Court's decision allowing victim-impact evidence was announced on June 27, 1991. Justice Marshall's dissenting opinion opened with the dramatic statement, "Power, not reason, is the new currency of this Court's decision-making." As he viewed the issue, the difference between the two victim-impact cases was not that the arguments Justice Powell had made had been shown to be wrong, but only that Justices Powell and Brennan had retired. Death penalty cases, in which the state exercises its ultimate power in response to a killer's actions, always tread the line between reason and emotion. The Court's recognition that the death penalty might be justified by retributivist reasons inevitably meant that emotion played a part in authorizing death sentences, and no one believed that juries in individual cases were unmoved by similar nonrational concerns. In attempting to guide the discretion of sentencers in capital cases, the Court attempted to place an overlay of rationality on what is always a somewhat emotional process.

The victim-impact and antisympathy cases show that the effort cannot fully succeed. Justice Scalia came to the position that the Court's capital punishment doctrine made no sense at all.41 The problem, as he saw it, was that the Court required states to narrow eligibility for the death penalty, which restricted a jury's discretion to impose the death penalty, and yet barred the states from keeping mitigating information from the jury, which expanded its discretion to decline to impose it. As a result, defendants could argue both that a state's death penalty statute unconstitutionally broadened jury discretion—through a vague "special circumstance," for example—and unconstitutionally narrowed jury discretion—by restricting mitigating evidence. Justice Scalia believed that such a structure of law was simply too arbitrary to endure (though the nature of the arbitrariness was different from the randomness that had led the Court to condemn the death penalty in 1972). From the Court's point of view, however, the degree of arbitrary decision that its new system allows is not so great as to invalidate the new death penalty system.

Delays in Carrying Out Executions: Habeas Corpus

The present system of capital punishment inevitably generates legal issues that make it impossible for states to carry out executions quickly. The Court tried to respond to that problem in a series of decisions aimed at accelerating the process of reviewing death sentences.

Once a defendant is convicted, he can appeal his conviction. (Prodded by the case of Gary Gilmore, the first person executed after the Court reauthorized capital punishment, the Court eventually held that states did not have to require appeals in capital cases. The argument in favor of requiring appeals was that higher courts were supposed to consider whether a particular death sentence was not out of line with the sentences imposed in other cases and that they could not make this sort of comparison if defendants kept cases from their view by accepting their death sentences.)[42]

In this appeal, the defendant can raise different kinds of issues. Some involve questions of state law, such as whether the judge's instructions to the jury accurately described the circumstances under which a person can use deadly force to defend himself. Most questions about the admission of evidence are state law questions. Other issues involve constitutional law. A defendant might claim, for example, that his constitutional rights were violated when the judge improperly placed the burden of proof on the defense, violating the constitutionally grounded presumption of innocence.

When a defendant appeals a conviction to a state's highest court, he can raise both state and constitutional law issues. Once the state's courts decide the state law issues, though, they drop out of the case. When a defendant moves to the next stage—seeking review by the United States Supreme Court, in what is called a direct appeal—he can raise only constitutional issues.

And while the Constitution is of course important to us all, defendants win cases much more often by pointing out errors of state law than by showing that their constitutional rights were violated.

Generally a case is closed after the state courts uphold a conviction and the United States Supreme Court either declines to hear the case or affirms the state courts. There are good reasons, though, to give defendants a chance to try again. The clearest examples occur when the defendant claims that something happened between the time of the first appeal and the time he tries again. The defendant might say, for example, that he has found new evidence that prosecutors deliberately concealed, evidence that would have persuaded the jury not to convict, or evidence that someone else committed the crime. Obviously the defendant could not have raised these claims during the first appeal, but equally obviously it would be unfair to deny the defendant the chance to show that his rights had been violated.

Responding to these sorts of concerns, states have set up systems of postconviction remedies. These are commonly known as habeas corpus, a technical term that merely describes methods of getting courts to consider criminal cases after they have gone through the first round of appeals. So, in capital cases, defendants might raise some issues on their first appeals and new issues—those that they could not have raised earlier—in a state postconviction proceeding.

That, however, is not the end of the story. After the Civil War, Congress was suspicious of how fair state courts would be in criminal cases, and it expanded what had previously been a rather narrow federal habeas corpus remedy. Congress allowed defendants in state cases to go into federal court to have their constitutional claims considered. (They file their cases using what are usually called "habeas petitions.") Shortly after that the Supreme Court held that defendants had to exhaust their state remedies before they could get federal habeas corpus. So under this system, defendants go up from their trial courts to the state's highest court and then can go over to the federal court, which will reconsider only the claims they have already made.

The Supreme Court struggled for many years to define which habeas cases the federal courts should hear. In 1953, though, the Court settled on a simple rule. The federal courts could freely reconsider any constitutional claim a defendant made; it did not matter what the state courts had said about it. And of course, defendants could appeal habeas cases from the federal trial courts to the federal courts of appeal and eventually to the Supreme Court.

In the abstract, there are good reasons for this apparently awkward setup. Many defendants do have decent constitutional claims, but often what happened to them is unique to their cases. The Supreme Court could in theory decide their cases on direct appeal, but doing so would not do much to develop constitutional law: The decision would be confined to the unique facts of the cases, and the Supreme Court has to devote its limited time to cases that have a reasonably broad impact. By making federal habeas corpus available, Congress in essence made the federal trial courts "little Supreme Courts" in criminal cases, relieving the burden on the Supreme Court while still insuring that some federal court would decide constitutional claims.

This does not come free, though. It takes time for defendants to exhaust their state remedies, particularly because state courts are usually fairly careful when a capital sentence is involved. And presenting the habeas claim and appealing it through the federal system takes still more time. Even under ordinary circumstances, appeals and habeas petitions can delay an execution for many years. (Federal habeas corpus is available to prisoners who have received prison terms, but the Court has been most concerned about delays in capital cases; where all that is at stake is a prison sentence that the habeas petitioner is already serving, delay does not make much difference.)

Even worse, as the Supreme Court came to see it, too often capital defendants were able to create extraordinary circumstances that caused even longer delays. This happened in three ways. First, there is the problem of new rules: Whenever the Supreme Court held that some procedure violated a defendant's constitutional right, everyone convicted in the past would claim that the same thing had happened in his case; because we now knew that his constitutional rights were violated, the defendant said, his conviction or death sentence should be vacated. Second, there is the problem of successive petitions: After a defendant's first habeas petition was denied, the defendant would come forward with a second, and then a third, petition, saying in each one that something new had happened, making it necessary to take up the case again. Third, there is the problem of abusive petitions: After the first habeas claim was denied, a defendant could bring a second petition raising exactly the same claim. The reason for this was quite technical. The Court said that habeas corpus was a remedy that ignored every prior judgment that any court had made—a sensible position when you think about why the federal court can freely reconsider what the state courts had done, but an invitation to incredible delay when applied to prior habeas decisions as well. Of course, the chances that a court would grant a second petition raising claims that it had denied in the first go-round were extremely small, but they did serve to keep the case—and in capital cases, the defendant—alive.

After about a decade of experience with the new death penalty, the Supreme Court became concerned that states were being blocked from carrying out executions because of habeas corpus. It worked out a set of rules that sharply limited defendants' ability to delay execution indefinitely. The Court encouraged lower courts to develop special procedures to deal quickly with capital cases,[43] but it devoted its greatest attention to the three problems of new rules, successive petitions, and abusive petitions.

The Court dealt with the new rules problem first. The Supreme Court under Chief Justice Earl Warren had revolutionized the constitutional law of criminal procedure. As it did, however, it wanted to avoid letting out of prison too many people convicted under procedures that had been constitutional when they were tried. The Warren Court dealt with this concern by saying that many new rules were not retroactive. If a new rule was not retroactive, people who had already been convicted could not claim its benefits. The Court gradually worked out its rules on retroactivity. Their core is that new constitutional rights are retroactive only if violating them appears likely to mean that someone who might not have committed a crime might still have been convicted—or if violating the rule is grossly unfair, not a mere technical violation of some arcane constitutional provision but a real and fundamental challenge to the fairness of the conviction.

Rules against retroactivity would appear to reduce the possibility of real delay as a result of new rules. One rather large difficulty remained, though. Suppose a defendant raises a claim on direct appeal that creates a new rule that the Court would find not retroactive. Of course, the Court cannot apply the rule against retroactivity to that very person; if it did, no one would ever have any reason to bring these claims to the Court, because they could not benefit from a victory. So, the Court said, it would give the benefit of the rule to the person who raised the claim.

Now, think about habeas corpus. We know that a defendant cannot get relief if he raises a claim the Court has said is not retroactive. So what he should do is raise a new claim: "My case is different from the nonretroactive one you just decided, so I'm not barred by its nonretroactivity. But, if you work out the principles of the Constitution you dealt with in that case, you'll discover that a different—though related—constitutional right was violated in my trial." If the Court was to cut down on habeas corpus, something had to be done about that sort of argument.

The Court responded by extending the idea that constitutional rules would not be retroactive. It said that defendants could not use habeas corpus to create new rules.[44] According to the Court, this had to mean more than barring nonretroactive claims from habeas corpus. Rather, a rule was new if a reasonable state court, considering the Supreme Court precedents when the defendant was tried and appealed his conviction, could have believed that no violation of the Constitution occurred.[45] This definition of new rules effectively eliminated the problem of delay as defendants tried to invoke newly found constitutional protections.

The Court cut back on habeas corpus in dealing with successive and abusive petitions as well. It applied the same rule to both kinds of problems. Basically, it said that in almost all cases defendants had only one chance to present their cases on habeas corpus to the federal courts. They could bring a second petition, or raise a claim a second time, only in very restricted circumstances. They could bring a second petition if they showed what the Court called "cause and prejudice." By "cause," the Court meant that defendants had to show that they had been unable to bring the claim the first time or perhaps that they had been unable to provide sufficient support for it the first time, because state officials interfered with their ability to present the claim, or—though this still remains unclear—because their lawyer was so grossly inadequate that the constitutional rights to effective assistance of counsel was violated when the claim was made the first time. And the Court was pretty unsympathetic to claims about interference. When Warren McCleskey's case came back to the Supreme Court, it was on a petition claiming that prosecutors had concealed from him evidence that they had placed an informant with him in prison, who got a confession from McCleskey. (Once a defendant has been indicted and has a lawyer, using informants in that way violates his constitutional rights.) The Court said that Mc-

Cleskey had made that claim before and could not make it again because his counsel, who the Court found was competent, had not investigated it carefully enough at first.[46]

But even if a defendant shows cause, he also has to show prejudice. That means that he has to show that the jury probably would not have convicted him or that he probably would not have been given a death sentence if there had been no constitutional violation—if, for example, the confession to McCleskey's jail-house companion had not been admitted.

The Court opened a final loophole, but it was quite small. Even if the defendant could not show cause and prejudice, still he might be able to get habeas corpus if he showed that he was actually innocent. Obviously the standard of actual innocence has to be higher than the standard for prejudice. According to the Court, a defendant can get habeas by showing that, if no constitutional violation had occurred, no reasonable juror would have convicted or imposed the death sentence. That is almost never going to be true.

The Supreme Court has done what it can to expedite carrying out death sentences. The Court's recent decisions about habeas corpus have substantially cut back on the scope of habeas. Although there are still proposals for legislation aiming to cut the time between conviction and execution even more, there is not that much leeway left. It is still going to take a fair amount of time to get from conviction to execution. Whatever problems there are in habeas corpus, they have nothing to do with the delays that occur within the state systems, when defendants appeal their convictions directly. And unless Congress eliminates habeas corpus entirely, which seems unlikely, there is still going to be the time consumed in the first round of habeas corpus.

Conclusion

What happened to the movement against the death penalty? Perhaps the Court would have arrived at the position it is now in no matter what. It may have arrived there, however, because of the route it took. Public support for capital punishment grew at least in part as a response to the Court's 1972 decision against capital punishment. Perhaps the Court would have been able to defer that opposition by nibbling away at capital punishment rather than attempting to abolish it: by ruling against the death penalty for rape and robbery first (in *Maxwell* and *Boykin*) and by requiring bifurcated trials and standards. The public might have become accustomed to living with fewer and fewer executions, until the time came to eliminate it entirely—either by legislative decision or by a constitutional decision to abolish a penalty that, by then, would have fallen into disuse.

Those were decisions that could have been made before the conservative transformation of the Supreme Court. Even afterwards, perhaps the public might have accepted abolition if the Court had said in 1976 that guided discretion statutes could not satisfy the Constitution. It could have relied on *McGautha* to say that attempting to confine discretion by statutory guidelines was a futile endeavor. Had the Court said in 1976 that it really meant it when it said that capital punishment was unconstitutional, the issue might have dropped out of politics.

In short, the Court itself was largely responsible for creating a situation in 1992 that no one found acceptable: Death penalty opponents were upset that the penalty remained on the books and that it was occasionally, but apparently randomly, carried out; death penalty proponents were upset that the penalty remained on the books but was only occasionally carried out.

The present Court believes that it is on the way to constructing an acceptable legal structure for the administration of the death penalty. Whether judges in the next century, having more experience with how the new system actually works, will share that view is an open question.

4

Death Stories

Tales of murder and execution have always captured the American public's imagination. Lizzie Borden, Joe Hill, Sacco and Vanzetti, Leopold and Loeb—acquitted of murder, sentenced to life imprisonment, or executed—live on in our memories because we are fascinated by their confrontation with death. The revival of the death penalty has generated a new set of public stories about life and death. As the moment of execution nears, sometimes cases become public events. The accounts that follow try to illuminate the aspects that made these cases fascinating. It deserves noting at the outset, though, that all the murderers whose fate caught public attention have been white.

Gary Gilmore

"Let's do it." With those words on January 17, 1977, Gary Gilmore encouraged his executioners to get on with the nation's first execution in a decade. Gilmore "chose" to be executed: After his conviction, he fired his lawyers and refused to authorize an appeal or any other challenges to his conviction or sentence. The strain of reinstituting the death penalty was so great, though, that the Supreme Court divided five-to-four over whether to respect Gilmore's choice.

Like many murderers, Gilmore was a drifter and an alcohol and drug abuser, unable to hold a job and in trouble with the law from his teenage years. And like many murderers, Gilmore thought that his desires should come before anyone else's. But unlike most murderers, Gilmore had something of a genius for publicity. He stage-managed his own execution to make him the center of attention for several months in 1976 and 1977. Even more, he lives on as the central figure in Norman Mailer's *The Executioner's Song.*

Gilmore's criminal career started when he was fourteen. He spent nearly eighteen of the succeeding 20 years in prison, where he was a notably violent inmate. In April 1976, Gilmore was released on parole and came home to Provo, Utah, where he lived with his uncle and aunt. He lost his job after only ten days and spent the next few weeks floundering around, frustrated at his inability to adjust to life outside prison. He started committing petty crimes—stealing some skis and stereos—and eventually stole some guns to pay off his debts. Meanwhile, Gilmore had resumed a romance with Nicole Barrett, but there too he became violent.

On July 19, Gilmore went to Nicole's house. Failing to find her, Gilmore persuaded Nicole's sister to go with him. Gilmore drove to a gas station and forced the attendant Max Jensen to give him the station's cash. Then Gilmore forced Jensen into the gas station's restroom and shot him twice in the head. Afterward, he took Nicole's sister to a motel and tried to rape her. The next night Gilmore looked for Nicole again. And again, after he could not find her, Gilmore went out robbing, this time a motel near his uncle's home. Gilmore ordered Bennie Bushnell, the night clerk, to lie down and shot him. Attempting to throw the gun away, Gilmore accidentally shot himself in the hand. When a gas station attendant noticed blood on Gilmore's hand, he called the police, and Gilmore was arrested.

Gilmore's trial was routine; the jury took only three days to convict Gilmore of murdering Bushnell and to sentence him to death. His execution by firing squad was then scheduled for November 15. A posttrial hearing was held on November 1. Gilmore's lawyers told the judge that, although they informed Gilmore that there were substantial grounds for appealing, Gilmore did not want to appeal. Gilmore told the judge that he did not "care to languish in prison for another day." The judge also considered several psychiatric reports. Some were prepared before Gilmore's trial and found no evidence then of mental illness or insanity. Another was a report from the Utah prison psychiatrist, who spent an hour with Gilmore and concluded that Gilmore had not "become insane or mentally ill." On November 4, the judge found that Gilmore understood what he was doing.

When posttrial motions were denied, Gilmore fired his lawyers. Nonetheless, the lawyers filed an appeal to the Utah Supreme Court. Gilmore sent two handwritten letters to that court saying that he "wish[ed] to be executed on schedule" and asking that the court consider the appeal his former lawyers filed "null and void." With these letters before it, the Utah court entered a stay of execution, which lasted four days. Utah's governor then stayed the execution until the state's board of pardons could meet. The board was supposed to meet on November 17, after the initial execution date. On November 16, the day after he was supposed to have been executed, Gilmore, in prison, and Nicole Barrett, in her apartment, attempted to commit suicide. Although Nicole almost died, Gilmore apparently took too few sleeping pills to have much effect, and he recovered quickly.

On November 28, the board of pardons refused to extend the Governor's stay, and a new execution date was set for December 6.

On December 2, Bessie Gilmore, Gary's mother, applied to the United States Supreme Court for a stay of execution. Bessie Gilmore was assisted by lawyers from the American Civil Liberties Union (ACLU). In her application, Bessie Gilmore argued that the Utah death penalty statute was unconstitutional, an issue no court had considered (the trial judge did not address that issue and was prepared to certify an appeal so that the Utah Supreme Court could). Over three dissents, the Court granted a temporary stay, until it received an answer from Utah. Utah replied on December 7, and the next day Gilmore, through new attorneys, also filed a reply, claiming that his mother had no legal rights at stake that would allow her to delay the execution. On the same day, though, Gilmore also filed an action in state court saying that the state had forfeited its right to execute him at all by failing to execute him on time, apparently undercutting his asserted desire to be executed as soon as possible.

The Supreme Court lifted its temporary stay on December 13.[1] The justices divided over two questions. The Court's brief order simply said that the material presented to it "convinced" a majority that Gilmore "made a knowing and intelligent waiver of any and all federal rights he might have." Justice White, joined by Justices Brennan and Marshall, said that "the consent of a convicted defendant. . . does not privilege a State to impose a punishment otherwise forbidden by the Eighth Amendment." (Justice Blackmun also dissented.) For them, the Eighth Amendment restricted government power to protect all citizens; it did not merely give individuals rights they could choose to exercise or not. As Justice Marshall put it in his separate dissent, "the Eighth Amendment not only protects the right of individuals not to be the victims of cruel and unusual punishment, but. . .also expresses a fundamental interest of society in ensuring that state authority is not used to administer barbaric punishments." Marshall was skeptical as well about concluding that Gilmore's "waiver" of his rights was "intelligent." "Less than five months have passed," he wrote, since the murder, and only two months since sentencing. Marshall found Gilmore's behavior, including his suicide attempt and the new state court challenge to the execution, "erratic." The evidence on which the majority relied was suspect, too, because there had never been an adversary hearing and because some portions of the hearings had not been transcribed because of a bad recording device.

The second issue that troubled the Court was Bessie Gilmore's "standing," that is, her personal entitlement to challenge the death sentence imposed on her son. Of course, he could challenge the sentence, but, some members of the Court believed, the rights at stake were his. Bessie Gilmore appeared before the Court as Gary's "next friend." But Chief Justice Burger wrote, she could do that only if Gary was incompetent to represent his own interests. The state courts had properly found him competent and that, for Burger, was the end of the matter. If Gilmore was willing to submit to execution, his mother could not appear as his "next friend." (No one on the Court addressed the possibility that Bessie Gilmore had her own rights in the matter, although Justice White suggested that the state, or its officials, might face a "wrongful-death action" against it, presumably brought by Bessie Gilmore to vindicate either her or Gary's rights.)

Gilmore was outraged at the efforts to save his life. He told the ACLU to "butt out of my life" and castigated those who feared his execution would open the door to more executions as people who "chose to live in abject fear that haunts and surrounds their meager existence." People who were "dumb enough" to get sentenced to death should "accept [it] graciously and quietly." For Gilmore, "you don't kill or torture or maim somebody, then start snivelling because you were dumb enough to get caught and the going gets rough."

Henry Schwarzschild of the ACLU replied that he "won't let you turn us into killers." Death penalty opponents "believe that the killing of human beings is an act so appalling that we would not have the state do that in our name." They did not, Schwarzschild wrote, "share your destructive contempt for the life of your victims, for your own life, for the life of other people on death row in Utah and elsewhere."

Those who sought Supreme Court review in Gilmore's case feared that his execution would open the doors to massive numbers of executions. It did not. The attention the case received, though, meant that Gary Gilmore became a figure in American history. In *The Executioner's Song,* Norman Mailer used Gary Gilmore, the efforts to save him, and his execution as a metaphor for American life in the 1970s.

John Spenkelink

On May 25, 1979, John Spenkelink became the first person executed involuntarily under the application of the modern death penalty. For many, the murder Spenkelink committed seemed "ordinary," even understandable. And Spenkelink's case showed, even more than Gilmore's, how flawed the judicial system can be under stress.

Spenkelink got into trouble with the law as a teenager, when he was convicted of vandalism. One night he robbed six stores. He was convicted and sentenced to an indeterminate term in prison. He escaped and traveled in Canada and the United States. In early 1973, he picked up Joseph Szymankiewicz, a hitchhiker, in Nebraska. That decision led to Szymankiewicz's death and Spenkelink's execution. Both men were convicted felons, but Szymankiewicz was particularly vicious. As the two men traveled east, Szymankiewicz raped Spenkelink, forced him to play Russian roulette, and eventually stole all Spenkelink's money.

On reaching Tallahassee, Florida, Spenkelink decided he had had enough. Leaving Szymankiewicz at their motel, Spenkelink took his car to be washed. On his way back, he picked up Frank Bruum, another hitchhiker, and agreed to take him to New Orleans. He told Bruum that they had to stop at the motel first. Spenkelink planned to get his money back. He told Bruum to wait "a little ways from the motel" because Szymankiewicz was probably drunk and would be mad that Spenkelink had been gone so long. He also told Bruum that "if he should happen to hear a gunshot or something," it would be coming from the motel room.

Spenkelink returned to the motel with a gun. There he shot Szymankiewicz in the head and then again through his spine and aorta. Later Spenkelink claimed he took the gun with him because he was afraid of Szymankiewicz and that the gun went off while the two men were struggling in the motel room. After the murder, Spenkelink eventually wound up in California, where he and two other men were arrested for armed robbery. He was returned to Florida for the murder trial. After the Supreme Court's 1972 decisions invalidating existing death penalty statutes, Florida adopted a new one that its legislature thought was consistent with the 1972 decisions. Spenkelink was convicted and sentenced to death in December 1973, under Florida's new death penalty statute.

A lawyer for the state later said, "[Spenkelink] was probably the least obnoxious individual on death row in terms of the crime he committed... I didn't have some hideous monster... who strangled three generations of women. We had a guy who killed a faggot." (Jack Greenberg of the Legal Defense Fund notes that "[t]he egregious language... illustrates the role that irrelevant factors play in the imposition of the death penalty.")[2]

The Florida Supreme Court, affirming Spenkelink's conviction and death sentence in 1975, nonetheless called the murder "especially cruel, atrocious, and heinous." It pointed out that Spenkelink had voluntarily returned to the motel room, armed with his gun and intending to get his money back and, as his statement to Bruum indicated, expecting to use the gun. One judge dissented, finding it impossible to conclude that the evidence showed that Spenkelink had planned to kill. He suggested that this was at most an ordinary murder, not a particularly vicious one. The verdict, he said, reflected "subconscious prejudices and local mores," the jury's hostility to "underprivileged drifters" with "foreign and strange" names.

The Supreme Court declined to review Spenkelink's case, and he then filed a habeas corpus action in federal court. The case proceeded normally until Spenkelink's execution was imminent. The lower federal courts considered Spenkelink's claims extensively, upholding his sentence, and the Supreme Court again denied review in March 1979. Florida's governor denied executive clemency on May 18, 1979, and set the execution date for May 23. On May 21, Spenkelink filed another federal habeas corpus action, raising a new constitutional claim and seeking a stay of execution. The federal district court rejected the claim the same day, and Spenkelink appealed. To stop the execution, he needed the appellate court to issue a "certificate of probable cause" indicating the appellate court's belief that Spenkelink's new claim had some potential for winning. The appellate court refused to issue that certificate, over the dissent of Judge Elbert Tuttle, a highly respected judge appointed to the court by President Dwight Eisenhower, and planning went ahead for the May 23 execution.

Spenkelink then applied to the Supreme Court for a stay of execution. Justice William Rehnquist got the application. After consulting some of his colleagues, he found it extremely unlikely that four justices would vote to review Spenkelink's latest claim, which he found to be an implausible theory for extending some recent decisions. He concluded, "Applicant has had not merely one day in court. He has had many, many days in court." Rehnquist therefore denied Spenkelink's application.

The Supreme Court's rules allow litigants to go from one justice to another seeking stays like the one Spenkelink needed. Spenkelink went next to Justice Lewis Powell, who also refused. Finally Spenkelink got to Justice Thurgood Marshall. Relying on the fact that Judge Tuttle had dissented, Marshall granted a stay of execution, until the full Court could consider the case 36 hours later.

Meanwhile Spenkelink's lawyers managed to persuade Judge Tuttle to stay the execution, relying on their quite strained argument that Spenkelink's lawyers up to that point had not given him effective assistance of counsel. The stay outraged Florida's attorney general. He took the case to the U.S. Supreme Court, but a majority refused to vacate this new stay, which Justice Rehnquist later called a "clear abuse" of Judge Tuttle's power. He was concerned that repeated stays of execution, issued on the eve of scheduled executions, could leave states "powerless to carry out a death sentence." On May 24, after a series of telephone conferences in which the lawyers had to argue their positions without giving the judges any written briefs, the court of appeals itself vacated the stay. And when the Supreme Court took up the case on the same day, it vacated Marshall's stay. Spenkelink was executed at 10:12 on the morning of May 25.

In Spenkelink's case, the Court faced the reality of a contested execution for the first time since the moratorium on executions had begun nearly a decade earlier. The frenzied activity, with telephone conferences and oral arguments, and judge-shopping of the most obvious sort, heightened the tensions within the Court over the propriety of actually carrying out an execution. That the courts found the case so difficult, even though Spenkelink's purely legal arguments were not that strong, indicates their ambivalence about seeing a death sentence actually imposed.

Joseph Giarratano

Sometime early on the morning of February 5, 1979, Joseph Giarratano awakened from a night of heavy drug use in an apartment in Norfolk, Virginia, to discover the bodies of two women. Toni Kline, who had let Giarratano live with her for a couple of weeks, was dead in the bathroom with her throat cut. Her fifteen-year-old daughter Michelle was in bed, strangled after having been raped. Giarratano had started using drugs ten years earlier and had been an alcohol abuser for many years. He had a criminal record and a record of suicide attempts.

Giarratano quickly concluded that, although he could not remember what had happened, he must have killed the two women. He ran—to Jacksonville, Florida. Already suffering from suicidal depression and hallucinations because of his drug and alcohol use, on the bus to Florida Giarratano decided that, because he had killed the women, he did not deserve to live. As he later put it, "I was convinced that I was evil, and had to be punished for what I did." As soon as he arrived in Jacksonville, he went up to a police officer and said he had killed two people and wanted to turn himself in. He gave two statements to the Jacksonville police, saying that he killed Toni Kline first, then raped and murdered Michelle. After he was returned to Virginia, Giarratano made several more statements. The most detailed confession went through the crime step-by-step, this time saying that Giarratano raped Michelle before killing Toni.

Giarratano's confessions were corroborated by some physical evidence: his fingerprints in the apartment, blood on his boots, and a hair consistent with his found on Michelle's body. Giarratano pleaded not guilty by reason of insanity, but the evidence against him was strong, and he was quickly convicted and sentenced to death.

As it turned out, the apparently strong evidence really did not amount to much, when examined closely. The physical evidence simply showed that he had been in the same apartment with the Klines at the time they died, which he never disputed but which did not itself show that he had murdered them. The evidence strongly suggested that the killer was right-handed, but Giarratano was left-handed and had a weak right hand because of a neurological disorder. Giarratano's confessions were inconsistent with each other. At first he said that he killed Toni first, then that he killed her after killing Michelle. And the reason for the inconsistencies became clear from examining his most detailed confession: The police essentially fed him the answers to construct a confession consistent with physical evidence showing that Michelle died "some hours" before her mother. When Giarratano confessed, he certainly did believe he had murdered the women, but the evidence raised substantial doubts about that.

During his first years on death row, Giarratano continued to believe he was guilty. In 1983 he decided, as Gary Gilmore had, to abandon his appeals. He made that decision, though, while he was receiving strong antipsychotic medicine. Preparing for his execution, he stopped the medication. Without the medication, Giarratano actually became more rational and decided to fight his execution. He began to study law, and by all accounts, truly rehabilitated himself. Cured of his drug dependency, he became a "jail-house lawyer" for himself and other inmates.

One case he brought ended up in the Supreme Court. It did not directly challenge his conviction. Instead, Giarratano argued, his constitutional rights were denied when Virginia failed to provide him with a lawyer to present his postconviction challenges. The Supreme Court held in 1956 and again in 1963 that states had to provide lawyers for defendants who were appealing their convictions. But postconviction challenges are different. In theory, defendants have already had one chance to appeal, and states have no duty to give them a second chance at all. Giarratano's lawyers argued, though, that postconviction challenges in death penalty cases were different from the ordinary run of cases. Often the reasons for challenging a conviction did not become apparent until the time for appeal had passed, and even more often the reasons were so complex that it was unfair to create a system of postconviction review that pretended to give prisoners a chance but that in fact was a farce because the prisoners did not have lawyers.

The Supreme Court rejected Giarratano's claim.[3] It did come close to saying that, in different circumstances, states would have to provide lawyers for postconviction proceedings. Chief Justice Rehnquist, writing for four justices, said that Virginia did not have to provide lawyers because it did not have to provide postconviction remedies at all. Four justices disagreed. The key vote was cast by Justice Anthony Kennedy. He believed that Virginia did have to provide "meaningful access" to its courts in postconviction proceedings. But, he thought, Virginia had done so: For Justice Kennedy, it was crucial that "no prisoner on death row in Virginia has been unable to obtain counsel to represent him in postconviction proceedings." Although Giarratano lost, the decision established the principle that states have to do something to make sure that capital defendants get a real hearing in their postconviction proceedings.

Giarratano's case attracted the attention of Marie Deans, a Virginia activist against the death penalty. She persuaded conservatives James J. Kilpatrick and Richard Vigurie that there were real doubts about Giarratano's guilt, and they helped organize a letter-writing campaign to Virginia governor Douglas Wilder. The appeal for clemency also got the support of traditional death penalty opponents like Amnesty International. Giarratano himself wrote numerous legal articles, including one published in the *Yale Law Journal.* Entitled "'To the Best of Our Knowledge, We Have Never Been Wrong': Fallibility versus Finality in Capital Punishment," the article argued against efforts to accelerate the imposition of death sentences because too often evidence had turned up late in the process that the defendant was in fact innocent. The article, notably, did not refer to Giarratano's own claim of innocence.

Governor Douglas Wilder, the nation's first African-American governor, had opposed the death penalty as a member of the Virginia legislature. He had national political ambitions, though, planning to run for president in 1992, and he knew that Michael Dukakis's opposition to capital punishment had been a serious political liability in the 1988 presidential campaign. Wilder had rejected appeals for executive clemency before, perhaps most notably in the case of Wilbert Lee Evans, who had saved the lives of prison guards taken captive during a large-scale escape from Virginia's death row.

The public campaign for executive clemency had its effect. Giarratano, his judicial appeals concluded, was scheduled to be executed on Friday, February 22, 1991. On Tuesday, February 19, Governor Wilder announced that he was commuting Giarratano's sentence to life imprisonment, with the possibility of parole after he served twenty-five years. Wilder claimed that his decision was "on the merits," not influenced by "popular appeal." Yet he did not point out the anomaly that the basis for clemency was the possibility that Giarratano was innocent and yet Giarratano was going to spend at least twenty-five years in prison for a crime Governor Wilder believed he may not have committed. Giarratano pleaded for a new trial, but the state's attorney general Mary Sue Terry, convinced that Wilder was wrong (and planning herself to run for governor in 1993), refused to try him again. Giarratano will be eligible for parole in 2004.

Roger Keith Coleman

An hour before midnight on March 10, 1981, Bradley McCoy came home from his second-shift job in the small mining town of Grundy, Virginia. Walking through the open door, he found his wife, Wanda, lying dead in the back bedroom. She had been raped and then murdered by a deep slash in her neck. Because there were no signs of a break-in, the police assumed that Wanda McCoy knew her killer. Suspicion quickly focused on Roger Keith Coleman, Mrs. McCoy's brother-in-law, who had a prior conviction for attempted rape.

The police questioned Coleman around noon on March 11. They knew that Mrs. McCoy had been killed around 10:30. Coleman gave a detailed account of his movements the night before—he went to a grocery store, he reported for his shift at a coal mine only to find that the night shift had been laid off, he chatted with a friend who punched a time clock just as their conversation ended, and he went to a bathhouse in town at 10:50. Coleman's account, which witnesses later corroborated, did not rule out the possibility that he killed Mrs. McCoy, although he would have had to move very fast to do it. He gave the police the clothes he was wearing the night before; there were a couple of blood spots on his jeans, which had damp legs.

Local pressure to find Mrs. McCoy's killer was intense, and the police decided to arrest Coleman in early April. Their case was supported by the blood spots, which matched Mrs. McCoy's blood type, by the presence of two hairs found on Mrs. McCoy, which a scientific witness testified almost certainly came from Coleman, and by a semen specimen found on Mrs. McCoy, which closely matched Coleman's blood type. Finally, a witness who was in jail with Coleman testified that Coleman told him that Coleman and another man raped Mrs. McCoy.

Coleman testified on his own behalf, but the jury did not believe him and sentenced Coleman to death. After his conviction and first appeal, Coleman filed a postconviction action, raising a number of federal constitutional claims that had not been considered in his first appeal. For example, he wanted to show that a juror had said he hoped to sit on the jury so he could "burn the s.o.b." He also wanted to argue that he had not been given a defense that met constitutional standards and that the prosecution had concealed evidence that would have shown him innocent.

The state trial court rejected his claims, and Coleman, through his lawyers, tried to appeal. His lawyers filed the appeal thirty-three days after the trial court's decision and that turned out to be fatal. For under Virginia's procedural rules, appeals have to be filed within thirty days. The Virginia Supreme Court refused to consider the merits of Coleman's appeal. Then, when Coleman went to the federal courts, they said that Virginia's supreme court had simply applied a reasonable general procedural rule. The federal courts, they said, could not undermine Virginia's procedural rules by taking up claims that the Virginia courts would not consider. The Supreme Court agreed.[4] Coleman could get the federal courts to consider his claims only if he showed, as he could not, that somehow the state had interfered with his lawyers' ability to file their appeal on time.

Although Coleman's case had not attracted much media attention until then, the prospect that Virginia would execute someone whose conviction might be unconstitutional began to bother some observers. Justice O'Connor's opinion for the Supreme Court ended up fueling media attention. Her opinion began, "This is a case about federalism," which struck Coleman's supporters as a callous and abstract way of describing a case in which a man's life might be forfeited because his lawyers made a mistake.

By this point, Coleman was represented by lawyers from a prominent Washington law firm, who had good contacts with the media. They began to present reporters with evidence, not just that Coleman had been unfairly denied a chance to challenge his conviction but that he might be innocent. The time sequence presented at the trial barely gave Coleman time to murder Wanda McCoy. And after the murder, Coleman had no scratches, even though Mrs. McCoy apparently had fought her attacker. Indeed, she had dirt underneath her fingernails, suggesting that she had been killed outside her house. On the prosecution's theory, for Coleman to commit the crime within the time sequence it suggested, he would have had to wade through a creek, and his clothes should have been wetter and muddier than they were. The prosecution relied on the drops of blood spattered on Coleman's jeans, which matched Mrs. McCoy's blood type. But the murder was quite violent, and whoever committed it probably had much more blood on him than that. The jail-house witness's mother submitted an affidavit saying that he told her he made it all up, although the witness himself denied recanting. In late 1991, another local resident signed an affidavit stating that another person had told her he, not Coleman, had murdered Mrs. McCoy. And, indeed, there was some evidence that another person had been present at Mrs. McCoy's house when she was killed.

In a flurry of activity before his scheduled execution on May 20, 1992, Coleman took a lie-detector test—and failed. His supporters said that the test had to be inconclusive because of the pressures of the impending execution. Coleman's case was damaged when his own DNA expert showed that the sperm found in Mrs. McCoy came from a group constituting about 2% of the population and that Coleman was in that group. Finally, Coleman filed a federal habeas corpus action seeking to delay his execution until the court held a hearing on whether he was actually innocent. The district judge, though, found that Coleman had not presented even a "colorable claim" of innocence. The Supreme Court, by a seven-to-two vote, denied a stay of execution, and Coleman went to the electric chair on May 20.

Coleman may well have been guilty; the state's case, though not overwhelming, was substantial, and Coleman's attempt to show he was innocent failed to persuade the only judge who considered the claim. Still, Coleman died without any appellate court considering his more substantial constitutional challenges to his conviction (about the biased juror, for example)—and they refused to do so because his lawyers filed his appeal a few days too late.

Robert Alton Harris

Although several hundred executions had taken place by early 1992, some cases could still provoke frenzied judicial action. Robert Alton Harris's case is an example. Harris was executed on April 21, 1992, after a series of extraordinary judicial actions, though Harris's case was not at all extraordinary in itself. It attracted attention largely because Harris was the first person executed in California since the death penalty moratorium ended in 1977.

After thinking about it for a couple of months, Harris and his brother Daniel decided to rob a bank. On July 2, 1978, Daniel stole two guns. The brothers practiced with the guns the next day and then bought knit caps for disguise. They needed a getaway car and found their target on July 5 at a hamburger stand, where John Mayeski and Michael Baker, two teenagers, were eating in their car. Harris got in the back of the car and forced them to drive it to where the Harrises had practiced shooting; Daniel followed in Robert's car. After learning that Harris planned to use the stolen car in a robbery, the boys offered to walk up a hill, wait until they heard the cars leave, and then report the car stolen, giving misleading descriptions of the thieves. According to testimony at the trial, Harris agreed, but as the boys were walking up the hill, he shot Mayeski in the back and then again in the head. He then ran after Baker and shot him four times. He then returned to Mayeski, shooting him twice more. Robert and Daniel returned home, where—in an action that drove home Harris's callousness—Robert finished eating the boys' hamburgers and laughed at Daniel for "not having the stomach" to kill the boys.

The Harrises robbed the bank on July 5 and were arrested the same day. Daniel told the police about the murders and blamed Robert. After hearing Daniel's confession, Robert also confessed, telling a psychiatrist who interviewed him that he had killed Mayeski and Baker after assuring Daniel that they would not be hurt. Harris later repeated these confessions, telling a fellow inmate, for example, "I couldn't have no punks running around that could identify me, so I wasted them."

Robert Harris was convicted of kidnapping and murder. At the sentencing hearing, the jury learned that Harris had been convicted of manslaughter in 1975 and that, while in prison, he had raped and threatened the life of another inmate. It also heard testimony about Harris's "dismal childhood," including the fact that his father had been convicted of molesting Harris's sisters. Harris testified that Daniel had fired the first shots. The jury sentenced Harris to death.

Harris appealed to the California Supreme Court. He had a good chance to win the appeal. The California Supreme Court, headed by Chief Justice Rose Bird, routinely vacated death sentences; indeed, Bird and two of her colleagues were later turned out of office largely because of their record in voting to reverse death sentences. Harris had the misfortune of being one of the handful of defendants whose death sentences were affirmed by the California Supreme Court, over the dissent of Chief Justice Bird and one other justice.

Harris then sought federal habeas corpus, raising a large number of challenges to his conviction and sentence. The federal courts first focused on his claim that California's death penalty system was unconstitutional because it did not provide "comparative proportionality" review. Harris argued, that is, that the Supreme Court's decisions upholding death penalty statutes against the claim that death sentences were handed down arbitrarily rested in large measure on the Court's belief that state supreme courts would compare death cases to each other to insure that a death penalty was indeed proportional to the offenses regarded as deserving a death penalty in the state.

The court of appeals agreed with Harris, but the Supreme Court did not.[5] According to Justice White, who wrote the Court's opinion, the focus of "proportionality" review had to be on the "abstract" question of whether the death penalty was an appropriate sentence for the crime for which it was imposed. He agreed that the Court's earlier opinions suggested that "comparative proportionality" review, in which Harris's case would be compared with others to see if juries imposed death sentences in similar cases, would be a good idea, as "an additional safeguard against arbitrary or capricious sentencing." But, he wrote, it was not a constitutional requirement.

The case went back to the lower federal courts, which considered and rejected Harris's other claims. Eventually the state scheduled his execution for April 3, 1990. Harris filed another federal habeas corpus action on March 26. He presented some substantial new claims. Some centered around his claim that Daniel committed the murders and that Harris's confessions were designed to protect Daniel. Others centered around the death sentence itself. Harris argued that the jury had failed to be given adequate psychiatric evidence supporting his claim that, because he had been abused as a child, he ought not receive a death sentence. A court-appointed psychiatrist testified at the sentencing hearing, but Harris had been unable to hire his own psychiatric expert. And according to Harris, he had now found evidence, unavailable at trial, that he had suffered organic brain damage that affected his ability to control himself.

The court of appeals rejected Harris's new claims. Two of the three judges on the panel that decided the case found that Harris had "abused" the writ of habeas corpus by delaying the presentation of these claims. They went on to address and reject the merits of the claims, though. Judge John Noonan, appointed to the court by President Ronald Reagan, dissented. He believed that Harris had shown a real possibility that he had received incompetent assistance from his psychiatric experts, a violation, in Judge Noonan's view, of a "constitutional right of 'bedrock' fairness." For Judge Noonan, Harris had alleged facts showing that his psychiatrists had completely failed to appreciate the significance of his organic brain damage. And that was crucial. Judge Noonan put the case in the larger context of capital punishment and mental disease:

> When monstrous deeds are done. . .there is a natural desire to avenge the outrage and to eliminate its perpetrator. At the time the suspicion. . .must occur to reasonable persons that the person who performed such awful deeds is, if not insane, at least laboring under an infirmity of mind. Normal human beings, one thinks, could not engage in such cruel and callous conduct. If these suspicions of mental abnormality were, in fact, confirmed by competent psychiatric testimony. . .a humane and civilized jury would undoubtedly consider such evidence in mitigation because a humane and civilized jury could not judge a

> mentally impaired person in the same way it would judge a person free of such tendencies.[6]

After proceedings in this case were over, California planned to execute Harris on Tuesday, April 21, 1992.[7] As he had before, Harris filed yet another habeas corpus petition, this time claiming directly that he was innocent. The courts rapidly lost sight of this petition, because another action was filed on Good Friday, April 17. This was a class action brought by and on behalf of all prisoners under sentence of death in California; Harris was of course a member of that class. The action claimed that California's gas chamber was a cruel and unusual *method* of carrying out death sentences. Only three states authorized execution by lethal gas; eight had abandoned the gas chamber for execution by lethal injection over the past fifteen years. Further, when Arizona carried out a gas chamber execution on April 6, only a few days earlier, the process was so "gruesome" that Arizona's attorney general recommended that Arizona stop using the gas chamber.

This new challenge, unlike Harris's challenge to his conviction, was obviously substantial, and Judge Marilyn Hall Patel of the federal district court decided to issue a temporary restraining order barring California from using the gas chamber for ten days, until she could decide the merits of the case. Obviously that order applied to Harris, the only person scheduled to be executed in California's gas chamber within the ten-day period.

Now things began to fall apart. California's attorney general wanted to appeal Judge Patel's decision. The rules of the court of appeals for California say that the group of judges that first hears a death penalty case will hear all later appeals in the same case. The three judges met on Easter evening and decided to hold a telephone oral argument immediately, rather than waiting for the next morning. This meant that the judges had no written material from Harris's lawyers when the argument occurred. After hearing argument, the judges gave Harris's lawyers ninety minutes to file their written brief. Immediately after receiving it, the panel vacated Judge Hall's stay, over Judge Noonan's dissent.

Obviously, the majority was annoyed at what it saw as a stalling device. But what it did was almost lawless. The majority took the view that the challenge to the gas chamber should be heard in a state court, not a federal court. In taking this position, the majority relied on legal doctrines that nearly everyone agrees were inapplicable to the problem—so inapplicable, indeed, that the majority decided not to publish its opinion, which is available now only through electronic reporting services. More important, temporary restraining orders like the one Judge Patel issued are almost never appealable. To get an appeals court to consider whether a temporary restraining order was entered improperly, the challenger—the state, in this case—has to show that the trial judge acted without any semblance of legal justification. And whatever might be said about Judge Patel's analysis—she might have been wrong or perhaps she ought to have excepted Harris from the order's operation— she clearly did not act with no justification whatever.

The panel's decision was issued on Monday afternoon, less than a day before Harris was to be executed. Again the appeals court's rules came into play. When a judge asks for a rehearing by the twenty-eight judges of the entire court, ordinarily the court takes a month to act, but the proceedings are not stayed until the entire court's decision. In death penalty cases, though, the period was shortened to seven days, and a seven-day stay of execution was automatically entered. Somewhat oddly, although Judge Patel's decision was enough of a challenge to a death sentence to be assigned to Harris's initial panel, it was *not* enough of a challenge to invoke the special rules for rehearings in death penalty cases. The full court, then, might consider the case, but Harris's execution would go on as scheduled.

This seemed wrong to a number of judges on the court. So the chief judge started phoning judges to see if they would vote to stay the order directing Judge Patel to vacate her restraining order. The phone calls were confusing because there were a lot of issues before the court. About thirty minutes before the scheduled execution, though, a majority voted to stay it.

Now the Supreme Court got into the act. Acting on an application from California's attorney general, at 6 A.M. on Tuesday morning, the justices voted seven-to-two to vacate the stay.[8] The majority called the challenge to the gas chamber "an obvious attempt to avoid" rules restricting repetitive habeas corpus cases. But, they continued, even if the Court treated the case as an ordinary civil class action, it would not allow a delay in Harris's execution. According to the majority, "this claim could have been brought more than a decade ago. There is no good reason for this abusive delay, which has been compounded by last-minute attempts to manipulate the judicial process."

Observers later noted, however, that the Court's Eighth Amendment jurisprudence rested on the notion of "evolving standards of decency," and the challenge to the gas chamber as a method of execution might not have matured until shortly before the 1992 challenge, particularly in light of the gradual erosion in the use of the gas chamber for executions and the early April incident in Arizona.

That, indeed, was the focus of Justice Stevens's dissent, which cited evidence that "execution by cyanide gas is extremely and unnecessarily painful." He mentioned, in particular, "the barbaric use of cyanide gas in the Holocaust." And he pointed out, the so-called "delay" in the challenge might be blamed on California as much as on Harris. In 1983, he noted, three justices indicated their view that the gas chamber might now be unconstitutional. Four states responded to that by abandoning the gas chamber. "In light of these events," Justice Stevens wrote, California "should have revisited its 55-year-old statute."

The Court's decision was not yet the end of the case, though. It was 3:00 A.M. on the West Coast. One of Harris's lawyers awakened Judge Harry Pregerson and told him that the Court had vacated the existing stay. As Judge Pregerson saw the problem, the original appeals panel's decision was now the law. And under that decision, the gas chamber challenge, while it might have merit, should be heard in state court. Judge Pregerson concluded that Harris should be given time to do what the appeals panel said he should do—go to state court. So, he entered a new stay of execution. It was received at the gas chamber just after Harris had been strapped in but before the cyanide pellets had been released.

When the state went back to the Supreme Court to object to Judge Pregerson's stay, the justices apparently believed that he was simply defying their first ruling. In addition to vacating Judge Pregerson's stay two hours after it was entered, the Court entered an order without precedent: It said that "no further stays of Robert Alton Harris' execution shall be entered by the federal courts except upon order of this Court."[9] Technically, the Court may have had the power to enter that order; one statute allows any federal court, including the Supreme Court, to enter orders "in aid of their. . .jurisdiction[s]," and the Court's order might fit into that category. But it was by any account an extraordinary order. After this order, Harris was executed as scheduled, and in the gas chamber, at 6:21 A.M. on April 21.

By 1992, of course, a solid majority of the Supreme Court had become impatient with the status of the death penalty. Since 1976 it was clear that capital punishment was constitutional, yet executions were carried out only sporadically. As a majority of the justices saw it, lawyers for convicted defendants were "manipulating" the procedural system to thwart the expressed desire of the American public for more executions. Yet the extraordinary events surrounding the Harris case suggest that the public, and its judges, are more ambivalent about the death penalty than the Court's majority may believe.

Conclusion

What accounts for the public fascination with these death stories? In part, it is simply that some of the cases were "firsts"—the first execution in a decade, the first involuntary execution, the first execution in a major state outside the South. After Gilmore, other prisoners sentenced to die "volunteered" for execution as Gilmore had, but their names—Steven Judy, Frank Coppola—are not familiar as Gilmore's is. And of course, involuntary executions are now frequent enough to be relegated to small paragraphs on the inside pages of our newspapers.

A second reason for public attention to these cases is media orchestration. Gilmore, Giarratano, and Coleman attracted attention from the public in part because their supporters had access to the media. And Giarratano and Coleman had access in part because they could make credible claims that they were innocent. The prospect of executing an innocent person is frightening enough to ensure public attention to such cases.

But, beyond all this, death penalty cases combine elements to make them persistently fascinating. The public, it seems, is deeply ambivalent about the death penalty. The thought of deliberately killing someone—even someone who has deliberately killed another—is horribly threatening and yet alluring. The possibility that the person we are about to kill might be innocent only heightens the fascination and ambivalence and adds to the court's confusion about how to proceed in these capital cases.

5

The Death Penalty in the Twenty-first Century

By the early 1990s, capital punishment had been restored to the criminal justice system. Public opinion polls demonstrated widespread public support for capital punishment in the abstract. Perhaps more important, executions had become rather routine. Occasionally a death penalty case would reach the front pages, usually when lawyers generated a flurry of activity and publicity immediately before an execution was scheduled. More often, though, the broadcast media did not even mention executions, and they were relegated to the back pages of national newspapers.

Capital Punishment in Today's Supreme Court

Capital punishment is likely to be part of the criminal justice system for the foreseeable future. The Supreme Court will still decide some death penalty cases. For example, in 1991–92, the Court decided seven death penalty cases.[1]

Dawson v. Delaware[2] After escaping from prison, David Dawson stole two cars to confuse the police, then broke into two houses to steal some money. Madeline Kisner was at home in the second house, and Dawson stabbed her to death. He was arrested early the next morning, after he abandoned yet another car he had stolen. The prosecution wanted to introduce evidence in the penalty phase of his case that Dawson was a member of the Aryan Brotherhood, expert testimony showing that the Aryan Brotherhood was a racist prison gang, photographs of swastika tattoos on Dawson's back, and testimony that he called himself "Abaddon," which Dawson said meant "one of Satan's disciples." To avoid an extended battle over whether this evidence could be admitted, though, the prosecution eventually agreed to introduce *only* a statement that the Aryan Brotherhood was a white racist prison gang that began in California and that separate gangs calling themselves the Aryan Brotherhood existed in many state prisons, including Delaware's. The prosecution added no expert testimony explaining what the Aryan Brotherhood actually did.

Dawson claimed that the Aryan Brotherhood evidence violated his right of association under the Constitution. The Supreme Court disagreed with that broad claim, but it did agree that introducing the evidence violated Dawson's constitutional rights. The problem, the Court said, was that the evidence was completely unexplained. It might be true that the Aryan Brotherhood elsewhere was associated with drugs, escape attempts, and murders, Chief Justice Rehnquist wrote, and if the jury knew that it might have drawn some inferences about Dawson's character from his membership in Delaware's. But the prosecution's agreement meant that none of that information was presented to the jury. As it stood, nothing that the jury got was related to Dawson's case: "For example, the Aryan Brotherhood evidence was not tied in any way to the murder of Dawson's victim." At most, the evidence showed Dawson's "abstract beliefs," which could not be relied on in a sentencing proceeding. Dawson had to be resentenced.

Stringer v. Black[3] James Stringer planned the robbery of the Jackson, Mississippi, home of Ray and Nell McWilliams, a competitor of Stringer's in the business of selling jewelry, who Stringer knew kept jewelry and money in the house. Four people accompanied Stringer to the McWilliams house. Stringer was armed with a .357 magnum revolver, and his son had a "riot" shotgun. Stringer had planned to cut the McWilliams's throats, but when Stringer revealed his gun to Ray McWilliams, a fight broke out. One of the other robbers came in, put his own pistol to McWilliams's head, said "You're a dead man," and killed him. Stringer's son put the riot gun to the back of Nell McWilliams's head and killed her. James Stringer was convicted of capital murder. The jury found three aggravating circumstances, including that the murders were "especially heinous, atrocious, and cruel." In Mississippi, juries are instructed to balance the aggravating circumstances against whatever mitigating circumstances they find.

In habeas corpus proceedings, Stringer argued that the "especially heinous" aggravating circumstance was unconstitutionally vague and that he was therefore entitled to have his death sentence reconsidered. The lower courts refused to consider his claim because he was seeking to apply a new rule on habeas corpus. The Court had already held that similar language was unconstitutionally vague, and—in a second decision, rendered after Stringer's conviction became final—it had applied the vagueness doctrine to sentencing in a Mississippi case where the jury had found several aggravating circumstances including one vague one. The issue, then, was whether that second decision merely applied the existing rule against vagueness, in which case Stringer would win, or announced a new rule, in which case he would lose. The decision turned on an intensive analysis of whether Mississippi's sentencing system was different enough from the ones in states where the Court had invalidated similar aggravating circumstances *before* Stringer's conviction became final. The Court ruled for Stringer and said that the Mississippi Supreme Court had to consider carefully whether the two remaining aggravating circumstances outweighed the mitigating ones. The state court might still uphold the sentence, the Supreme Court said, but it had to look at the case again.

Riggins v. Nevada[4] David Riggins stabbed Paul Wade to death. Riggins claimed that after using cocaine he went to Wade's apartment and got into a fight. He testified that he had heard voices in his head telling him that killing Wade would be justifiable homicide. But Riggins testified under unusual circumstances. He had been arrested for Wade's murder in November 1987. A few days after his arrest he told a jail psychiatrist that he was hearing voices and having trouble sleeping. The doctor prescribed 800 milligrams of Mellaril, an antipsychotic drug. And although the dosage varied over the next several months, during his trial Riggins was still taking 800 milligrams of Mellaril. In June his lawyers asked a judge to order the jail to stop giving Riggins the medicine. The drug makes people drowsy and, at dosages like the one Riggins was getting, sometimes made them seem "confused." Riggins's lawyers believed that a jury that saw Riggins while he was affected by the medicine would be unable to evaluate fairly his claims about hearing voices and might believe him to be more cold-blooded and calm than he really was. The jury convicted Riggins and sentenced him to death.

The Supreme Court agreed with Riggins that he should not have been tried while he was involuntarily receiving Mellaril. The problem, according to Justice O'Connor, was not that the Mellaril made it impossible for the jury fairly to assess Riggins's true behavior and appearance. The difficulty, instead, was that the state courts had not found that giving him the medicine was "essential" to protect the public or Riggins or to ensure a fair trial. The courts should have considered whether there were alternatives to continuing the high doses of Mellaril and should not simply have assumed that there was a high chance that, if taken off the drugs, Riggins would not be competent to stand trial.

Sochor v. Florida[5] Dennis Sochor tried to rape a woman he had met in a bar on New Year's Eve. When she resisted, he choked her to death. The jury was instructed that it could find an aggravating circumstance that the murder "was committed in a cold, calculated and premeditated manner, without any pretense of moral or legal justification." The jury recommended a death sentence, and the judge agreed, finding four aggravating circumstances and no mitigating ones. The state supreme court found that the "coldness" factor, which required more than the usual premeditation and planning, was not supported by the evidence against Sochor. It affirmed the conviction anyway, though, because three aggravating circumstances remained.

Sochor claimed that the Florida Supreme Court affirmed his death sentence without finding, as it should have, that the judge's mistaken reliance on the "coldness" factor was harmless error. The Supreme Court examined each sentence in the state court's discussion of the consequences of striking the "coldness" factor and agreed with Sochor. It sent the case back to the state supreme court for it to decide whether the error was indeed harmless.

Morgan v. Illinois[6] This was a follow-up to the Witherspoon case that had been part of the initial attack on capital punishment. *Witherspoon* held that the government could not automatically exclude from a jury someone who expressed qualms about imposing the death penalty, as long as the juror indicated that he or she would follow the judge's instructions. Derrick Morgan was on trial for murdering a drug dealer who competed for business with the El-Rukn gang in Chicago. The evidence showed that Morgan was paid $4,000 to kill the dealer, a "friend," who Morgan shot in the head six times. During jury selection, the trial judge asked the initial *Witherspoon* question: "Would you automatically vote against the death penalty no matter what the facts of the case were?" Morgan's lawyer requested that they be asked a reverse question: "Would you automatically vote to impose the death penalty no matter what the facts are?" The trial judge refused to ask that question but did ask whether the jurors would follow his instructions "even though you may not agree" or, for some jurors, simply whether they would be "fair and impartial" or "give both sides a fair trial." The jury convicted Morgan and sentenced him to death.

The Supreme Court agreed that Morgan was entitled to have jurors asked specifically about their views on capital punishment. According to Justice White, "a juror who will automatically vote for the death penalty in every case will fail in good faith to consider the evidence of aggravating and mitigating circumstances," and therefore would not be "impartial." And to allow the defense "to exercise intelligently" its power to challenge jurors for cause, a specific question was required, because "a juror could in good conscience swear to uphold the law and yet be unaware that maintaining such dogmatic beliefs about the death penalty would prevent him or her from doing so."

Medina v. California[7] Teofilo Medina went on a crime spree in 1984. After stealing a gun, he held up two gas stations, a drive-in, and a market, killed three people working at the places he robbed, and shot at two people who tried to follow his getaway car. Before he went on trial for murder, Medina's lawyer sought a determination that he was incompetent to stand trial—that is, unable to understand the proceedings or help his lawyer in conducting a defense. California statutes say that a defendant has the burden of persuading a jury, by a "preponderance of the evidence," that he is incompetent to stand trial. Medina's incompetence hearing took six days. Six doctors testified. One said that Medina was schizophrenic and incompetent to stand trial; another agreed that Medina was schizophrenic but thought that he could stand trial. Two others doubted that Medina was schizophrenic—one refused to give an opinion on competence, the other "leaned toward a finding of competence." A fifth doctor had treated Medina for knife wounds and gave no opinion on competence. The sixth thought that Medina might have been "malingering" and was competent. During the hearing, Medina "engaged in several verbal and physical outbursts" and once "overturned the counsel table." The jury found Medina competent to stand trial.

After his conviction and death sentence by a different jury, Medina appealed, claiming that California could not require him to prove that he was not competent to stand trial; instead, the government had to show that he was competent. The Supreme Court disagreed. It relied on long-established cases that had allowed states to treat insanity as a defense that the defendant had to prove. The only issue, according to Justice Kennedy, was whether putting the burden of persuasion on the defendant was fundamentally unfair. Although everyone agreed that incompetent defendants could not be tried, the historical evidence about who had the burden of showing incompetence was mixed, and the states vary even today about what to do.

Sawyer v. Whitley[8] In 1979 Robert Sawyer and Charles Lane returned from a night of drinking to the house Sawyer shared with his girlfriend and her two young children. Frances Arwood, the former wife of the girlfriend's stepbrother, was there. Sawyer and Lane argued with Arwood, accusing her of giving pills to the children. They beat her and kicked her into the bathroom, where they held her under the water in the bathtub and poured scalding water over her; Lane probably raped her around this time. After dragging her back into the living room, Sawyer poured lighter fluid over Arwood and lit it. His girlfriend testified that, just before this, Sawyer told Lane that he would show Lane "just how cruel" he could be. After watching her burn, Sawyer and Lane sat around listening to records. Arwood was in a coma for two months before she died. In separate trials, Lane and Sawyer were convicted of murder; Lane received a life sentence, and Sawyer was sentenced to death. After a long series of appeals, Sawyer's first habeas corpus petition was denied in 1990. Then he filed a second petition. He claimed that his constitutional rights had been violated because the jury had not considered evidence, which the prosecution should have made available, that one of the children had told a police officer that Lane rather than Sawyer used and lit the lighter fluid and other evidence about Sawyer's stays at mental institutions as a teenager.

Under the Court's habeas corpus doctrine, Sawyer could get relief only if he showed that he was "actually innocent." It is easy to understand what it means to say that someone is actually innocent of a crime. The issue before the Supreme Court in *Sawyer* was what it meant to say that a defendant was "actually innocent" of the death penalty. The Court divided over that question, with a majority holding that Sawyer could get relief only if he showed that, with the new evidence, no reasonable juror could have found him eligible for execution—that is, that the new evidence showed that no aggravating circumstance existed. But, Chief Justice Rehnquist said, the mental health evidence simply went to mitigation, not aggravation. Because the crime was so aggravated, Sawyer was clearly eligible for the death sentence, and that, according to the Chief Justice, meant that he was not "actually innocent" of the penalty. There was a lot of evidence that Sawyer himself had used the lighter fluid, and even if Lane had done so, Sawyer would be guilty for helping him. Finally, the child's testimony did not undermine the evidence supporting a finding of cruelty through beating and scalding Arwood with boiling water. Justice Stevens would have applied a different standard—was it "clearly erroneous" to sentence Sawyer to death?—but he reached the same conclusion: The sentence was not unjust, and habeas corpus could be denied.

Of course, these cases were important to the defendants, and some—the jury inquiry case (*Morgan*) and the burden of proof case (*Medina*), for example—might have some impact on more than a handful of cases. But mostly the cases involved cleaning up some details about the administration of statutory systems authorizing capital punishment. None went anywhere near the heart of the death penalty system.

Yet there was a remarkable stability in the Court's approach to capital punishment. In 1976 only three justices on the Court would have required guided discretion statutes that took account of both aggravating and mitigating circumstances. By 1990 that was entirely conventional. Only Justice Scalia saw a tension between guiding discretion through specifying aggravating circumstances and allowing discretion through unrestrained consideration of mitigating ones. Further, no one explicitly sought to deregulate or deconstitutionalize the death penalty issue by remitting it completely to the states.

Finally and perhaps most remarkably, despite the dramatic changes in the Court's composition, even the accession of a new "Rehnquist Court" did not bring about major changes in death penalty jurisprudence. The Court remained closely divided over death penalty issues: When Justice Brennan left the Court in 1990, Justice Blackmun became more concerned about the administration of the death penalty. From 1986 through 1991, the Court decided thirty-nine capital punishment cases and vacated the death sentences in nineteen. Here is the division in the seven cases the Court decided in 1991–92:

- *Dawson*—eight to one to vacate the death sentence
- *Stringer*—six to three to vacate the death sentence
- *Riggins*—seven to two to vacate the conviction
- *Sochor*—eight to one to vacate the death sentence
- *Morgan*—six to three to vacate the death sentence
- *Medina*—seven to two to uphold the conviction and death sentence
- *Sawyer*—unanimous to uphold the death sentence

Over the next several years, some cases that would have been decided by a vote of five-to-four in 1978 will still be decided by a vote of five-to-four, although in 1978 the government might lose and now it might win.

The Court's continuing division almost certainly reflects its sense that, all things considered, the decision for death is an extremely close one. Until a new movement against the death penalty arises, this situation is unlikely to change. Paradoxically, the reconstructed death penalty system will probably retard the emergence of such a new movement.

Public Support for Capital Punishment

Abolitionist sentiment peaked in 1966, when only 42% of the public supported capital punishment.[9] Since then, public support has steadily grown, essentially without interruption. By the early 1990s, surveys typically reported support for capital punishment at levels around 75%. And although support was greatest among whites, males, and conservatives, it was high among all demographic groups: By a slight margin, African-Americans and self-described liberals favored the death penalty. Further, the trends were the same among all groups. And the results were unusually stable: Giving people more information about capital punishment did not change their answers much; support declined a bit, but not dramatically.

With support for capital punishment at these levels, the prospects for a renewed abolitionist movement were small. Yet the crude survey statistics conceal important information. For example, sometimes people explain the growth in death penalty support by pointing out that crime rates have grown too. But in fact, death penalty support grew during the 1980s despite a decline in the homicide rate during that decade. Of course, the crime rate statistics do not really tell us whether the rate of crimes for which people believe the death penalty is appropriate has declined too. What matters is public *belief* about crime rates. And although crime rates declined, people did not believe that. One reason may be increased media attention to horrible murders: We know more about more murders than we used to, and so we may believe that they are more common than they really are.

Justice Marshall suggested in 1972 that crude surveys were not really helpful because what mattered was what people with accurate information about the death penalty believed. More sophisticated studies have provided some modest support for Marshall's hypothesis.[10] Information does lead to a small decline in support for the death penalty. And news reports that a "killer" has been released on parole apparently have led many people to believe that those who would otherwise be sentenced to death will actually serve relatively short prison terms. In fact, those murderers are almost never released on parole until a very substantial period has passed. In one survey, 90% of those asked reported their belief that murderers were eligible for parole in less than twenty-five years; of those, nearly half indicated that they would be less inclined to support the death penalty if murderers could not be paroled until they served at least twenty-five years. In fact, in their state, murderers *did* have to serve twenty-five years before they were eligible for parole.

Justice Marshall's "informed public" hypothesis suggests that public support for the death penalty may be as high as it is precisely because people have not experienced a criminal justice system with a regularly imposed death penalty for almost twenty years. As the capital punishment becomes more routine, public perception of its importance—or, more accurately, of the fact that it has little to do with deterring murder—is, if Justice Marshall was correct, likely to lead to a decline in support for the death penalty.

Challenging the New Death Penalty System

Having failed to abolish capital punishment because it was cruel and barbarous, death penalty opponents today supplement their basic arguments against the death penalty with arguments against the way the death penalty is administered. To convert those arguments into a case for abolition, they must show that the difficulties they identify are systemic, that is, that the difficulties cannot be eliminated by tinkering with the system.[11] Criticisms of the present death penalty system follow.

Reversal Rates Compared to what happens in noncapital cases, the rates at which appellate courts reverse convictions or vacate sentences are extraordinarily high. The Supreme Court's decisions in 1991–92—five out of seven death sentence cases vacated—suggest the dimensions of this phenomenon. From 1972 to 1980, the reversal rate in death penalty cases in all appellate courts was about 60%; from 1982 to 1985 the rate was about 45%, taking state appeals and federal habeas corpus together; today the rate is probably around 30%. In contrast, the reversal rate in ordinary criminal cases is about 5%. Opponents of the death penalty believe that the extraordinarily high reversal rates in death penalty cases show that something is wrong with the system. As professor Robert Burt puts the point, "[I]t is difficult to avoid the suspicion that our criminal justice system impeaches its own integrity" with reversal rates so high in cases "where—one might assume—front-line dispensing officers would be more careful in their conduct."[12]

Execution Rates Juries are willing to send people to death row, but the overall system is quite reluctant to execute them. By mid-1992, only 178 people had actually been executed since 1972. Between 1972 and 1992, the greatest number of executions in any year was twenty-five.

And consider the implications of continuing to sentence people to death. Let's assume that there are now 2,500 people already sentenced to death but that 40% of the sentences are eventually vacated. That leaves 1,500 who have to be executed. And assume that 200 people are sentenced to death each year and again that 40% of those sentences will be vacated. Each year, 120 more people would actually face execution. Even to keep the death row population stable, 120 people a year would have to be executed—four times as many each year as have been executed recently. And to reduce death row populations over a ten-year period by carrying out executions, something like 250 people a year would have to be executed—almost one each weekday. Yet, in the 1930s—the decade with the highest recorded number of executions—the annual rate was a little over 150 executions per year, and the highest number was 199 in 1935. Of course, a large part of this calculation involves eliminating a large backlog. Still, recent execution rates have not approached what would be needed to keep the backlog from growing, much less what would be needed to reduce it.

Death Row Conditions Death row used to be a place where people sentenced to death were confined for the few months before they were executed. Security was extremely tight for the very few people on death row at any one time because prison wardens believed that death row prisoners had every reason in the world to try to escape and no reason to avoid killing guards and anyone else who got in their way. Today, death rows still exist, with similarly tight security. Often, prisoners are allowed to leave their cells for exercise for only thirty minutes each day. When they move through the prison, they must wear handcuffs and leg shackles. As one death row prisoner put it, "Imagine being locked up in your bathroom all day, year after year." In Texas, guards call, "Dead man comin' through," when a death row prisoner moves through the prison.[13]

Now, though, death rows are places for the long-term confinement of a rather large population. Conditions on death row might well be regarded as unconstitutionally cruel if they were inflicted on anyone other than people under sentence of death. And given low execution rates and high reversal rates, maybe those conditions are unconstitutional anyway.

Irrationality and Arbitrariness Low execution rates, death penalty opponents say, make the system irrational and arbitrary. It is irrational because it cannot possibly serve the goals of deterrence and retribution that might perhaps justify capital punishment. Just as in 1972, actually being executed is, in Justice Stewart's phrase, unusual in the sense that being struck by lightning is unusual. And it is arbitrary because, even if we put aside the troubling statistics about the impact of race and wealth on who gets sentenced to death, nothing but chance distinguishes those who are executed from those who are not. In the Sawyer case decided by the Supreme Court in 1992, for example, no one could plausibly say that Sawyer deserved to die more than Lane did: Sawyer may have used the lighter fluid, but Lane fully participated in the atrocious events.

In some cases, the arbitrariness of the system becomes bizarre. In one case, the Supreme Court appears to have held that the death penalty is an appropriate sanction for breach of contract. *Ricketts v. Adamson* grew out of the notorious Arizona murder of Donald Bolles, an investigative reporter who died when his car exploded while he was working on a story about organized crime.[14] John Harvey Adamson was arrested and charged with first-degree murder for planting the bomb. In the middle of his trial, he reached a plea agreement with the prosecutor. The prosecutor accepted Adamson's plea to second-degree murder, and Adamson agreed to testify against two men who had hired him to kill Bolles. They agreed that if Adamson refused to testify, the first-degree murder charge would be reinstated.

Adamson did testify, and the two men were convicted, but their convictions were reversed on appeal. Adamson then took the position that he had fully complied with his agreement and did not have to testify at their retrial. At that point, the prosecutor was faced with the prospect that no one would be convicted of first-degree murder. Hoping to salvage something, he said that Adamson's plea agreement required his testimony at the two men's second trial and prosecuted Adamson for first-degree murder. Adamson appealed the decision to put him on trial to the state supreme court. When it rejected his appeal, Adamson finally indicated that he was willing to testify. Now, though, the prosecutor refused to go along and obtained a death sentence. The Supreme Court held that prosecuting Adamson did not violate his constitutional rights because the state supreme court's interpretation of the plea agreement was reasonable. The Court conceded that Adamson's interpretation was reasonable too, and we might wonder how Adamson could have tested the meaning of the agreement other than by refusing to testify and then, when his interpretation was rejected, offering to testify. In the end, Adamson was sentenced to death because the prosecutor needed a death sentence in a notorious case and because Adamson misinterpreted the contract he had made with the prosecutor.

The case becomes even more peculiar. The Supreme Court sent the case back to the lower courts so they could consider other constitutional claims Adamson made. The lower court then concluded that the Arizona death penalty statute was unconstitutional. The Supreme Court granted review in another Arizona case to consider *that* decision and held off on deciding the state's appeal in Adamson's case. Eventually, the Supreme Court upheld the Arizona statute by a five-to-four vote. Ordinarily, the next step would be to grant the state's appeal and send Adamson's case back to the lower courts. Under the Court's rules, though, that is an action that requires five votes. Justices Kennedy and O'Connor, both of whom had voted to uphold Arizona's statute, were disqualified in the Adamson case. That meant that the four dissenters outvoted the three remaining justices from the majority, and the lower court's decision vacating Adamson's sentence on grounds the Supreme Court held inadequate nonetheless remained in effect.[15]

Regional Concentration There is no particular reason to think that murderers in the South deserve to die more than murderers in the North and West do, but there is a striking concentration of death sentences in the South: In 1991, for example, about 72% of all those facing death sentences were in Texas, Louisiana, Alabama, Georgia, and Florida. Death penalty opponents suspect that this concentration results, if not from race discrimination in any direct sense, then from the cultural legacy of the Deep South's system of race discrimination.

Barbarism Death penalty opponents have often criticized the means used to carry out death sentences. For example, dissenting from the Court's refusal to delay an execution in a case called *Gray v. Lucas,* Justice Marshall described the process of execution by lethal gas in graphic detail.[16] Marshall found the method "cruel" because it involved "extreme pain" over a ten-minute period and because lethal injections were equally effective and "though equally barbaric in [their effects], involve[d] far less physical pain." Justice Stevens took up the refrain in the flurry of cases surrounding California's execution of Robert Alton Harris in April 1992, the state's first execution in more than twenty years.[17] After quoting from affidavits describing the convulsions, writhing, and pain felt while inhaling cyanide gas, Justice Stevens said that "moral progress" had transformed the gas chamber, once "a humane method of execution," into an "unnecessarily cruel" one. By 1992, he noted, only three states retained the gas chamber. For him, execution by lethal injection was now the only constitutionally permissible method of execution.

The most troubling aspect of the new system of capital punishment, though, is how badly defendants charged with capital crimes are defended.

Defective Assistance of Counsel

Too often, many argue, defendants are represented by inexperienced lawyers. In some noted cases, defendants faced with the possibility of a death sentence have been represented by lawyers who had not tried a criminal case in years, much less a capital case. Professor Vivian Berger provides this catalogue of "horror stories":

> defense counsel who refer to the accused as a "nigger" in front of the jury, who indicate that they are representing the client with reluctance, who absent themselves from court while a prosecution witness takes the stand, who adduce no evidence in favor of the client at the penalty phase, or who file no brief on appeal.[18]

According to Berger, "*one-quarter* of Kentucky's death row inmates had trial attorneys who have since been disbarred or resigned rather than face disbarment." And compensation for appointed attorneys can be extraordinarily low—"as little as $1,000 per case" in some states. These problems are compounded because low compensation rates and inadequate counsel systems are typical of the states of the Deep South, precisely where death penalty cases are concentrated.

Some of these difficulties are not unique to capital cases. Public defenders are always overworked, and appointed counsel are typically underpaid. The problems are exacerbated in capital cases, though. The defendants are particularly unpopular, and appointed counsel may want to maintain some distance from their clients to preserve relations with the community. And capital cases, particularly in the penalty phase, are a new specialty in criminal law. Even experienced criminal lawyers find them different. When they take cases to trial, they concentrate on getting the defendant off or convicted of some crime that does not carry the death sentence. If they fail, they are often unprepared, either emotionally or in terms of the evidence they might produce, for the sentencing phase of the trial, which may occur immediately after the guilt phase.

Although prosecutors at the penalty phase legalize the issue, or appeal to generalized concerns about deterrence and fear, defense counsel must "humanize" the defendant—show his unique human characteristics that may make jurors reluctant to impose the death penalty on this particular human being. Professor Robert Weisberg quotes counsel who open their penalty phase arguments by saying, "It is, I feel, an awesome responsibility that I have, but my responsibility is nothing, nothing at all compared to the responsibility that you bear." The argument continues by describing the defendant's up-bringing in a home of alcoholics "who locked him and his siblings into their house when they would go downtown to drink" and his mother who said, "Take this one. I can't stand the sight of him," when he was four: "What happened to the so misshapen spirit on some primordial level at an age beyond control, at an age before reason, at an age when he didn't have a choice? Human frailty."[19]

Often, though, defense counsel fail even to try to humanize the defendant. They may simply give up. Berger quotes one penalty phase argument in its entirety:

> May it please the Court, ladies and gentlemen of the jury, any lawyer who finds himself in this position cannot help but feel somewhere along the way there must be something that he could have done to have brought about a different decision, he always does. I must admit I have never been

> in this position before.
> I think there has been enough dramatics already, and all I would like to leave with you for your own sake is, "Venge[a]nce is mine, saith the Lord." Thank you.[20]

Or, having expended their efforts at the guilt phase, they may have failed to investigate evidence bearing on the penalty phase. As Berger puts it, investigating and presenting mitigating facts "smacks more of social work than law," and attorneys "who feel comfortable with traditional trial work. . . are devastated when the client is convicted and afterward just throw in the towel."

When defense attorneys are grossly inadequate, as in some of Berger's horror stories, the defendant's constitutional rights might be violated. *Strickland v. Washington* gave the Court an opportunity to discuss what the Constitution required of defense counsel in death cases.[21] The Sixth Amendment requires that defendants have the assistance of counsel, and the Court has held that this means that they must have "effective assistance." Determining what constitutes effective assistance has been difficult, however. Lawyers have to make many decisions in the heat of a trial, some of which will turn out in hindsight to have been quite bad. Yet a defendant is entitled to a lawyer who has some grasp of the law applicable to the case and some insight into possible defense strategies. The Supreme Court does not want a doctrine of ineffective assistance of counsel that routinely allows courts to second-guess the strategic decisions defense lawyers make, but it should not develop a doctrine that leaves defendants simply with a warm body next to them—more than a "potted plant," as Oliver North's lawyer put it.

The facts of *Strickland* suggest some of the difficulties faced by defendants and their attorneys in capital cases. Washington committed an extended series of crimes in September 1976, including three murders, kidnapping, attempted murder, and assaults. Eventually he surrendered and gave the police a lengthy confession. An experienced criminal lawyer was appointed to defend him. The lawyer was active in the early stages of the defense but became "hopeless" when he discovered that Washington had confessed to all three murders. Against the lawyer's advice, Washington pleaded guilty and waived his right to a jury determination of sentence. To prepare for the sentencing hearing, the lawyer spoke with Washington and telephoned his wife and mother but did not meet them or seek any other character witnesses. At the hearing, the lawyer urged that the fact that Washington had confessed showed that he did not deserve a death sentence. After being sentenced to death, Washington argued that his lawyer had not given him effective assistance of counsel. The lawyer, Washington said, did not try to get a psychiatric evaluation or to present character witnesses and did not offer the judge a meaningful argument against a death sentence.

The Supreme Court, in its first and so far only extended consideration of the requirement of effective assistance, rejected Washington's claim. Instead of providing detailed guidelines for acceptable attorney behavior, the Court adopted a general standard. The Constitution was violated, according to the Court, when defense attorneys "made errors so serious that counsel was not functioning as the 'counsel'" required by the Constitution, if those errors deprived the defendant of "a fair trial, a trial whose result is reliable." The Court said that "the proper measure of attorney performance remains simply reasonableness under prevailing professional norms." It emphasized that courts should be "highly deferential" to the attorneys themselves and "must indulge a strong presumption that counsel's conduct falls within the wide range of reasonable professional assistance."

Although it went largely unstated, the Court had an obvious concern: Trials are fast-moving, and no one can expect that lawyers will always make the best decisions all the time. Whenever a defendant loses, we will be able to identify some decisions the lawyers made that, had they been made differently, might have led to a different result. To reverse convictions simply because we think that the lawyer could have done a better job would be to reverse nearly every conviction.

Only Justice Marshall dissented from the Court's approach to the issue of effective assistance. His opinion opened by pointing to the "unfortunate but undeniable fact that a person of means. . . usually can obtain better representation" than poor people, who have to rely on appointed counsel with "limited time and resources to devote to a given case." Then his opinion asked, "Is a 'reasonably competent attorney' a reasonably competent adequately paid retained lawyer or a reasonably competent appointed attorney?" For Marshall, some aspects of criminal defense were clear enough that the courts could develop appropriate guidelines: The lawyer should confer with his or her client and should object to "significant, arguably erroneous rulings."

Marshall did not mention an additional problem with the Court's approach. It relies on an assessment of whether the attorney made reasonable strategic decisions. Sometimes, though, it might seem as if the attorney made no decision at all but simply drifted. When the attorney's competence is challenged, the state will ask soft-ball questions of the attorney. The state will ask, "Did you have strategic reasons for failing to pursue this or that aspect of the case?" Because answering "no" would cast doubt on the attorney's competence to practice law, what can we expect the answer to be?

Problems with Attacking the New Capital Punishment System

Supporters of capital punishment would not find the attacks on the new system very persuasive. Some of the challenges may not be that strong in themselves, and others can be handled without doing away with the death penalty.

Consider, for example, the high reversal rates in capital cases. Some, perhaps a large number, of the reversals occur because states are adjusting to new rules. As the Supreme Court's constitutional rulings stabilize the system, the reversal rates will decline. And, even if they remain high compared to noncapital cases, that would show only that appellate courts were taking extraordinary care when the extreme penalty was involved. How can we fault them for that?

The problems of arbitrariness and irrationality are also not so severe, a supporter of capital punishment would maintain. So long as we execute only people who deserve to die, why should it matter that we do not execute some other people? Sawyer clearly did deserve to die, on this view, and the fact that Lane "got off" with a life sentence does not do anything to undermine the validity of Sawyer's sentence.

Supporters of capital punishment are rightly suspicious of claims about the barbarism of particular methods of execution. They believe, almost always correctly, that people who argue that the gas chamber is barbaric will be back arguing that lethal injections are barbaric too, as soon as the gas chamber is taken apart.[22] What drives the argument against the gas chamber, that is, is opposition to the death penalty itself, not concern about any particular method of execution. And to the concern that death rows are overcrowded and barbarous, the reply might be to wonder whether abolition would improve conditions: Prisoners with life sentences would have nothing to lose and would have to be controlled under quite severe restrictions for the rest of their lives.

Finally, the objections based on regional concentration and defective assistance of counsel meet similar responses. There is nothing wrong about the fact that a group of states decide to respond to the crime problem similarly, unless that response really is rooted in race discrimination. If death penalty opponents could show that death penalty systems were infected with race discrimination, they ought to prevail. But, as *McCleskey* shows, modern death penalty systems do satisfy the constitutional standards the Supreme Court has set out.

As with race discrimination, so with defective assistance of counsel: If the assistance is so bad as to violate the Constitution, the remedy is clear—provide effective assistance. Doing away with the death penalty does not respond to the constitutional problem. And if the assistance is below the most desirable standard even if it does not violate the Constitution, the remedy is to train more lawyers to handle death penalty cases well. Several states have created capital punishment resource centers to represent defendants on appeal, and although these centers are themselves understaffed, the possibility of enhancing training for trial counsel does exist.

The fundamental problem with the systemic challenge to modern death penalty statutes is simple. The challenge identifies a number of discrete problems with the death penalty system. None of those problems, though, are inherent in having a death penalty. The challenge could succeed only if death penalty opponents could show that there was no way to eliminate the problems: that, for some reason, training defense attorneys for death cases would never be sufficient, that all methods of execution really are barbaric, and so on through the list of objections. That might be possible, but it has not been done persuasively yet.

A New Abolition Movement?

Historically, opposition to the death penalty had been fueled by three main factors: a principled concern that the state should not deliberately kill, concern that the death penalty discriminated against African-Americans, and outrage over what death penalty opponents believed were serious miscarriages of justice—the execution of innocent defendants who, opponents believed, had not even committed the crime or the execution of defendants who, even if guilty, surely did not deserve the ultimate penalty. The modern death penalty system transformed some of these reasons for opposing the death penalty.

Race Discrimination The McCleskey case rejected a race discrimination challenge to the death penalty, but what was more important in the politics of capital punishment was that the race discrimination argument had been transformed. The argument there was not that African-Americans received an unfair share of death sentences. Instead, it was that prosecutors, juries, and judges treated African-American *and* white killers of whites more severely than they treated those who killed African- Americans. Rhetorically, opponents could say that this showed that the system of capital punishment devalued African-American lives as compared to white lives, just as the earlier system devalued those lives by executing more African-Americans than deserved execution. But the rhetoric had less effect. An obvious response was that this sort of inadequacy was not an argument against capital punishment but was instead an argument that death sentences should be handed out more often. The problem, it could be said, was that the system failed to impose the death sentence often enough.

Miscarriages of Justice The miscarriage of justice argument also became more difficult for death penalty opponents. In a fair number of cases—running in the 1980s at a rate of less than a half-dozen a year—people sentenced to death were released when information came out showing that they were innocent. This happened not only as a result of appeals in their cases but sometimes because of unrelated and chance events, like the confession of the real killer who was arrested for some other crime and decided to clear his conscience. The cases of Randall Adams and Clarence Brantley are good examples. Both were sentenced to death for brutal murders. During the extended appeals period, however, other people confessed to the murders. Eventually, both men were released.

Death penalty opponents could not make much ground with these cases because, after all, in the end Adams and Brantley were not executed. True, they were not released because the death penalty system operated "correctly," but the fact that they were released undermines the claim that the death penalty system has already resulted in the execution of innocent people. Even strong supporters of the miscarriage of justice argument were able to discover only 23 cases of executions of people they believed clearly innocent, all of which occurred before 1943.[23] And in fact, it is unusual for murder defendants to claim innocence; for example, in one study, only 8% of those arrested for homicide "disputed responsibility for the killing."[24] The overall revolution in criminal procedure meant that the chance that an innocent person would be arrested, prosecuted, convicted, sentenced to death, and actually executed had been substantially reduced.

The reconstructed death penalty system also shrunk the other class of "miscarriages of justice," the execution of guilty people who did not deserve to die. Oddly, the first person who resisted his execution under the new regime, John Spenkelink, is one of the few real candidates for this sort of miscarriage of justice. Spenkelink was the drifter who killed a man he had been traveling with, after the victim beat him, raped him, and stole his money.

Spenkelink's case is unusual, though.[25] None of the murderers involved in the seven Supreme Court cases in 1991–92 were clearly inappropriate subjects for the death penalty. The Court's requirement that the death-eligible class be narrowed appears to have worked to constrain juries, and they appear to have done a reasonably good job of considering all mitigating evidence. Under these circumstances, frequently the most that could be said is that juries imposed death sentences in cases where people could fairly argue over whether the defendant deserved to die but not that they sentenced people to die who clearly ought not be executed.

Against this, there are several longer-term factors that may help give birth to a new movement against the death penalty. First is the sheer number of people sentenced to death. Inevitably, a "miscarriage of justice" will occur: Eventually states will execute people who, many observers agree, might well not have committed the crimes for which they died and who, even more will agree, certainly should not have been executed when serious questions of innocence remained open. As doubts gradually accumulate in connection with different defendants, the movement to abolish the death penalty will regain some momentum.

Second, of more immediate impact, the Supreme Court's effort to shorten the time between sentencing and execution, sometimes encouraged by supporters in Congress and state legislatures, may backfire. For as the Adams and Brantley cases show, one reason that the death penalty system today produces fewer gross miscarriages of justice than the earlier system is precisely that the appeals period is quite long. If the Court and its supporters succeed in making it possible to execute someone relatively soon after sentencing, the chance that an innocent person will be executed increases.

Third, and perhaps most important, the chance of a miscarriage of justice is also increased by what is now widely regarded as the inadequate provision of attorneys for defendants in capital cases. The Supreme Court's concern about delay exacerbates the problem of inadequate counsel. Roger Coleman, for example, was executed in 1992 even though he had some plausible arguments that his constitutional rights had been violated at his trial.[26] His lawyer, though, had failed to file some legal papers in time, and the state courts said that, because his lawyer had not followed the rules, they would not consider his constitutional claims. The Supreme Court held that this also barred the federal courts from considering the claims in Coleman's habeas corpus case.[27] When defendants have inadequate lawyers *and* are rushed from sentencing to execution, the chance of a gross miscarriage of justice increases.

The United States in International Perspective Finally, the position of the United States in the world community will affect the future course of the death penalty here. No other industrialized Western society uses the death penalty to anything like the degree to which the United States does. Canada and the United Kingdom, with legal traditions similar to ours, abolished the death penalty in the mid-1960s, yet it continues in the United States. There are reasons for that, of course: the higher crime rate, the wider availability of guns that criminals can use, and the racial and cultural diversity in the United States population, which exacerbates the tensions that lead to violence. Yet it may not be possible in the long run to avoid some embarrassing facts: that only South Africa and China employ the death penalty to anything like the degree the United States does, that an early step in the democratization of Central and Eastern Europe and the states of the former Soviet Union was the repudiation of capital punishment.

The Supreme Court, in the juvenile death penalty case, said that facts like these had no bearing on the underlying constitutional analysis. As Franklin Zimring and Gordon Hawkins point out, they do show that the public demand for retribution can be satisfied by penalties other than death, at least once abolition has become a settled fact of life. They also note that typically the death penalty has been abolished when polls indicate substantial public support for the penalty and that public support declines as the people become accustomed to a criminal justice system without the death penalty.[28]

In short, the international experience suggests, though it does not prove, that Justice Stewart was wrong to believe that abolition would lead to vigilante justice. And although the international experience is not directly relevant to the constitutional issue in the United States, international factors will affect the development of a new movement against the death penalty, and that new movement will in turn affect the way in which the Supreme Court understands the Constitution.

Conclusion

It is easy to exaggerate public support for the death penalty. Notably, the governing bodies of nearly all the major religious denominations in the country—the Roman Catholic bishops, the National Council of Churches and a number of the churches that are its members, and major Jewish groups—have stated their opposition to capital punishment. And the long-term historical trends are sharply against capital punishment: Ever since Beccaria, the world's people have increasingly been persuaded that capital punishment is unwise because it is unnecessary or immoral.

As Justice Marshall said when the Court restored capital punishment, it is one thing to believe in capital punishment as an abstract proposition and quite another to support its application as a matter of routine, in real cases involving real defendants (and of course, real victims). It seems likely that one reason opinion polls show such great support for capital punishment in the early 1990s is that the death penalty still remains a largely abstract proposition. The newspapers report executions, especially when an execution becomes controversial. They almost never report decisions vacating death sentences, and such decisions almost never become controversial. As death penalty opponent Hugo Adam Bedau puts it, "[T]he average person seems convinced the death penalty is an important legal threat, abstractly desirable as part of society's permanent bulwark against crime, but. . .is relatively indifferent to whether a given convict is. . . ever executed."[29]

As the Court removes obstacles to carrying out death sentences, not only will executions become even more routine than they have, but the number of executions will increase dramatically. In 1991 there were 2,500 people under sentence of death. Each year many more people have been sentenced to death than have been executed. If executions begin to take place at rates like one a day, capital punishment will change from an abstract question of criminal justice policy to a real part of experience of people throughout the society. And if that happens, support for the death penalty is likely to diminish.

In 1983 law professor Robert Weisberg described a condition that has persisted to this day:

> We will sentence vast numbers of murderers to death, but execute virtually none of them. Simply having many death sentences can satisfy many proponents of the death penalty who demand capital punishment, because in a vague way they want the law to make a statement of social authority and control. . .And we can at the same time avoid arousing great numbers of people who would vent their moral and political opposition to capital punishment only on the occasion of actual executions.[30]

Weisberg may underestimate the public frustration that occurs when death sentences are not carried out. If the courts respond to that frustration by increasing the rate of execution, though, the compromise Weisberg describes would break down, and opponents of capital punishment would again be mobilized. In the end, as the number of executions rises, pressure to abolish the death penalty is likely to increase again, as it did in the 1950s and 1960s.

Chapter Notes

CHAPTER ONE

1. California v. Ramos, 463 U.S. 992 (1983).
2. Thorsten Sellin, *The Penalty of Death* (Beverly Hills, Calif.: Sage, 1980), pp. 120, 110. Other studies are reported in Jonathan Sorensen and James Marquart, "Working the Dead," in *Facing the Death Penalty: Essays on a Cruel and Unusual Punishment,* Michael Radelet, ed. (Philadelphia: Temple University Press, 1989), pp. 170–1; Wendy Phillips Wolfson, "The Deterrent Effect of the Death Penalty Upon Prison Murder," in *The Death Penalty in America,* Hugo Alan Bedau, ed. (3d. ed., New York: Oxford University Press, 1982), pp. 159–73.
3. Richard Lempert suggests another difficulty, arising from the passage of time, for retributive justifications of the death penalty: Murderers may deserve to die at the moment they kill, but "it does not follow that they deserve death at the time it arrives" because they may have changed so that it would be unjust to execute them. Richard Lempert, "Desert and Deterrence: An Assessment of the Moral Bases of the Case for Capital Punishment," *Michigan Law Review* 79 (1981): 1177, at p. 1184. One response is that executive clemency is designed for precisely these cases.
4. Walter Berns, *For Capital Punishment: Crime and the Morality of the Death Penalty* (New York: Basic Books, 1979), pp. 186, 176.
5. An overview of the studies is provided in Franklin Zimring and Gordon Hawkins, *Capital Punishment and the American Agenda* (Cambridge: Cambridge University Press, 1986), pp. 167–86, and Lempert, "Desert and Deterrence," pp. 1197–1222.
6. The studies are reported in Sellin, *Penalty of Death,* pp. 91–97.
7. For critiques of Ehrlich's work, see William J. Bowers, with Glenn L. Pierce and John F. McDevitt, *Legal Homicide: Death as Punishment in America, 1864–1982* (Boston: Northeastern University Press, 1984), ch. 9; Hans Zeisel, "The Deterrent Effect of the Death Penalty: Facts v. Faith," *Supreme Court Review* 1976 (1976): 317; Lawrence Klein, Brian Forst, and Victor Filatov, "The Deterrent Effect of Capital Punishment: As Assessment of the Evidence," in *The Death Penalty in America,* Hugo Adam Bedau, ed., pp. 138–59.
8. Lempert, "Desert and Deterrence," pp. 1224–25.

9. This argument could be countered if, instead of deterring murder, the death penalty actually caused it. Some studies have suggested that the death penalty does have this "brutalization" effect, but the evidence is quite thin.
10. Barron v. Mayor & City Council of Baltimore, 32 U.S. (7 Pet.) 243 (1833).
11. Palko v. Connecticut, 302 U.S. 319 (1937). The earlier rejection was Twining v. New Jersey, 211 U.S. 78 (1908).
12. Robinson v. California, 370 U.S. 660 (1962).
13. Furman v. Georgia, 408 U.S. 238, 263 (1972).
14. *In re* Kemmler, 136 U.S. 436 (1890).
15. 217 U.S. 349 (1910).
16. The same point had been made in an earlier case by three dissenting justices. O'Neil v. Vermont, 144 U.S. 323 (1892). The Court in *O'Neil* did not reach the question.
17. 356 U.S. 86 (1958).

CHAPTER TWO

1. Good overviews of these developments are William J. Bowers, with Glenn L. Pierce and John F. McDevitt, *Legal Homicide: Death as Punishment in America, 1864–1982* (Boston: Northeastern University Press, 1984), ch. 1, and Philip English Mackey, editor, *Voices Against Death: American Opposition to Capital Punishment, 1787–1975* (New York: Burt Franklin, 1976), pp. xi–liii.
2. For a contemporary study of jury resistance to mandatory death sentences, see Hugo Adam Bedau, *Death Is Different: Studies in the Morality, Law, and Politics of Capital Punishment* (Boston: Northeastern University Press, 1987), ch. 9.
3. For a study of the ending of public executions, see Louis Masur, *Rites of Execution: Capital Punishment and the Transformation of American Culture, 1776–1865* (New York: Oxford University Press, 1989).
4. Stein v. New York, 346 U.S. 156 (1953).
5. For a detailed study, see Dan T. Carter, *Scottsboro: A Tragedy of the American South* (New York: Oxford University Press, 1969).
6. 287 U.S. 45 (1932).
7. Betts v. Brady, 316 U.S. 455 (1942); Gideon v. Wainwright, 372 U.S. 335 (1963).
8. 297 U.S. 278 (1936). For a study, see Richard Cortner, *A "Scottsboro" Case in Mississippi: The Supreme Court and* Brown v. Mississippi (Jackson: University Press of Mississippi, 1986).
9. Louisiana ex rel. Francis v. Resweber, 329 U.S. 459 (1947). For a comprehensive examination of the case, see Arthur S. Miller and

Jeffrey Bowman, *Death By Installments: The Ordeal of Willie Francis* (New York: Greenwood Press, 1988).
10. William J. Brennan, "Constitutional Adjudication and the Death Penalty: A View from the Court," *Harvard Law Review* 100 (1986): 313, 314.
11. Rudolph v. Alabama, 375 U.S. 889 (1963).
12. Michael Meltsner, *Cruel and Unusual: The Supreme Court and Capital Punishment* (New York: Random House, 1973), describes the development of the Inc. Fund's program. For a modest revision of Meltsner's account, see Eric L. Muller, "The Legal Defense Fund's Capital Punishment Campaign: The Distorting Influence of Death," *Yale Law & Policy Review* 4 (1985): 158.
13. Samuel Gross and Robert Mauro, *Death and Discrimination: Racial Disparities in Capital Sentencing* (Boston: Northeastern University Press, 1989), p. 122.
14. Witherspoon v. Illinois, 391 U.S. 510 (1968).
15. Later the Court found more extensive survey evidence on that issue still inconclusive. Lockhart v. McCree, 476 U.S. 162 (1986).
16. Adams v. Texas, 448 U.S. 38 (1980).
17. 469 U.S. 412 (1985).
18. For a discussion of the *Maxwell* litigation, see Meltsner, *Cruel and Unusual,* pp. 86–105, 149–67, 199–213.
19. The Court's deliberations are detailed in Bernard Schwartz, *The Unpublished Opinions of the Warren Court* (New York: Oxford University Press, 1985), ch. 10.
20. Maxwell v. Bishop, 398 U.S. 262 (1970). On December 29, 1970, shortly before he left office, Governor Laurence Rockefeller commuted Maxwell's death sentence, along with those of all the other men on Arkansas's death row.
21. McGautha v. California, 402 U.S. 183 (1971).
22. For this discussion, see Bob Woodward and Scott Armstrong, *The Brethren: Inside the Supreme Court* (New York: Simon & Schuster, 1979), pp. 206–7; William J. Brennan, "Constitutional Adjudication and the Death Penalty: A View From the Court," *Harvard Law Review* 100 (1986): 313, 321–22.
23. 395 U.S. 238 (1969).
24. Meltsner, *Cruel and Unusual,* p. 168.
25. Brennan, "Constitutional Adjudication," p. 322.

CHAPTER THREE

1. Bob Woodward & Scott Armstrong, *The Brethren: Inside the Supreme Court* (New York: Simon & Schuster, 1979), p. 219.

2. *Id.*, pp. 430–44.
3. Robert Burt, "Disorder in the Court: The Death Penalty and the Constitution," *Michigan Law Review* 85 (1987): 1741, at 1770.
4. Woodson v. North Carolina, 428 U.S. 280 (1976). Justices Brennan and Marshall reiterated their opposition to capital punishment in all circumstances, so there was a majority of five against mandatory death penalties.
5. Roberts v. Louisiana, 428 U.S. 325 (1976).
6. 483 U.S. 66 (1987).
7. The Court noted that only three murderers had been sentenced to death under mandatory death statutes like Nevada's.
8. Blystone v. Pennsylvania, 494 U.S. 299 (1990).
9. Jurek v. Texas, 428 U.S. 262 (1976).
10. 486 U.S. 367 (1988).
11. Caldwell v. Mississippi, 472 U.S. 320 (1985).
12. For a discussion, see Welsh S. White, *The Death Penalty in the Nineties* (Ann Arbor: University of Michigan Press, 1991), pp. 115–29.
13. 486 U.S. 356 (1988).
14. See, for example, Zant v. Stephens, 462 U.S. 862 (1983); Cabana v. Bullock, 474 U.S. 376 (1986).
15. 468 U.S. 447 (1984).
16. 463 U.S. 939 (1983).
17. Godfrey v. Georgia, 446 U.S. 420 (1980).
18. See, for example, Maynard v. Cartwright, 486 U.S. 356 (1988).
19. See White, *Death Penalty in the Nineties,* ch. 6.
20. Robert Weisberg, "Deregulating Death," *Supreme Court Review* 1983 (1983): 305, at 375.
21. 438 U.S. 586 (1978).
22. Compare Penry v. Lynaugh, 492 U.S. 302 (1989) (instructions inadequate), with Franklin v. Lynaugh, 487 U.S. 164 (1988). These are Texas cases. The primary Florida case is Hitchcock v. Dugger, 481 U.S. 393 (1987).
23. Coker v. Georgia, 433 U.S. 584 (1977).
24. 458 U.S. 782 (1982). The issue had been raised, but not answered by the Court, in Lockett v. Ohio, 438 U.S. 586 (1978), which is discussed earlier in the chapter.
25. 481 U.S. 137 (1987).
26. Justice White, *Enmund*'s author, joined Justice O'Connor's opinion.
27. Eventually the prosecutor decided not to seek the death penalty during the Tison brothers' resentencing.
28. 487 U.S. 815 (1988).
29. Stanford v. Kentucky, 492 U.S 361 (1989).

30. For an analysis of international law and its relation to the constitutional question here, see Joan Hartman, "'Unusual' Punishment: The Domestic Effects of International Norms Restricting the Application of the Death Penalty," *University of Cincinnati Law Review* 52 (1983): 655.
31. 477 U.S. 399 (1986). Justice Rehnquist, joined by Chief Justice Burger, argued that the common-law prohibition against executing the insane did not establish the existence of a similar constitutional right, an argument with which Justice O'Connor, writing separately, agreed.
32. In the remainder of the opinion, Marshall wrote for a plurality holding that the state's procedures for determining whether the prisoner was insane were inadequate. Rectifying those defects would require the state to develop a reasonably elaborate, quasi-judicial process, and Justice Powell, who agreed that the state could not execute an insane prisoner, would have allowed the state to use a more streamlined procedure. Because four justices found no constitutional violation in executing an insane prisoner, Justice Powell's description of the procedures required, not Justice Marshall's, probably represents the current state of the law on the question.
33. Penry v. Lynaugh, 492 U.S. 302 (1989).
34. 481 U.S. 279 (1987).
35. The study is reported in Samuel Gross and Robert Mauro, *Death and Discrimination: Racial Disparities in Capital Sentencing* (Boston: Northeastern University Press, 1989), p. 114.
36. Gross & Mauro, p. 212 (chapter title).
37. Booth v. Maryland, 482 U.S. 496 (1987).
38. South Carolina v. Gathers, 490 U.S. 805 (1989).
39. Payne v. Tennessee, 111 S.Ct. 2597 (1991).
40. California v. Brown, 479 U.S. 538 (1987).
41. Walton v. Arizona, 110 S.Ct. 3047 (1990).
42. Whitmore v. Arkansas, 495 U.S. 149 (1990).
43. Barefoot v. Estelle, 463 U.S. 880 (1983).
44. Teague v. Lane, 489 U.S. 288 (1989).
45. Butler v. McKellar, 494 U.S. 407 (1990).
46. McCleskey v. Zant, 111 S.Ct. 1454 (1991).

CHAPTER FOUR

1. Gilmore v. Utah, 429 U.S. 1012 (1976).
2. Quoted in Jack Greenberg, "Capital Punishment as a System," *Yale Law Journal* 91 (1982): 908.
3. Murray v. Giarratano, 492 U.S. 1 (1989).

4. Coleman v. Thompson, 111 S.Ct. 2546 (1991).
5. Pulley v. Harris, 465 U.S. 37 (1984). Justices Brennan and Marshall dissented.
6. Harris v. Vasquez, 913 F. 2d 606 (9th Cir. 1990).
7. The events and law surrounding this phase of the *Harris* case are discussed in three essays in the *Yale Law Journal* 102 (1992): 205–79.
8. Gomez v. District Court, 112 S. Ct. 1652 (1992).
9. Vasquez v. Harris, 112 S.Ct. 1713 (1992).

CHAPTER FIVE

1. In addition to the cases listed in the text, the Court reversed a number of death sentences from Florida because the jury, whose recommendation of a death sentence is given "great weight" by judges who actually impose the sentence, had considered an invalid aggravating circumstance. Espinosa v. Florida, 112 S.Ct. 2926 (1992).
2. 112 S.Ct. 1093 (1992).
3. 112 S.Ct. 1130 (1992).
4. 112 S.Ct. 1810 (1992).
5. 112 S.Ct. 2114 (1992).
6. 112 S.Ct. 2222 (1992).
7. 112 S.Ct. 2572 (1992).
8. 112 S.Ct. 2514 (1992).
9. I have relied on James Alan Fox, Michael L. Radelet, and Julie L. Bonsteel, "Death Penalty Opinion in the Post–*Furman* Years," *New York University Review of Law & Social Change* 18 (1990–91): 499, for the survey data here.
10. Austin Sarat and Neil Vidmar, "Public Opinion, the Death Penalty, and the Eighth Amendment: Testing the Marshall Hypothesis," *Wisconsin Law Review* 1976 (1976): 171.
11. A good presentation of this sort of argument is Jack Greenberg, "Against the American System of Capital Punishment," *Harvard Law Review* 99 (1986): 1670.
12. Robert Burt, "Disorder in the Court: The Death Penalty and the Constitution," *Michigan Law Review* 85 (1987): 1741, at 1793.
13. Quoted by Russell Canan, "Burning at the Wire: The Execution of John Evans," in *Facing the Death Penalty: Essays on a Cruel and Unusual Punishment,* Michael Radelet, ed. (Philadelphia: Temple University Press, 1989), p. 62; Jonathan Sorensen and James Marquardt, "Working the Dead," in *id.,* pp. 172–4. The conditions on Texas's death row are somewhat less restrictive (three hours of recreation a day, five days a week) than the ones Canan describes.
14. 483 U.S. 1 (1987).

15. Lewis v. Adamson, 110 S.Ct. 3287 (1990).
16. 463 U.S. 1237 (1983).
17. Gomez v. United States District Court, 112 S.Ct. 1652 (1992).
18. Vivian Berger, "Justice Delayed or Justice Denied?—A Comment on Recent Proposals to Reform Death Penalty Habeas Corpus," *Columbia Law Review* 90 (1990): 1665, at 1670.
19. Robert Weisberg, "Deregulating Death," *Supreme Court Review* 1983 (1983): 305, at 381–2.
20. Vivian Berger, "The Chiropractor as Brain Surgeon: Defense Lawyering in Capital Cases," *New York University Review of Law and Social Change* 18 (1990–91): 245, at 247.
21. 466 U.S. 668 (1984).
22. This may not be true of Justice Stevens, however.
23. Hugo A. Bedau and Micahel Radelet, "Miscarriages of Justice in Potentially Capital Cases," *Stanford Law Review* 40 (1987): 33.
24. Barry Nakell and Kenneth Hardy, *The Arbitrariness of the Death Penalty* (Philadelphia: Temple University Press, 1987), pp. 93, 95.
25. Victor L. Streib, "Executions Under the Post-*Furman* Capital Punishment Statutes: The Halting Progression from 'Let's Do It' to 'Hey, There Ain't No Point in Pulling So Tight,'" *Rutgers Law Journal* 15 (1984): 443, comes to a different conclusion, finding that six of the first eleven people executed after *Furman* committed "fairly ordinary killings that occurred during armed robberies" and that only three—child-murders and a premeditated ambush—were "particularly heinous." Streib's conclusions, though, sometimes require him to ignore the events associated with, though not directly part of, the armed robberies; three of his six "fairly ordinary killings" occurred during crime sprees committed by career criminals.
26. Coleman's supporters also claimed that he might well be innocent, but that claim was strongly contested.
27. Coleman v. Thompson, 111 S.Ct. 2546 (1991).
28. Franklin Zimring and Gordon Hawkins, *Capital Punishment and the American Agenda* (Cambridge: Cambridge University Press, 1986), pp. xvi, 13. For an earlier survey of public opinion, see Neil Vidmar and Phoebe Ellsworth, "Public Opinion and the Death Penalty," *Stanford Law Review* 26 (1974): 1245.
29. *The Death Penalty in America,* Hugo Alan Bedau, ed. (3d. ed., New York: Oxford University Press, 1982), p. 68.
30. Weisberg, "Deregulating Death," at 387.

Appendixes

TABLE OF CONTENTS

A. *Weems v. United States, 1910*

B. Memorandum to the Conference Re: Capital Punishment, 1963

C. *Maxwell v. Bishop, 1968*
(Draft opinions of Justices Douglas, Black, Fortas, Harlan)

D. *McGautha v. California, 1970*
(Excerpt)

E. *Furman v. Georgia, 1972*
(Opinions of Justices Stewart and White—excerpts)

F. *Gregg v. Georgia, 1976*
(Joint opinion of Justices Stewart, Powell and Stevens—excerpts)

G. *McCleskey v. Kemp, 1987*
(Excerpts)

H. *Payne v. Tennessee, 1991*

Appendix A

WEEMS V. UNITED STATES

217 U.S. 349 (1910)

MR. JUSTICE MCKENNA delivered the opinion of the court.

This writ of error brings up for review the judgment of the Supreme Court of the Philippine Islands, affirming the conviction of plaintiff in error for falsifying a "public and official document."

In the "complaint," by which the prosecution was begun, it was charged that the plaintiff in error, "a duly appointed, qualified and acting disbursing officer of the Bureau of Coast Guard and Transportation of the United States Government of the Philippine Islands," did, as such, "corruptly and with intent, then and there, to deceive and defraud the United States Government of the Philippine Islands, and its officials, falsify a public and official document, namely, a cash book of the captain of the Board of Manila, Philippine Islands, and the Bureau of Coast Guard and Transportation of the United States Government of the Philippine Islands," kept by him as disbursing officer of that bureau. The falsification, which is alleged with much particularity, was committed by entering as paid out, "as wages of employes of the Light House Service of the United States Government of the Philippine Islands," at the Capul Light House of 208 pesos, and for like service at the Matabriga Light House of 408 pesos, Philippine currency. A demurrer was filed to the "complaint," which was overruled.

He was convicted, and the following sentence was imposed upon him: "To the penalty of fifteen years of Cadena, together with the accessories of section 56 of the Penal Code, and to pay a fine of four thousand pesetas, but not to serve imprisonment as a subsidiary punishment in case of his insolvency, on account of the nature of the main penalty, and to pay the costs of this cause."...

The assignment of error is that "A punishment of fifteen years' imprisonment was a cruel and unusual punishment, and, to the extent of the sentence, the judgment below should be reversed on this ground." Weems was convicted, as we have seen, for the falsification of a public and official document, by entering therein, as paid out, the sums of 208 and 408 pesos, respectively, as wages to certain employes of the Light House service. In other words, in entering upon his cash book those sums as having been paid out when they were not paid out, and the "truth," to use the language of the statute, was thereby perverted "in the narration of facts."

By other provisions of the code we find that there are only two degrees of punishment higher in scale than cadena temporal, death, and cadena perpetua. The punishment of cadena temporal is from twelve years and one day to twenty years (arts. 28 and 96), which "shall be served" in certain "penal institutions." And it is provided that "those sentenced to cadena temporal and cadena perpetua shall labor for the benefit of the state. They shall always carry a chain at the ankle, hanging from the wrists; they shall be employed at hard and painful labor, and shall receive no assistance whatsoever from without the institution." Arts. 105, 106. There are besides certain accessory penalties imposed, which are defined to be (1) civil interdiction; (2) perpetual absolute disqualification; (3) subjection to surveillance during life. These penalties are defined as follows:

> "Art. 42. Civil interdiction shall deprive the person punished as long as he suffers it, of the rights of parental authority, guardianship of person or property, participation in the family council, marital authority, the administration of property, and the right to dispose of his own property by acts inter vivos. Those cases are excepted in which the law explicitly limits its effects.
>
> "Art. 43. Subjection to the surveillance of the authorities imposes the following obligations on the persons punished.
>
> "1. That of fixing his domicil and giving notice thereof to the authority immediately in charge of his surveillance, not being allowed to change it without the knowledge and permission of said authority in writing.
>
> "2. To observe the rules of inspection prescribed.
>
> "3. To adopt some trade, art, industry, or profession, should he not have known means of subsistence of his own.
>
> "Whenever a person punished is placed under the surveillance of the authorities, notice thereof shall be given to the government and to the governor general."

The penalty of perpetual absolute disqualification is the deprivation of office, even though it be held by popular election, the deprivation of the right to vote or to be elected to public office, the disqualification to acquire honors, etc., and the loss of retirement pay, etc.

These provisions are attacked as infringing that provision of the bill of rights of the islands which forbids the infliction of cruel and unusual punishment. It must be confessed that they, and the sentence in this case, excite wonder in minds accustomed to a more considerate adaptation of punishment to the degree of crime. In a sense the law in controversy seems to be independent of degrees. One may be an offender against it, as we have seen, though he gain nothing and injure nobody. It has, however, some human indulgence—it is not exactly Draconian in uniformity.

Though it starts with a severe penalty, between that and the maximum penalty it yields something to extenuating circumstances. Indeed, by article 96 of the Penal Code the penalty is declared to be "divisible," and the legal term of its "duration is understood as distributed into three parts forming the three degrees—that is, the minimum, medium, and maximum," being respectively from twelve years and one day to fourteen years and eight months, from fourteen years eight months and one day to seventeen years and four months, from seventeen years four months and one day to twenty years. The law therefore allows a range from twelve years and a day to twenty years, and the Government in its brief ventures to say that "the sentence of fifteen years is well within the law." But the sentence is attacked as well as the law, and what it is to be well within the law a few words will exhibit. The minimum term of imprisonment is twelve years, and that, therefore, must be imposed for "perverting the truth" in a single item of a public record, though there be no one injured, though there be no fraud or purpose of it, no gain or desire of it. Twenty years is the maximum imprisonment, and that only can be imposed for the perversion of truth in every item of an officer's accounts, whatever be the time covered and whatever fraud it conceals or tends to conceal. Between these two possible sentences, which seem to have no adaptable relation, or rather in the difference of eight years for the lowest possible offense and the highest possible, the courts below selected three years to add to the minimum of twelve years and a day for the falsification of two items of expenditure, amounting to the sums of 408 and 204 pesos. And the fine and "accesories" must be brought into view. The fine was four thousand pesetas, an excess also over the minimum. The "accesories" we have already defined. We can now give graphic description of Weems' sentence and of the law under which it was imposed. Let us confine it to the minimum degree of the law, for it is with the law that we are most concerned. Its minimum degree is confinement in a penal institution for twelve years and one day, a chain at the ankle and wrist of the offender, hard and painful labor, no assistance from friend or relative, no marital authority or parental rights or rights of property, no participation even in the family council. These parts of his penalty endure for the term of imprisonment. From other parts there is no intermission. His prison bars and chains are removed, it is true, after twelve years, but he goes from them to a perpetual limitation of his liberty. He is forever kept under the shadow of his crime, forever kept within voice and view of the criminal magistrate, not being able to change his domicil without giving notice to the "authority immediately in charge of his surveillance," and without permission in writing. He may not seek, even in other scenes and among other people, to retrieve his fall from rectitude. Even that hope is taken from him and he is subject to tormenting regulations that, if not so tangible as iron bars and stone walls, oppress as much by their continuity, and deprive of essential liberty. No circumstance of degradation is omitted. It may be that even the cruelty of pain is not omitted. He must bear a chain night and day. He is condemned to painful as well as hard labor. What painful labor may mean we have no exact measure. It must be something more than hard labor. It may be hard labor pressed to the point of pain. Such penalties for such offenses amaze those who have formed their conception of the relation of a state to even its offending citizens from the practice of the American commonwealths, and believe that it is a precept of justice that punishment for crime should be graduated and proportioned to offense.

Is this also a precept of the fundamental law? We say fundamental law, for the provision of the Philippine bill of rights, prohibiting the infliction of cruel and unusual punishment, was taken from the Constitution of the United States and must have the same meaning. This was decided in *Kepner v. United States,* 195 U.S. 100, 122; and *Serra v. Mortiga,* 204 U.S. 470. In *Kepner v. United States* this court considered the instructions of the President to the Philippine Commission and quoted from them the admonition to the commission that the government that we were establishing was not designed "for our satisfaction or for the expression of our theoretical views, but for the happiness, peace and prosperity of the people of the Philippine Islands, and the measures adopted should be made to conform to their customs, their habits, and even their prejudices, to the fullest extent consistent with the accomplishment of the indispensable requisites of just and effective government." But, it was pointed out, a qualification accompanied the admonition, and the commission was instructed "to bear in mind" and the people of the islands "made plainly to understand" that certain great principles of government had been made the basis of our governmental system which were deemed "essential to the rule of law and the maintenance of individual freedom." And the President further declared that there were "certain practical rules of government which we have found to be essential to the preservation of those great principles of liberty and law." These he admonished the commission to establish and maintain in the islands "for the sake of their liberty and happiness," however they might conflict with the customs or laws of procedure with which they were familiar. In view of the importance of these principles and rules, which the President said the "enlightened thought of the Philippine Islands" would come to appreciate, he imposed their observance "upon every division and branch of the government of the Philippines."

Among those rules was that which prohibited the infliction of cruel and unusual punishment. It was repeated in the act of July 1, 1902, providing for the administration of the affairs of the civil government in the islands, and this court said of it and of the instructions of the President that they were "intended to carry to the Philippine Islands those principles of our government which the President declared to be established as rules of law for the maintenance of individual freedom." The instructions of the President and the act of Congress found in nominal existence in the islands the Penal Code of Spain, its continuance having been declared by military order. It may be there was not and could not be a careful consideration of its provisions and a determination to what extent they accorded with or were repugnant to the "great principles of liberty and law" which had been "made the basis of our governmental system." Upon the institution of the government of the commission, if not before, that consideration and determination necessarily came to the courts and are presented by this record.

What constitutes a cruel and unusual punishment has not been exactly decided. . .

It appears, therefore, that Wilson, and those who thought like Wilson, felt sure that the spirit of liberty could be trusted, and that its ideals would be represented, not debased, by legislation. Henry and those who believed as he did would take no chances. Their predominant political impulse was distrust of power, and they insisted on constitutional limitations against its abuse. But surely they intended more than to register a fear of the forms of abuse that went out of practice with the Stuarts. Surely, their jealously of power had a saner justification than that. They were men of action, practical and sagacious, not beset with vain imagining, and it must have come to them that there could be exercises of cruelty by laws other than those which inflicted bodily pain or mutilation. With power in a legislature great, if not unlimited, to give criminal character to the actions of men, with power unlimited to fix terms of imprisonment with what accompaniments they might, what more potent instrument of cruelty could be put into the hands of power? And it was believed that power might be tempted to cruelty. This was the motive of the clause, and if we are to attribute an intelligent providence to its advocates we cannot think that it was intended to prohibit only practices like the

Stuarts, or to prevent only an exact repetition of history. We cannot think that the possibility of a coercive cruelty being exercised through other forms of punishment was overlooked. We say "coercive cruelty," because there was more to be considered than the ordinary criminal laws. Cruelty might become an instrument of tyranny; of zeal for a purpose, either honest or sinister.

Legislation, both statutory and constitutional, is enacted, it is true, from an experience of evils, but its general language should not, therefore, be necessarily confined to the form that evil had theretofore taken. Time works changes, brings into existence new conditions and purposes. Therefore a principle to be vital must be capable of wider application than the mischief which gave it birth. This is peculiarly true of constitutions. They are not ephemeral enactments, designed to meet passing occasions. They are, to use the words of Chief Justice Marshall, "designed to approach immortality as nearly as human institutions can approach it." The future is their care and provision for events of good and bad tendencies of which no prophecy can be made. In the application of a constitution, therefore, our contemplation cannot be only of what has been but of what may be. Under any other rule a constitution would indeed be as easy of application as it would be deficient in efficacy and power. Its general principles would have little value and be converted by precedent into impotent and lifeless formulas. Rights declared in words might be lost in reality. And this has been recognized. The meaning and vitality of the Constitution have developed against narrow and restrictive construction. . .

An extended review of the cases in the state courts interpreting their respective constitutions we will not make. It may be said of all of them that there was not such challenge to the import and consequence of the inhibition of cruel and unusual punishments as the law under consideration presents. It has no fellow in American legislation. Let us remember that it has come to us from a government of a different form and genius from ours. It is cruel in its excess of imprisonment and that which accompanies and follows imprisonment. It is unusual in its character. Its punishments come under the condemnation of the bill of rights, both on account of their degree and kind. And they would have those bad attributes even if they were found in a Federal enactment and not taken from an alien source. . .

From this comment we turn back to the law in controversy. Its character and the sentence in this case may be illustrated by examples even better than it can be represented by words. There are degrees of homicide that are not punished so severely, nor are the following crimes: misprision of treason, inciting rebellion, conspiracy to destroy the Government by force, recruiting soldiers in the United

States to fight against the United States, forgery of letters patent, forgery of bonds and other instruments for the purpose of defrauding the United States, robbery, larceny and other crimes. Section 86 of the Penal Laws of the United States, as revised and amended by the act of Congress of March 4, 1909, c. 321 (35 Stat. 1088), provides that any person charged with the payment of any appropriation made by Congress who shall pay to any clerk or other employe of the United States a sum less than that provided by law and require a receipt for a sum greater than that paid to and received by him shall be guilty of embezzlement, and shall be fined in double the amount so withheld and imprisoned not more than two years. The offense described has similarity to the offense for which Weems was convicted, but the punishment provided for it is in great contrast to the penalties of cadena temporal and its "accesories." If we turn to the legislation of the Philippine Commission we find that instead of the penalties of cadena temporal, medium degree, (fourteen years eight months and one day to seventeen years and four months, with fine and "accessories"), to cadena perpetua, fixed by the Spanish penal code for the falsification of bank notes and other instruments authorized by the law of the kingdom, it is provided that the forgery of or counterfeiting the obligations or securities of the United States or of the Philippine Islands shall be punished by a fine of not more than ten thousand pesos and by imprisonment of not more than fifteen years. In other words, the highest punishment possible for a crime which may cause the loss of many thousand of dollars, and to prevent which the duty of the State should be as eager as to prevent the perversion of truth in a public document, is not greater than that which may be imposed for falsifying a single item of a public account. And this contrast shows more than different exercises of legislative judgment. It is greater than that. It condemns the sentence in this case as cruel and unusual. It exhibits a difference between unrestrained power and that which is exercised under the spirit of constitutional limitations formed to establish justice. The State thereby suffers nothing and loses no power. The purpose of punishment is fulfilled, crime is repressed by penalties of just, not tormenting, severity, its repetition is prevented, and hope is given for the reformation of the criminal. . .

Appendix B

MEMORANDUM TO THE CONFERENCE

RE: CAPITAL PUNISHMENT, OCTOBER TERM, 1963

ARTHUR J. GOLDBERG*

INTRODUCTION

The current Conference list includes at least six capital cases.[1] In the discussion of these cases, I propose to raise the following issue: Whether, and under what circumstances, the imposition of the death penalty is proscribed by the Eighth and Fourteenth Amendments to the United States Constitution.

In none of these cases has the cruel and unusual punishment issue been explicitly presented to this Court; nor does it appear that the issue was raised in the lower courts.[2] But in knowingly sustaining the death penalty in each of these cases, the courts necessarily passed on the legality of its imposition; and considering the nature of the issue, petitioners' failure to urge it should not preclude this Court from considering this matter. Cf. *Weems v. United States,* 217 U.S. 349, 362.

I circulate this memorandum—which simply raises some of the relevant considerations and does not purport to be definitive—to afford an opportunity for consideration of the matter prior to our discussion.

BACKGROUND

The proscription against cruel and unusual punishment [that] first appeared in the English Bill of Rights of 1688 was included

---

* Associate Justice of the Supreme Court of the United States. This memorandum is published in the exact form it was circulated to the Conference.

1. *Walker v. Nevada* (felony murder) 85 Misc.; *Arnold v. North Carolina* (murder) 138 Misc.; *Snider v. Cunningham* (rape of a young girl) 169 Misc.; *White v. Washington* (murder) 232 Misc.; *Rudolph v. Alabama* (rape) 308 Misc.; and *Smith v. Bomar* (felony murder) 336 Misc.

2. The legality of the penalty was alluded to, however, by the Washington Supreme Court in *White v. Washington* and the Alabama Supreme Court in *Rudolph v. Alabama.*

in the Virginia Declaration of Rights of 1776 and was approved by Congress, with little debate, as part of the Eighth Amendment.

The first significant case raising the issue was *Wilkerson v. Utah,* 99 U.S. 130 (1878). The accused had been found guilty by a federal territorial court of "wilful, malicious and premeditated murder," and sentenced to "be publicly shot until. . .dead." He did not challenge the death penalty as such, but rather the mode of execution, claiming that it was not authorized by the governing statutes. The Court held that it was authorized and that shooting—a traditional method of executing certain types of offenders—was not cruel and unusual. In arriving at the latter conclusion, the Court said:

> Difficulty would attend the effort to define with exactness the extent of the constitutional provision which provides that cruel and unusual punishments shall not be inflicted; but it is safe to affirm that punishments of torture. . .and all others in the same line of unnecessary cruelty, are forbidden by that amendment. . . . *Id.,* at 135–136.

Whereas *Wilkerson* involved a federal territory, the next significant case—*In re Kemmler,* 136 U.S. 436 (1890)—challenged the power of a State to take the life of a murderer by electrocution. It was not then contended, and in the opinion of the Court "it could not be, that the Eighth Amendment was intended to apply to the states."[3] It was urged, however, that the Due Process Clause prohibited the States from imposing cruel and unusual punishments. The Court held that reversal would be proper only if the State "had committed an error so gross as to amount in law to a denial. . .of due process," and that the State's conclusion—based as it was on "a voluminous mass of evidence"—that electrocution was a most humane mode of execution was not such an error. The Court quoted the above-cited paragraph from *Wilkerson* and added the following dictum:

> Punishments are cruel when they involve torture or a lingering death; but the punishment of death is not cruel, within the meaning of that word as used in the Constitution. It implies there something inhuman and barbarous, something more than the mere extinguishment of life. 136 U.S., at 447.

Up to this time therefore, the only challenged violations of the cruel and unusual punishment proscription involved not the extent of the punishment (*e.g.,* death), but the mode of inflicting assumedly valid punishments (*e.g.,* shooting, electrocution).

3. In *Francis v. Resweber,* 329 U.S. 459, it was assumed, and in *Robinson v. California,* 370 U.S. 660, it was decided that the Eighth Amendment is applicable to the State through the Fourteenth Amendment.

Two years after *Wilkerson* in *O'Neil v. Vermont,* 144 U.S. 323 (1892), extent of punishment was challenged in the context of a long prison term and heavy fine, and the Court divided for the first time over the meaning and application of the Eighth Amendment. A jury found O'Neil guilty of 307 separate offenses of illegally selling intoxicating liquor, under a statute which made each sale a separate offense. He was sentenced to pay an aggregate fine of $6,140, and if that fine were not paid within a designated period of time, "he should be confined at hard labor, in the house of correction. . .for the term of 19,914 days." The Court declined to consider whether this punishment was cruel and unusual "because as a Federal question, it is not assigned as error, nor even suggested in the brief. . .," and because, in any event, the Eighth Amendment did not apply to the States.

Justice Field, dissenting, would have applied the Eighth Amendment to the States through the "privileges and immunities" clause of the Fourteenth Amendment. He also rejected the traditional reading of the Eighth Amendment which would limit its application "to punishments which inflict [such] torture" as "were at one time inflicted in England." He concluded that:

> The inhibition is directed, not only against punishments of the character mentioned, but against all punishments which by their excessive length or severity are greatly disproportioned to the offense charged. The whole inhibition is against that which is excessive either in the bail required, or fine imposed, or punishment inflicted. 14 [4] U.S., at 339–340.
>
> It is against the excessive severity of the punishment, as applied to the offenses for which it is inflicted, that the inhibition is directed. *Id.,* at 364.

Justices Harlan and Brewer would also have applied the Eighth Amendment to the States; and they too deemed the penalty in issue cruel and unusual.

In the next case—*Weems v. United States,* 217 U.S. 349 (1910)—the Court adopted the basic principles adumbrated in Justice Field's dissent. An officer of "the United States Government of the Philippine Islands" had been convicted of falsifying a public document, and sentenced to 15 years of "*cadena temporal.*" This ominous sounding punishment, of Spanish origin, required the prisoner "always [to] carry a chain at the ankle, hanging from the wrists; [to] be employed at hard and painful labor, and [to] receive no assistance whatsoever from without the institution." In addition, the prisoner was to suffer "civil interdiction" which denied him the rights of "parental authority, guardianship of person or property, participation in the family counsel, marital authority, the administration of property, and the right to dispose of his own property by acts inter vivos." He was also subject to "surveillance" during his entire lifetime.

The severity of the penalty was not challenged in the courts below, but the Court considered it under the "plain error" rule, stating that it has "less reluctance to disregard prior examples in the criminal cases than in civil cases, and less reluctance to act under [the plain error rule] when rights are asserted which are of such high character as to find expression and sanction in the Constitution or Bill of Rights."

After a careful analysis of the historical experience which formed the basis for the Eighth Amendment, the Court observed that:

> Legislation, both statutory and constitutional, is enacted, it is true, from an experience of evils, but its general language should not, therefore, be necessarily confined to the form that evil had theretofore taken. Time works changes, brings into existence new conditions and purpose. Therefore a principle to be vital must be capable of wider application than the mischief which gave it birth. This is peculiarly true of constitutions. They are not ephemeral enactments, designed to meet passing occasions. They are, to use the words of Chief Justice Marshall, 'designed to approach immortality as nearly as human institutions can approach it.' The future is their care and provision for events of good and bad tendencies of which no prophecy can be made. In the application of a constitution, therefore, our contemplation cannot be only of what has been but of what may be. Under any other rule a constitution would indeed be as easy of application as it would be deficient in efficacy and power. Its general principles would have little value and be converted by precedent into impotent and lifeless formulas. Rights declared in words might be lost in reality.

After analyzing the earlier authorities—including a 1689 case where the King's Bench struck down a 30,000-pound fine for assault as "excessive and exorbitant, against Magna Charta, the right of the subject and the law of the land,"[4] the Court stated that:

> The clause of the Constitution in the opinion of learned commentators may be therefore progressive, and is not fastened to the obsolete but may acquire meaning as public opinion becomes enlightened by a humane justice.

In setting out the standards for applying the Cruel and Unusual Punishment Clause, the Court, of course, disclaimed the right "to assert a judgment against that of the legislature of the

4. Lord Devonshire's Case, 11 State Trials 1354.

expediency of the laws or the right to oppose the judicial power to the legislative power to define crimes and fix their punishment. . . [because] for the proper exercise of such power there must be a comprehension of all that the legislature did nor could take into account, that is, a consideration of the mischief and the remedy." The States have a "wide range of power. . . to adapt its penal laws to conditions as they may exist and punish the crimes of men according to their forms and frequency."

The Court then examined the penalty in question against the evil sought to be mitigated and concluded that: the "sentence in this case [was] cruel and unusual." In doing this, the Court noted that "The state thereby suffers nothing and loses no power. The purpose of punishment is fulfilled, crime is repressed by penalties of just, not tormenting, severity, its repetition is prevented, and hope is given for the reformation of the criminal."

Justice White filed a dissenting opinion which was concurred in by Justice Holmes. The dissent accused the Court of considering the punishment in the abstract:

> I say only abstractly considered, because the first impression produced by the merely abstract view of the subject is met by the admonition that the duty of defining and punishing crime has never in any civilized country been exerted upon mere abstract considerations of the inherent nature of the crime punished, but has always involved the most practical consideration of the tendency at a particular time to commit certain crimes, of the difficulty of repressing the same, and of how far it is necessary to impose stern remedies to prevent the commission of such crimes. And, of course, as these considerations involve the necessity for a familiarity with local conditions in the Philippine Islands which I do not possess, such want of knowledge at once additionally admonishes me of the wrong to arise from forming a judgment upon insufficient data or without a knowledge of the subject matter upon which the judgment is to be exerted.

The dissent concluded that the proscription was intended as a limitation only upon the infliction of "unnecessary bodily suffering through a resort to inhuman methods. . . ." *Id.,* at 409.

The *Weems* decision stands as the turning point in the construction of the Cruel and Unusual Punishment Clause. To be sure, the earlier cases used words such as "unnecessary" and "excessive." But in those cases, attention was focused on the mode of effecting punishments, the extent of which were not challenged. For example, on the assumption that death is a valid punishment for murder, the question was whether shooting produces unnecessary or excessive pain in producing death. The question posed (and apparently answered) in *Weems* was whether the *extent* of a given punishment was unnecessarily or excessively harsh, considering the admitted legislative power to "repress" crime, prevent its repetition, and reform the criminal.

In light of its antecedents, the *Weems* case can be read as recognizing the following tests: (1) Giving full weight to reasonable legislative findings, a punishment is cruel and unusual, if a less severe one can as effectively achieve the permissible ends of punishment (*i.e.,* deterrence, isolation, rehabilitation, or whatever the contemporary society considers the permissible objectives of punishment). (2) Regardless of its effectiveness in achieving the permissible ends of punishment, a punishment is cruel and unusual if it offends the contemporary sense of decency (*e.g.,* torture). (3) Regardless of its effectiveness in achieving the permissible ends of punishment, a punishment is cruel and unusual if the evil it produces is disproportionally higher than the harm it seeks to prevent (*e.g.,* the death penalty for economic crimes).

In the half century that has followed *Weems v. United States,* this Court has never abandoned the tests there recognized.[5] Individual Justices have implied their agreement with one or the other of them.

In *Trop v. Dulles,* 356 U.S. 86 (1958), for example, THE CHIEF JUSTICE, writing for Justices BLACK, DOUGLAS and WHITTAKER, concluded that the Eighth Amendment "must draw its meaning from the evolving standards of decency that mark the progress of a maturing society."[6]

Louisiana ex rel. Francis v. Resweber, 329 U.S. 459 (1947)—like the cases prior to *Weems*—dealt with the "cruelty inherent in the method of punishment, not the necessary suffering involved in any method employed to extinguish life humanely." *Id.,* at 464. The Court

---

5. Since *Weems,* there have been but three significant cases raising the cruel and unusual punishment issue. Two of these were decided without an opinion of the Court. *Louisiana ex rel. Francis v. Resweber,* 329 U.S. 459; *Trop v. Dulles,* 356 U.S. 86. The third case, *Robinson v. California,* 370 U.S. 660—which was decided by an opinion of the Court—did not purport to be announcing standards or tests of cruel and unusual punishment; it simply reasoned by analogy that since physical diseases could not constitutionally be made a crime, it follows that addiction—which is also a disease—could not be made criminal without running afoul of the Eighth and Fourteenth Amendments (regardless of the extent or severity of the punishment).

6. The opinion also contained the following observation: "Whatever the arguments may be against capital punishment, both on moral grounds and in terms of accomplishing the purposes of punishment—and they are forceful—the death penalty has been employed throughout our history, and, in a day when it is still widely accepted, it cannot be said to violate the constitutional concept of cruelty." *Id.,* at 99.

there held that the State could constitutionally execute a murderer who it had once failed to execute through no fault on its part.

In concurring in the result, MR. JUSTICE BRENNAN seemed to give recognition to the test under which a punishment is not cruel and unusual unless a less severe one can as effectively achieve the permissible ends of punishment. He said:

> In view of the manifest severity of this sanction [expatriation], I feel that we should look closely at its probable effect, to determine whether Congress' imposition of expatriation as a penal device is justified in reason. Clearly the severity of the penalty, in the case of a serious offense, is not enough to invalidate it where the nature of the penalty is rationally directed to achieve the legitimate ends of punishment.[7]

After reviewing the probable effects of expatriation, and concluding that they would probably be insubstantial when measured against the ends at which punishments are generally directed, MR. JUSTICE BRENNAN observed that "in the light of these considerations, it is understandable that the Government has not pressed its case on the basis of expatriation of the deserter as punishment for his crime."

MR. JUSTICE DOUGLAS has also implied agreement with the "less severe" punishment test. In concurring in *Robinson v. California,* 370 U.S. 660 (1962), he said:[8]

> A prosecution for addiction, with its resulting stigma and irreparable damage to the good name of the accused, cannot be justified a means of protecting society, *where a civil commitment would do as well.*
>
> *Id.*, at 677. (Emphasis added.)

IS CAPITAL PUNISHMENT, AS SUCH, UNCONSTITUTIONAL UNDER THE TESTS RECOGNIZED BY THIS COURT?

A. The Evolving Standards Of Decency

This Court has never explicitly considered whether, and under what circumstances, the Eighth and Fourteenth Amendments to the United States Constitution proscribes the imposition of the

7. In addition to rehabilitation, MR. JUSTICE BRENNAN included deterrence and insultation of the offender among the permissible purposes of punishment.
8. Justice Frankfurter has implied agreement with this test as well. He said in *Lambert v. California,* 355 U.S. 225, 231 (dissent), that: "Cruelly disproportionate relation between what the law requires and the sanction for its disobedience may constitute. . . cruel and unusual punishment."

death penalty. The Court has, of course, implicitly decided (in every case affirming a capital conviction) that the death penalty is constitutional. But in light of the worldwide trend toward abolition, I think this Court should now request argument and explicitly consider this constantly recurring issue.

I am convinced that whatever may be said of times past, "the evolving standards of decency that mark the progress of [our] maturing society" now condemn as barbaric and inhuman the deliberate institutionalized taking of human life by the state.

Many, if not most, of the civilized nations of the western world have abolished the death penalty; and few that have abolished it have ever restored it. The worldwide trend is unmistakenly in the direction of abolition.[9]

Moreover, in this country (where Wisconsin, Maine, Minnesota, Alabama, Delaware, Michigan, Rhode Island, North Dakota, Hawaii, Virgin Islands and Puerto Rico have abolished the death penalty),[10] it seems that public opinion (at least as measured by public

---

9. The United Nations' Report on Capital Punishment (1962) lists the following jurisdictions as having abolished capital punishment completely: Argentina (1922), Australia (Queensland), Austria (1945), Brazil (1889), Columbia (1910), Costa Rica (1882), Denmark (1930), Dominican Republic (1924), Ecuador (1897), Federal Republic of Germany (1949), Finland (1949), Greenland (1954), Iceland (1950), Italy (1944), Mexico (25 states out of 29 and the federal territory [)](Constitution, 1931), Norway (1905), Netherlands (1870), Netherlands Antilles (1957), New Zealand (1961), Portugal (1867), Republic of San Marino (1865), Sweden (1921), Switzerland (1937), Uruguay (1907), Venezuela (1863), Belgium (1867), Liechtenstein (1798), Lu[x]embourg, Vatican City State. The following jurisdictions are listed as having abolished capital punishment "almost completely": "Australia; New South Wales, where the death penalty is abolished for murder but not for treason or piracy; it is not, however, applied in fact. Nicaragua: the death penalty is applicable only if the crime is committed with one or more aggravating circumstances."

The following jurisdictions have retained capital punishment: "Afghanistan, Australia (except two states), Burma, Canada, Cambodia, Central African Republic, Ceylon, Chile, China (Taiwan), Cuba, Czechoslovakia, Dahomey, El Salvador, France, Gambia, Ghana, Gibraltar, Greece, Guatemala, Hong Kong, India, Indonesia, Iran, Iraq, Ireland, Ivory Coast, Japan, Laos, Lebanon, Liberia, Federation of Malaya, Mauritius, Mexico (four states out of 29—i.e., the states of Morelos, Oaxaca, San Luis Potosi and Tabasco), Morocco, Netherlands New Guinea, Nigeria, Northern Rhodesia, Myasaland, Pakistan, Philippines, Poland, Senegal, Seychelles, Somalia (Northern), Somalia (Central and Southern), Spain, Republic of South Africa, Sudan, Surinam, Tanganyika, Thailand, Togo, Turkey, United Arab Republic, Union of Soviet Socialist Republics, United Kingdom, Republic of Viet-Nam, Western Pacific Islands, Yugoslavia, Zanzibar."

10. Michigan and Rhode Island have retained—but never impose the death penalty for treason. Cf. *Pennsylvania v. Nelson,* 350 U.S. 497. Rhode Island has retained it also for murder committed by a prisoner under sentence of life imprisonment.

opinion polls, of whose general unreliability we are all aware) does not strongly favor the retention of the death penalty. The most recent Roper survey indicates that only 42% of those polled favored the retention of capital punishment; 50% opposed it; and 8% were undecided. The most recent Gallup survey indicates that 51% of those polled favored the retention of capital punishment; 36% opposed it; and 13% were undecided. (The comparable figures seven years earlier were 68%, 25% and 7%.)[11]

It may be suggested that since the death penalty is a mode of punishment "about which opinion is fairly divided," a state does not violate the Constitution when it "treats [the prisoner] by [such] a mode." *Louisiana ex rel. Francis v. Resweber* (Frankfurter, J., concurring). With all deference, this reasoning does not seem persuasive here. In certain matters—especially those relating to fair procedures in criminal trials—this Court traditionally has guided rather than followed public opinion in the process of articulating and establishing progressively civilized standards of decency. If only punishments already overwhelmingly condemned by public opinion came within the cruel and unusual punishment proscription, the Eighth Amendment would be a dead letter; for such punishments would presumably be abolished by the legislature. The Eighth Amendment, like the others in the Bill of Rights, was intended as a countermajoritarian limitation on governmental action; it should be applied to nurture rather than to retard our "evolving standards of decency." Can there be any doubt that if this Court condemns the death penalty as cruel and unusual—whatever the initial effect—before too long that penalty will no longer be "a mode of punishment about which opinion is fairly divided." As the Court recognized in *Weems:* "Our contemplation cannot be only of what has been but of what may be."

There is another consideration which, in all frankness, enters into my thinking on this subject. Whenever capital punishment is considered, concern is expressed about the possibility of mistakenly and irremedially executing an "innocent" man. The concept of innocence has, of course, at least two meanings when used by a court. A person is "innocent" if he is not the one who committed the crime. A person is also innocent, regardless of whether or not he is the one who committed the crime, if his conviction was improperly secured. The thought of innocent men—in the first sense—being executed in any substantial number would certainly be enough to condemn the penalty of death in most people's eyes. This Court is equally concerned with the possibility of innocent men—in the second sense—being executed. Our evolving concepts of due process and fundamental

11. The Roper Poll was conducted in 1958, the Gallup Poll in 1960.

fairness (apart from those relating to punishment) require this Court—not infrequently—to hold that what was considered permissible yesterday is prohibited today; that what was viewed as a limitation solely on the Federal Government yesterday, is a limitation also on the States today; that what this Court felt itself precluded from reviewing yesterday, it may review today. Moreover, these same concepts require us to reverse and vacate today, criminal convictions which were deemed constitutional when secured. But when such convictions resulted in the penalty of death, they cannot be reversed and vacated. Of course in law, as in life generally, a price must be paid for progress. But when this price is in human life, we must surely make every effort to avoid unnecessary sacrifice. Compare, for example, the cases of *Williams v. Georgia,* 349 U.S. 375, and *Fay v. Noia,* 372 U.S. 391. In each case, the accused was convicted of first degree murder by a process which was not deemed unconstitutional at the time it was conducted;[12] in each case the process was subsequently declared unconstitutional; in each case the accused did not properly raise constitutional objections to the process. The only difference was that Williams was sentenced to death and executed (see Prettyman, Death and the Supreme Court (1961), 211 ff.) while Fay was sentenced to life imprisonment. Fay is now free; so undoubtedly would Williams have been (after the decision in *Fay v. Noia* which would have permitted Williams collaterally to attack his conviction) but for the finality of his sentence.

I conclude therefore that under the "evolving standard of decency" test, punishment by death is cruel and unusual.

B. Unnecessary And Excessive Punishment

Even if it could be said that our "evolving standards of decency" do not yet condemn the death penalty, I suggest nevertheless that this penalty is unconstitutional under the following additional test derived from the *Weems* case: Giving full weight to reasonable legislative findings, a punishment is cruel and unusual if a less severe one can as effectively achieve the permissible ends of punishment.

Little discussion need be devoted to rehabilitation and isolation (*i.e.,* removal from the community): capital punishment obviously does not rehabilitate; nor could a State be heard to argue that the death penalty better serves the isolation goal of punishment

12. Williams was indicted by a grand jury whose composition was determined by the drawing of tickets whose color differed with the race of the person named on the ticket; Fay's conviction was secured with the help of a coerced confession.

(because it is cheaper to execute than safely and securely to imprison for life). Moreover, vengeance is no longer considered an acceptable goal of punishment. Cf. *Williams v. New York,* 337 U.S. 241, 249.

Thus the crucial question is whether capital punishment has any uniquely *deterrent* effect upon potential criminals. If it does not, then a less severe punishment (*e.g.,* life imprisonment) would as effectively deter; and it would follow that the death penalty is unconstitutional under the above test.[13]

Much research has recently been conducted in an effort to learn whether capital punishment is a unique deterrent to capital crime; and many claims (favoring abolition) have been predicated upon the results of this research. The most that can be said, however, is that "there is no clear evidence in any of the figures. . . that the abolition of capital punishment has led to an increase in the homicide rate, or that its reintroduction has led to a fall." Royal Comm. Report on Capital Punishment (1953) 23.[14]

Thus, the meaningful question—at least at this point in the development of our methods of studying the relationship between punishments and crimes—is not whether capital punishment really deters crime (for we do not know the answer to this question); it is: "where [does] the onus of proof [lie] in this matter of the death penalty."[15] If the State must affirmatively show that capital punishment has a unique deterrent impact, then it has failed. If the advo-

---

13. Many thoughtful commentators suggest that if it could be shown that the death penalty really does prevent murders, then capital punishment for murder is justified. For then the State would not be "taking" a life; it would merely be choosing to save one life at the cost of another. As Michael and Wechsler put it: "We need not pause to reconsider the universal judgment that there is no social interest in preserving the lives of aggressors at the cost of their victims. Given the choice that must be made, the only defensible policy is one that will operate as a sanction against unlawful aggression." A Rationale of the Law of Homicide, 37 Col. L. Rev. 701.

Or as more recently stated:

"the only conceivable moral ground which a state can have that will justify it in taking a citizen's life...is simply that one man's life is necessary and indispensable for the protection and preservation of many other citizen's lives." Morris, Thoughts on Capital Punishment, 35 Wash. L. Rev. 335 (1960).

14. As Professor H.L.A. Hart has warned, this conclusion (and the statistics upon which it is based) should be taken to mean only that "there is no evidence from the statistics that the death penalty is a superior deterrent to imprisonment;" it should not be taken to mean (as some have argued) that "there is evidence that the death penalty is not a superior deterrent to imprisonment." Hart, Murder and its Punishment, 12 N.W.L. Rev. 433, 457 (1957). Professor Francis Allen has joined this caveat; Review, 10 Stan. L. Rev. 595 (1958) ("[S]uch inquiries rarely approach any minimum standards of decent scientific rigor." *Id.,* at 600). Professor Richard Donnelly has expressed similar caution. Capital Punishment in Connecticut, 35 Conn. Bar J. 39 (1961).

15. Hart, *supra,* 460.

cates of abolition must prove that capital punishment lacks a unique deterrent impact, then they have failed.

Whatever standard is generally applicable in passing on legislative findings based on conflicting evidence, the State must, in my opinion, show an overriding necessity before it can take human life.[16] This principle was recognized as long ago as 1794, when the preamble to the Pennsylvania criminal statutes announced that ". . .the punishment of death ought never to be inflicted, where it is not *absolutely necessary* to the public safety. . . ." (Emphasis added.) The Court has frequently held that doubts should always be resolved against the application of the death sentence. See, *e.g., Andres v. United States,* 333 U.S. 740, 752.

I conclude therefore that since there is no persuasive evidence that capital punishment uniquely deters capital crime, and since doubts should be resolved against the death penalty, this penalty runs afoul of the *Weems* test which proscribes punishments unnecessarily severe in relation to the permissible goals of punishment.[17]

---

16. Cf. *Schneider v. State,* 308 U.S. 147, 161.

17. The views of the Reporter (Professor Wechsler) and Advisory Committee to the American Law Institute's Model Penal Code are summarized as follows:

"[J]udgment of death is executed in a trivial fraction of the cases in which it might legally be imposed; and that there is no quantitative evidence that either its availability or its execution has noticeable influence upon the frequency of murder. This conclusion is not surprising when it is remembered that murders are, upon the whole, either crimes of passion, in which a calculus of consequences has small psychological reality, or crimes of such depravity that the actor reveals himself as doubtfully within the reach of influences that might be especially inhibitory in the case of an ordinary man. There is, therefore, room for substantial doubt that any solid case can be maintained for the death penalty, as it is employed in the United States, as a deterrent to murder. The social need for grievous condemnation of the act can be met, as it is met in abolition states, without resorting to capital punishment.

"Apart from the efficacy of the death penalty as a deterrent, its possible imposition has, we believe, a discernible and baneful effect on the administration of criminal justice. A trial where life is at stake becomes inevitably a morbid and sensational affair, fraught with risk that public sympathy will be aroused for the defendant without reference to guilt or innocence of the crime charged. In the rare cases where capital sentence is imposed, this unwholesome influence carries through the period preceding execution, reaching a climax when sentence is carried out.

"The special sentiment associated with judgment of death is reflected also in the courts, lending added weight to claims of error in the trial and multiplying and protracting the appellate processes, including post-conviction remedies developed during recent years. As astute and realistic an observer as Mr. Justice Jackson, observed to the Reporter shortly prior to his death that he opposed capital punishment because of its deleterious effects on the judicial process and stated that he would appear and urge the Institute to favor abolition.

"Beyond these considerations, it is obvious that capital punishment is the most difficult of sanctions to administer with even rough equality. A rigid legislative

IS CAPITAL PUNISHMENT UNCONSTITUTIONAL AS APPLIED TO CERTAIN TYPES OF CRIMES AND CERTAIN TYPES OF CRIMINALS?

I recognize that my Brethren may not agree with the reasoning set forth in the preceeding portion of the memorandum in support of my view that capital punishment, as such, is unconstitutional. I submit for consideration therefore, the proposition that the infliction of death at least for certain types of crimes and on certain types of offenders violates the Eighth and Fourteenth Amendments.

Consider, for example, the constitutionality of death as a penalty for sexual crimes which do not endanger life (*e.g.*, rape). A persuasive argument can be made—much more persuasive than can be made in relation to murder considered as a general category—that the threat of capital punishment is not a unique deterrent to sexual crimes. Again, there is no convincing statistical data. But the psychiatric and psychological observations about the motivation of sexual offenses seem persuasive of the conclusion that if these crimes can be deterred at all, they can be deterred as well by the threat of a long prison sentence as by the threat of death.

Moreover, even assuming that sexual crimes not endangering life are uniquely deterred by the threat of death, there remains the question posed by the third test derived from the *Weems* case: May human life constitutionally be taken by the State to protect a value other than human life? Certainly, if the value sought to be preserved was economic, the taking of human life would be unconstitutional regardless of the efficacy of the deterrent. Here, however, the value sought to be preserved is undoubtedly considered much more important than economic values. I believe, nevertheless, that the general consensus is that the value is less than life. When this consensus is coupled with the questionable efficacy of capital punishment as a unique deterrent to sexual crimes, they result in a persuasive argument against the constitutionality of death as a punishment for sexual crimes not endangering human life.[18]

---

definition of capital murders has proved unworkable in practice, given the infinite variety of homicides and possible mitigating factors. A discretionary system thus becomes inevitable, with equally inevitable differences in judgment depending on the individuals involved and other accidents of time and place. Yet most dramatically when life is at stake, equality is, as it is generally felt to be, a most important element of justice.

"Finally, there is the point that erroneous convictions are inevitable and beyond correction in the light of newly discovered evidence when a capital sentence has been executed."

18. This would also eliminate the well-recognized disparity in the imposition of the death penalty for sexual crimes committed by whites and nonwhites. See, *e.g.*, National Prison Statistics, April 1952, which indicates that between 1937 and 1951, 233 Negroes and 26 whites were executed for rape in the United States.

The Court—consistent with its approach in *Robinson v. California*—should also consider the constitutionality of death as a penalty for certain types of offenders, such as those incapable of exercising any volition (or control) over their conduct (and who are consequently nondeterrable themselves and not likely to serve as models for each other potential offenders who might be deterrable).

The cases of *White v. Washington,* 374 P.2d 942 (232 Misc.), and *Snider v. Cunningham* (169 Misc.), presently before this Court on petitions for certiorari, seem to raise this issue. In *White,* the highest court of the State sanctioned the imposition of the death penalty on a murderer, about whom the psychiatric evidence was unanimous that he could not possibly have been deterred by the threat of any penalty no matter how severe, and about whom the court concluded that: "There was substantial evidence from which the jury could have found that appellant could not control his own behavior. . . ." In *Snider,* the District Court, after a hearing on federal habeas, found that the accused "has an irresistible sex urge which he is, at times, unable to control." And the Court of Appeals concluded that "he has little or no control of his sex urges in the presence of a female under his control in a secluded place." Thus, it seems clear that although the accused may have had some control over the situations in which he might find himself, once he was alone with a female, the fear of capital punishment would not uniquely deter an attempt to satisfy his "sex urge."

It seems clear that for this type of offender capital punishment is not a unique deterrent; thus, under the test previously outlined, the imposition of the death penalty on such an offender would violate the constitutional proscription on cruel and unusual punishments.

CONCLUSION

The foregoing expresses my substantial doubts concerning the constitutionality of the death penalty.

Appendix C

MAXWELL v. BISHOP (OCTOBER TERM, 1968)

DRAFT OPINIONS OF JUSTICES DOUGLAS, BLACK, FORTAS, AND HARLAN

SUPREME COURT OF THE UNITED STATES

William L. Maxwell, Petitioner, *v.* O. E. Bishop, Superintendent, Arkansas State Penitentiary. On Writ Of Certiorari To The United States Court Of Appeals for The Eighth Circuit.
[April ———, 1969.]

MR. JUSTICE DOUGLAS delivered the opinion of the Court.

Petitioner, a Negro, was convicted of rape of a white woman, a crime which Arkansas makes punishable by death. Ark. Stat. Ann. § 41-3403. Arkansas, however, gives discretion to the jury to impose life imprisonment instead: "The jury shall have the right in all cases where the punishment is now death by law, to render a verdict of life imprisonment in the State penitentiary at hard labor."[1]

The jury elected punishment by death. The Supreme Court of Arkansas affirmed. 236 Ark. 694, 370 S.W. 2d 113. No review of that decision was sought here. A federal habeas corpus proceeding was then filed; but it brought no relief. *Maxwell* v. *Stephens,* 279 F. Supp. 205, aff'd 348 F. 2d 325 (one judge dissenting). We denied

1. This type of statute is kin to the Federal Act adopted in 1897. See *Andres* v. *United States,* 333 U.S. 740. As stated by Mr. Justice Frankfurter "The statute reflects the movement, active during the nineteenth century, against the death sentence. The movement was impelled both by ethical and humanitarian arguments against capital punishment, as well as by the practical consideration that jurors were reluctant to bring in verdicts which inevitably called for its infliction. Almost every State passed mitigating legislation." 333 U.S., at 753 (concurring opinion). And see *Cotton* v. *Utah,* 130 U.S. 83, 86–87.

Arkansas' present law appeared in 1915 in the following form: "That the jury shall have the right in all cases where the punishment is now death by law, to tender a verdict of life imprisonment in the State penitentiary at hard labor." Acts 1915, p. 775.

certiorari. 382 U.S. 944. The present habeas corpus proceeding was commenced by a second federal petition. The District Court denied petitioner's application for the writ. 257 F. Supp. 710. The Court of Appeals affirmed. 398 F. 2d 138. The case is here on a petition for a writ of certiorari which we granted. 394 U.S.———.

The criminal trial in Arkansas is a unitary trial, the same jury resolving the issues of guilt and punishment and rendering a verdict on each question at the same time.

There are standards to guide the jury in determining the question of guilt. But the legislature has provided no standards for guiding the jury on the penalty of death and no instructions limiting or directing the exercise by the jury of its absolute discretion were given by the judge in the trial of this case.

The initial question in this case is whether a unitary trial, as distinguished from a bifurcated trial, affords an accused in a capital case an effective and practical opportunity to tender evidence relevant to the issue of punishment as distinguished from the issue of guilt; and if so whether the choice between remaining silent to protect ones innocence and speaking out to encourage rational sentencing "needlessly penalizes the assertion of [ones] constitutional right[s]." *United States* v. *Jackson,* 390 U.S. 570, 583.

The difficulties of the accused in introducing evidence relevant to the issue of punishment are not as difficult in California as in Arkansas, because California has bifurcated trials.[2] In California—once guilt is determined—the jury turns to the wholly distinct issue of punishment. In a unitary trial, where guilt and punishment are decided at the same time by the same jury, the important question presented is whether a defendant receives that due process on this issue of punishment that is required by the Fourteenth Amendment.

I

A defendant in a state criminal trial need not take the stand, for the Self-Incrimination Clause of the Fifth Amendment applicable by reason of the Fourteenth protects him. *Malloy* v. *Hogan,* 378 U.S. 1. As a corollary, his failure to take the stand may not be used against him by the prosecutor. *Griffin* v. *California,* 380 U.S. 609. This privilege against self-incrimination may be important. Yet if the defendant is to escape death, his testimony may be essential. If he takes the stand in a unitary trial, Arkansas permits searching cross-

2. West's Ann. Calif. Code § 190.1. And see 39 McKinneys Consol. L. N. Y. Ann. § 125.35; 18 Pa. Stat. Ann. § 4701: Conn. Gen. Stat. Ann. § 53–10 (Supp. 1965).

examination as to whether he ever committed "other crimes and immoralities." See *Skaggs* v. *State,* 234 Ark. 510, 511, 353 S. W. 2d 3, 4 (1962); *Rayburn* v. *State,* 200 Ark. 914, 141 S. W. 2d 532 (1940); *Bevis* v. *State,* 209 Ark. 624, 192 S. W. 2d 113 (1946), and a host of prejudicial questions. *Gaines* v. *State,* 208 Ark. 293, 186 S. W. 2d 154 (1945); *McGraw* v. *State,* 184 Ark. 342, 42 S. W. 2d 373 (1931). Once the question of his character is opened prior to the determination of guilt or innocence, there may be introduced every prejudicial occurrence, real or imagined, in the accused's history. *Amos* v. *State,* 209 Ark. 55, 189 S. W. 2d 611.

Unless the accused testifies or opens up the question, evidence of prior crimes is inadmissible. *Bonds v. State*, 240 Ark. 908, 403 S. W. 2d 52; *Alford v. State*, 223 Ark. 330, 266 S. W. 2d 804 (1954). Yet on the issue whether an accused should live or die, the jury, like the judge who imposes the sentence, *Williams v. New York*, 337 U.S. 241, 247, may need to know much more about the accused than is likely or permissibly forthcoming on the trial of the issue of guilt. At times, his right of allocution may therefore be essential to the requirements of due process. See *Specht v. Patterson*, 386 U.S. 605, 610. *Hill v. United States*, 368 U.S. 424, 429. Yet a defendant can be subjected to the same withering cross-examination on character, misdeeds, reputation, and prior crimes, though he takes the stand in a unitary trial to tender mitigating circumstances. That is to say, though he uses his right of allocution in an attempt to obtain mercy rather than complete exoneration, his efforts to obtain a lesser punishment may only worsen his position on the issue of guilt. The law, as it developed, made taking the stand the great divide between immunity from attack on collateral matters that reflect on character or reputation on the one hand and relentless pursuit on the other. Yet crossing that great divide may indeed afford the only possible choice of obtaining a fair trial on the issue of punishment.

It may be that only by presenting his mitigating evidence may an accused make an impact on the jury's determination of the penalty. Yet he may not dare exercise his right of allocution at the unitary trial, lest he suffer irreparable harm on the guilt issue. He thus purchases a fair trial on the issue of guilt at the cost of sacrificing his right to a fair trial on the issue of punishment.

A unitary trial does not accommodate both the right of allocution and the right to silence; it forces the defendant to choose between them. In doing so, it is "inherently coercive," and "impose[s] an impermissible burden upon the assertion of a constitutional right." *United States* v. *Jackson,* 390 U.S., at 583.

II

And so we reach the *second* question whether lodging in a jury or in a judge an unlimited discretion that a defendant should live or die comports with the Fourteenth Amendment.

The law normally gives a jury guidelines:

Which party is at fault in an automobile accident?

Was the decedent insane when he made his will?

Was homicide justified because of self-defense?

The grant to a judge or a jury of an undefined and unreviewable discretion without any effective or practical opportunity to confine it is telling the judge or jury to send whomsoever they choose to death. That is lodging in its hands "a naked and arbitrary power," *Yick Wo.* v. *Hopkins,* 118 U.S. 356, 366, a power struck down in that case under the Equal Protection Clause because it permitted racial discrimination in the issuance of licenses to run a laundry. Our cases dealing with the Equal Protection Clause and economic issues give leeway where there is a rational foundation for discrimination. See *Loving* v. *Virginia,* 388 U.S. 1, 9. But we have been much stricter when "fundamental rights and liberties" are at issue. See *Harper* v. *Virginia Board,* 383 U.S. 663, 670. And there is, of course, no right more fundamental than the right to live.

In *Skinner* v. *Oklahoma,* 316 U.S. 535, a State sterilized those who robbed banks from the outside, exempting those who robbed banks from the inside; and we held the law to be violative of equal protection:

> "When the law lays an unequal hand on those who have committed intrinsically the same probity of offense and sterilizes one and not the other, it has made as. . . insidious discrimination as if it had selected a particular race or nationality for oppressive treatment." 316 U.S. 540–541.

A law, such as Arkansas', may in operation seriously implicate the Equal Protection Clause.

The Due Process Clause of the Fourteenth Amendment is also involved, as indicated by *Graccio* v. *Pennsylvania,* 382 U.S. 399, an opinion of the Court written by MR. JUSTICE BLACK. The case involved a Pennsylvania prosecution in which the defendant was found not guilty. Pursuant to a Pennsylvania statute the jury was directed to determine whether the defendant or the other side should pay the costs. The jury made the assessment against the defendant. We set it aside, saying that a law fails to meet the requirements of due process if it "leaves judges and jurors free to decide, without any legally fixed standards, what is prohibited and what is not in each particular case."[3] *Id.*, 402–403. We said:

> "Certainly one of the basic purposes of the Due Process Clause has always been to protect a person against having the Government impose burdens upon him except in accordance with the valid laws of the land. Implicit in this constitutional safeguard is the premise that the law must be one that carries an understandable meaning with legal standards that courts must enforce. This state Act as written does not even begin to meet this constitutional requirement." *Id.*, 403.

In a footnote we said, "In so holding we intend to cast no doubt whatever on the constitutionality of the settled practice of many States to leave to juries finding defendants guilty of a crime the power to fix punishment within legally prescribed limits." *Id.*, 405, n. 8. Some courts have relied on that footnote as sanction for granting the jury complete discretion to exercise the death or life choice.[4] But we read it as doing no more than reserving the important constitutional question now tendered, what are "legally prescribed limits" in capital cases?

Under Arkansas law those who should receive death and those who should not are undefined. There is no classification whatsoever, the choice being left completely to the discretion of the jury.

Where there are no guidelines or relevant evidence one jury may decide that one defendant is not "fit to live," *Witherspoon* v. *Illinois*, 391 U.S. 510, 521, n.20, because he is a black who raped a white woman, while another defendant is "fit to live" because he is a white who raped a black.[5] Or whatever the race of the defendant one

---

3. We held that the instructions given to this jury did not cure the "void for vagueness" defect in the statute:

"It may possibly be that the trial court's charge comes nearer to giving a guide to the jury than those that preceded it, but it still falls short of the kind of legal standard due process requires. At best it only told the jury that if it found appellant guilty of 'some misconduct' less than that charged against him, it was authorized by law to saddle him with the State's costs in its unsuccessful prosecution. It would be difficult if not impossible for a person to prepare a defense against such general abstract charges as 'misconduct,' or 'reprehensible conduct.' If used in a *statute* which imposed forfeitures, punishments or judgments for costs, such loose and unlimiting terms would certainly cause the statute to fail to measure up to the requirements of the Due Process Clause. And these terms are no more effective to make a statute valid which standing alone is void for vagueness." 382 U.S., at 404.

4. The Death Penalty Cases, 56 Calif. L. Rev. 1268, 1416 *et seq.* (1968).

5. Between 1930 and 1962, when petitioner was sentenced to die, 446 persons were executed for rape in this country. For the distribution of the cases by States and by race see United States Department of Justice, Bureau of Prisons, National Prisoner Statistics, No. 32, Execution 1962 (April 1963), Table 2.

jury may be seized by the spirit of the mob, while another, dealing with the same quality of offense, may be more reasoned and compassionate. As Attorney General Ramsey Clark recently said:[6]

> "A small and capricious selection of offenders have been put to death. Most persons convicted of the same crimes have been imprisoned. Experienced wardens know many prisoners serving life or less whose crimes were equally, or more atrocious, than those of men on death row."

We know from our own observations that the death penalty is seldom suffered by the affluent member of society; it is reserved, in practice, for the indigent and those otherwise inferior or somehow incapacitated, whether by education or mental instability.

When the issue of punishment is resolved after guilt is determined, the defendant is free to testify without restraint and to offer any evidence, if there be such, that is of a mitigating character. In noncapital cases the pre-sentence report to the judge covers early environment, religious training, education, employment record, and criminal history. Since the jury in the capital case performs the same function as the sentencing judge in the noncapital case, it is argued that the jury should have the same background information in some form or other.

The existence of standards and of a record makes possible at least a degree of judicial review.

The introduction of background evidence may help the defendant in some cases and hurt him in others.

If a State wants to leave to judges and juries discretion to take the life of a man who commits an offense, it must provide "legally fixed standards" lest the law become capricious or provide no understandable guidelines for the jury's or judge's decision.

What manner of men does a State want to execute? Is killing a policeman or a prison guard more heinous than killing a neighbor in an old feud? Is killing for a fee more monstrous than killing in a household quarrel?

The list of aggravating circumstances that one group thinks warrants imposition of the death penalty will be anathema to another group. There will likewise be a wide variety of opinions when it comes to mitigating circumstances.

Should the aggravating circumstances be those enumerated in § 201.6(3) of the Model Penal Code of the American Law Institute?

---

6. Hearings, Subcommittee on Criminal Laws and Procedures of the Senate Judiciary Committee on S. 1760, 1968.

> "(a) The murder was committed by a convict under sentence of imprisonment.
> "(b) The defendant was previously convicted of another murder or of a felony or felonies involving the use or threat of violence to the person.
> "(c) At the time the murder was committed the defendant also committed another murder or murders.
> "(d) The defendant knowingly created a great risk of death to many persons.
> "(e) The murder was committed while the defendant was engaged or was an accomplice in the commission of, or the attempt to commit, or flight after committing robbery, rape by force or intimidation, arson, burglary or kidnaping.
> "(f) The murder was committed for the purpose of avoiding or preventing a lawful arrest or effecting an escape from lawful custody.
> "(g) The murder was committed for hire or pecuniary gain.
> "(h) The murder was especially heinous, atrocious or cruel, manifesting exceptional depravity."

Should mitigating circumstances include those described in § 201.6(4) of the Model Penal Code?

> "(a) The defendant has no history of prior criminal activity.
> "(b) The murder was committed while the defendant was under the influence of extreme mental or emotional disturbance.
> "(c) The victim was a participant in the defendant's homicidal conduct or consented to the homicidal act.
> "(d) The murder was committed under circumstances which the defendant believed to provide a moral justification or extenuation for his conduct.
> "(e) The defendant was an accomplice in a murder committed by another person and his participation in the homicidal act was relatively minor.
> "(f) The defendant acted under duress or under the domination of another person.
> "(g) At the time of the murder, the capacity of the defendant to appreciate the criminality of his conduct or to conform his conduct to the requirements of law was impaired as a result of mental disease or defect or intoxication.
> "(h) The youth of the defendant at the time of the crime."

Should any substantial mitigating circumstances save the accused from the death penalty even if there are aggravating circumstances, as provided in § 201.6(2) of the Model Penal Code?

The draft provides that the jury should be instructed that it may not impose the death sentence "unless it finds there was an aggravating circumstance" as defined in the draft and further that "there were no substantial, mitigating circumstances." *Id.,* p. 77.

Should evidence of the prospects of rehabilitating the defendant be admissible?

Should the prosecution be allowed to show that the defendant is a psychotic beyond the reach of any known therapy?

These considerations present profound questions. The task is not for this Court but for the local legislatures. Standards or guidelines are necessary for as MR. JUSTICE BLACK said in *Graccio* v. *Pennsylvania, supra,* a law which "leaves judges and jurors free to decide without any legally fixed standards what is prohibitive and what is not in each case" violates the Fourteenth Amendment. 382 U.S. 402–403. Without the guidance of standards, the jury may unwittingly impose the death penalty for reasons which the State considers impermissible.[7] Without standards, the appellate courts are precluded from ensuring that the jury has performed its task. Without standards to guide him in preparing his testimony, the defendant has no notice of the reasons for which he may live or die.[8]

III

We reverse not on the issue of guilt but solely on the infliction of capital punishment. That was the effect of our reversal in *Witherspoon* v. *Illinois,* 391 U.S. 510. where we held that "a State may not entrust the determination of whether a man should live or die to a tribunal organized to return a verdict of death." *Id.,* at 521.

The state statute in that case[9] set the punishment at death, life imprisonment, or imprisonment for 14 years. It was a unitary trial, the jury being directed to "fix the punishment," once guilt was found.[10]

In the present case we follow the *Witherspoon* precedent and reverse on the issue of punishment only. Were this a case where guilt

7. Should "deterrence" be a standard? The California Supreme Court has concluded that the *deterrence* rationale of capital punishment is "unproven and illegitimate," *People* v. *Ketchel,* 59 Cal. 2d 503, 537–539, 381 P. 2d 394, 412–413 (1963). It therefore prohibits counsel from allowing the penalty jury to consider that standard.

8. In Arizona, the jury is precluded from considering evidence concerning the defendant's background, character, or prior criminal record, because the State has determined that the jury should punish the *crime* rather than the *criminal.* Accordingly, the defendant has notice that he will not be prepared to present evidence of "mitigating" circumstances. *State* v. *Narten,* 99 Ariz. 116, ———, 407 P. 2d 81 86 (1965).

9. Ill. Rev. Stat., c. 38, §§ 3360, 801 (1959).

10. § 360, n. 3, *supra.*

determination was prejudiced by a unitary trial, as where the accused waived his Fifth Amendment right to assert his right of allocution, a reversal on the finding of guilt would also be necessary. But Maxwell did not take the stand and no other evidence in the record suggests that the guilt determination was prejudiced by the unitary procedure.

This is a federal habeas corpus proceeding involving the constitutional rights of one convicted under a state law. The federal Act gives the District Court power to "dispose of the matter as law and justice require." 28 U. S. C. § 2243. See *Fay* v. *Noia,* 372 U. S. 391, 397, 438; *Sheppard* v. *Maxwell,* 384 U.S. 333, 363; *Jackson* v. *Denno,* 378 U. S. 368, 396; *Rogers* v. *United States,* 378 U. S. 549.

We reverse the judgment of the Court of Appeals and direct that the cause be remanded to the District Court for disposition in conformity with this opinion.

It is so ordered.

MR. JUSTICE BLACK, dissenting.

If this Court is determined to abolish the death penalty, I think it should do so forthrightly, and not by nibbles. See, e. g., *United States* v. *Jackson,* 390 U. S. 570, and *Witherspoon* v. *Illinois,* 391 U. S. 510. So far as I know, no opinion of the Court has ever suggested that any part of the Federal Constitution compels either the States or Federal Government to have bifurcated trials, that is, trials in which separate jury proceedings are held to determine guilt and punishment. This country has managed to get along without the constitutional requirement of such trials for around 180 years and it seems late in the day for this Court to announce such a constitutional rule.

So far as I am concerned, the question of whether the Fourteenth Amendment compels the States' to adopt a two-stage jury trial in capital cases or any others was convincingly answered just two Terms ago in our decision in *Spencer* v. *Texas,* 385 U.S. 554. In his opinion for the Court rejecting the argument that the Constitution should for the first time be construed as compelling the States to adopt such two-stage trials. MR. JUSTICE HARLAN concluded:

> "To say that the two-stage jury trial in the English-Connecticut style is probably the fairest, as some commentators and courts have suggested, and with which we might well agree were the matter before us in a legislative or rule-making context, is a far cry from a constitutional determination that this method of handling the problem is compelled by the Fourteenth Amendment. Two-part trials are rare in our jurisprudence; they have never been com-

> pelled by this Court as a matter of law, or even as a matter of federal procedure. With recidivism the major problem that it is, substantial changes in trial procedure in countless local courts around the country would be required were this Court to sustain the contentions made by these petitioners. This we are unwilling to do. To take such a step would be quite beyond the pale of this Court's proper function in our federal system. It would be a wholly unjustifiable encroachment by this Court upon the constitutional power of States to promulgate their own rules of evidence to try their own state-created crimes in their own state courts, so long as their rules are not prohibited by any provision of the United States Constitution, which these rules are not." 385 U. S., at 568–569.

Since I thought that this statement was constitutionally correct when it was written and since I still adhere to it, I would affirm this conviction.

MR. JUSTICE FORTAS.

I concur in the judgment of the Court and in Part I of its opinion.

I do not agree that we should rule, on the basis of the present state of our knowledge, that statutes which allow the judge or jury a choice of punishment to be imposed are unconstitutional unless explicit standards are prescribed to guide them in making the choice. I do not know, and the Court does not suggest, meaningful standards or a basis upon which a legislature could prescribe different punishments for the kaleidoscope of crime and the infinite variety of humans who commit them. Neither the refinement of moral criteria nor the progress of penology or of the arts of psychiatry, chemistry or environmental therapy enables me to envision the development of meaningful standards. In this area, we do not yet have the skills to produce words which would fit the punishment to the crime or to the criminal with more precision than would result if the judge or jury acted without standards. To assume otherwise, I think, is to delude ourselves and to insist upon a constitutional mandate which, at best, will be meaningless. The standards to be adopted will not really serve the purpose of administering justice more evenly, or more appropriately, or both better results. And I fear that insistence upon standards will cause legislatures to reduce the use of the flexible or alternative penalties which most modern penologists applaud, and to substitute for them more stringent, mandatory penalties. I am not prepared to say that due process of law requires these results.

On the other hand, I fully agree that due process requires that the defendant be given an adequate opportunity to present to the sentencing authority—judge or jury—material relevant to the sentence to be imposed. In the case of jury sentencing at least, this means that he is entitled to a bifurcated trial.

I think we should note that the thrust of the Court's opinion may not be confined to capital cases, but may apply in all cases involving major penalties, at least where the jury has sentencing power and alternatives are available to it.

MR. JUSTICE HARLAN, concurring in the result.

Until 1915, one convicted of rape in Arkansas was automatically sentenced to death. In that year, a statute gave the jury discretion to impose instead a sentence of life imprisonment at hard labor. See Ark. Stat. Ann. § 43-2153. Arkansas' reform was part of a nationwide dissatisfaction with mandatory death penalties, which eventuated in the repeal of all such provisions.

The State of Arkansas acknowledges that, due to the statutory bestowal of sentencing discretion upon the jury, there is at issue in an Arkansas capital case "something more than the guilt or innocence of the accused. . . ; the jury must decide whether the convicted will live or die." Once it is recognized that the jury may have to make this second, distinct decision, it becomes apparent that a capital defendant has the strongest imaginable interest in being accorded a hearing at which he may put before the jury in an effective manner any evidence which might operate to mitigate his punishment.

When the issue in a criminal trial is that of guilt or innocence, this Court has held that "[a] person's right to. . .an opportunity to be heard in his defense—a right to his day in court—[is] basic to our system of jurisprudence," and has stated that "there are certain immutable principles of justice which inhere in the very idea of a free government which no member of the Union may disregard, as that no man shall be condemned in his person or property without. . .an opportunity of being heard in his defense." In a variety of cases involving administrative tribunals, this Court has consistently held that when one's liberty or property is significantly affected by an adjudicative decision, "due process of law requires that at some stage of the proceedings. . .[he] shall have an opportunity to be heard," and that in such instances "a hearing in its very essence demands that he who is entitled to it shall have the right to support his allegations by argument, however brief, and, if need be, by proof, however informal."

No administrative or judicial decision could possibly have greater significance for a party than the determination of a jury whether he is to live or to die. I would hold that the principle of the foregoing cases does apply to capital sentencing when performed by a jury, and would hold that a capital defendant has a right, assured by the Due Process Clause of the Fourteenth Amendment, to present to the jury evidence in mitigation of his punishment. I would hold that the right encompasses not only the giving of personal testimony but the presentation of evidence by the testimony of other witnesses, by documents, and by physical exhibits.

I find no conflict between the existence of such a right and my view that, for reasons which appear *infra,* at ——— – ———, a State is not constitutionally required to promulgate specific standards to govern jury sentencing. My Brother BRENNAN argues that unless a State has established such standards a defendant will never be able effectively to exercise his right to present mitigating evidence, since otherwise he will not know what evidence is relevant. I think this objection ephemeral. Some States have gone part way toward establishing standards by decreeing that certain types of mitigating evidence are inadmissible. I find this perfectly proper, so long as the distinction between admissible and inadmissible evidence is not wholly arbitrary. In may view, a capital defendant in such a State would have a constitutional right to present all mitigating evidence which is relevant under the State's own criteria.

On the other hand, some States have ruled that the sentencing decision is to be within the jury's "absolute discretion." I take this to mean that the jury may fix the defendant's punishment on the basis of any or all evidence which seems to it relevant, in light of their own or the community's conceptions of punishment. In such a State, I would hold that the defendant has a constitutional right to introduce, within very broad limits, whatever evidence he thinks might induce the jury to mitigate his punishment. Exercise of the right would in no way contravene the State's policy of permitting the jury "absolute discretion" in sentencing—the only result would be that the jury would have more evidence upon which to base its discretionary decision.

Appendix D

McGAUTHA V. CALIFORNIA

402 U.S. 183 (1970) (EXCERPT)

We consider first McGautha's and Crampton's common claim: that the absence of standards to guide the jury's discretion on the punishment issue is constitutionally intolerable. To fit their arguments within a constitutional frame of reference petitioners contend that to leave the jury completely at large to impose or withhold the death penalty as it sees fit is fundamentally lawless and therefore violates the basic command of the Fourteenth Amendment that no State shall deprive a person of his life without due process of law. Despite the undeniable surface appeal of the proposition, we conclude that the courts below correctly rejected it.[8]

A

In order to see petitioners' claim in perspective, it is useful to call to mind the salient features of the history of capital punishment for homicides under the common law in England, and subsequent statutory developments in this country. This history reveals continual efforts, uniformly unsuccessful, to identify before the fact those homicides for which the slayer should die. Thus, the laws of Alfred, echoing Exodus 21: 12–13, provided: "Let the man who slayeth

---

8. The lower courts thus placed themselves in accord with all other American jurisdictions which have considered the issue. See, *e.g., In re Ernst,* 294 F. 2d 556 (CA3 1961); *Florida ex rel. Thomas* v. *Culver,* 253 F. 2d 507 (CA5 1958); *Maxwell* v. *Bishop,* 398 F. 2d 138 (CA8 1968), vacated on other grounds, 398 U.S. 262 (1970); *Sims* v. *Eyman,* 405 F. 2d 439 (CA9 1969); *Segura* v. *Patterson,* 402 F. 2d 249 (CA10 1968); *McCants* v. *State,* 282 Ala. 397, 211 So. 2d 877 (1968); *Bagley* v. *State,* 247 Ark. 113, 444 S. W. 2d 567 (1969); *State* v. *Walters,* 145 Conn. 60, 138 A. 2d 786, appeal dismissed, 358 U.S. 46 (1958); *Wilson* v. *State,* 225 So. 2d 321 (Fla. 1969); *Miller* v. *State,* 224 Ga. 627, 163 S.E. 2d 730 (1968); *State* v. *Latham,* 190 Kan. 411, 375 P. 2d 788 (1962); *Duisen* v. *State,* 441 S. W. 2d 688 (Mo. 1969); *State* v. *Johnson,* 34 N. J. 212, 168 A. 2d 1, appeal dismissed, 368 U. S. 145 (1961); *People* v. *Fitzpatrick,* 61 Misc. 2d 1043, 308 N. Y. S. 2d 18 (1970); *State* v. *Roseboro,* 276 N. C. 185, 171 S. E. 2d 886 (1970); *Hunter* v. *State,* 222 Tenn. 672, 440 S. W. 2d 1 (1969); *State* v. *Kelback,* 23 Utah 2d 231, 461 P. 2d 297 (1969); *Johnson* v. *Commonwealth,* 208 Va. 481, 158 S. E. 2d 725 (1968); *State* v. *Smith,* 74 Wash. 2d 744, 446 P. 2d 571 (1968).

another wilfully perish by death. Let him who slayeth another of necessity or unwillingly, or unwilfully, as God may have sent him into his hands, and for whom he has not lain in wait be worthy of his life and of lawful bot if he seek an asylum." Quoted in 3 J. Stephen, History of the Criminal Law of England 24 (1883). In the 13th century, Bracton set it down that a man was responsible for all homicides except those which happened by pure accident or inevitable necessity, although he did not explain the consequences of such responsibility. *Id.,* at 35. The Statute of Gloucester, 6 Edw. 1, c. 9 (1278), provided that in cases of self-defense or misadventure the jury should neither convict nor acquit, but should find the fact specially, so that the King could decide whether to pardon the accused. It appears that in time such pardons—which may not have prevented forfeiture of goods—came to issue as of course. 3 Stephen, *supra,* at 36–42.

During all this time there was no clear distinction in terminology or consequences among the various kinds of criminal homicide. All were *prima facie* capital, but all were subject to the benefit of clergy, which after 1350 came to be available to almost any man who could read. Although originally those entitled to benefit of clergy were simply delivered to the bishop for ecclesiastical proceedings, with the possibility of degradation from orders, incarceration, and corporal punishment for those found guilty, during the 15th and 16th centuries the maximum penalty for clergyable offenses became branding on the thumb, imprisonment for not more than one year, and forfeiture of goods. 1 Stephen, *supra,* at 459–464. By the statutes of 23 Hen. 8, c. 1, §§ 3,4 (1531), and 1 Edw. 6, c. 12, § 10 (1547), benefit of clergy was taken away in all cases of "murder of malice prepensed." 1 Stephen, *supra,* at 464–465; 3 *id.,* at 44. During the next century and a half, however, "malice prepense" or "malice aforethought" came to be divorced from actual ill will and inferred without more from the act of killing. Correspondingly, manslaughter, which was initially restricted to cases of "chance medley," came to include homicides where the existence of adequate provocation rebutted the inference of malice. 3 *id.,* at 46–73.

The growth of the law continued in this country, where there was rebellion against the common-law rule imposing a mandatory death sentence on all convicted murderers. Thus, in 1794, Pennsylvania attempted to reduce the rigors of the law by abolishing capital punishment except for "murder of the first degree," defined to include all "willful, deliberate and premeditated" killings, for which the death penalty remained mandatory. Pa. Laws 1794, c. 1777. This reform was soon copied by Virginia and thereafter by many other States.

This new legislative criterion for isolating crimes appropriately punishable by death soon proved as unsuccessful as the concept of "malice aforethought." Within a year the distinction between the degrees of murder was practically obliterated in Pennsylvania. See Keedy, History of the Pennsylvania Statute Creating Degrees of Murder, 97 U. Pa. L. Rev. 759, 773–777 (1949). Other States had similar experiences. Wechsler & Michael, A Rationale of the Law of Homicide: I, 37 Col. L. Rev. 701, 707–709 (1937). The result was characterized in this way by Chief Judge Cardozo, as he then was:

> "What we have is merely a privilege offered to the jury to find the lesser degree when the suddenness of the intent, the vehemence of the passion, seems to call irresistibly for the exercise of mercy. I have no objection to giving them this dispensing power, but it should be given to them directly and not in a mystifying cloud of words." What Medicine Can Do For Law, in Law and Literature 70, 100 (1931).[9]

At the same time, jurors on occasion took the law into their own hands in cases which were "willful, deliberate, and premeditated" in any view of that phrase, but which nevertheless were clearly inappropriate for the death penalty. In such cases they simply refused to convict of the capital offense. See Report of the Royal Commission on Capital Punishment, 1949–1953, Cmd. 8932, ¶¶ 27–29 (1953); *Andres* v. *United States,* 333 U. S. 740, 753 (1948) (Frankfurter, J., concurring); cf. H. Kalven & H. Zeisel, The American Jury 306–312 (1966).

In order to meet the problem of jury nullification, legislatures did not try, as before, to refine further the definition of capital homicides. Instead they adopted the method of forthrightly granting juries the discretion which they had been exercising in fact. See Knowlton, Problems of Jury Discretion in Capital Cases, 101 U. Pa. L. Rev. 1099, 1102 and n. 18 (1953); Note, The Two-Trial System in Capital Cases, 39 N. Y. U. L. Rev. 50, 52 (1964). Tennessee was the first State to give juries sentencing discretion in capital cases.[10] Tenn.

9. In context the emphasis is on the confusing distinction between degrees of murder, not the desirability of juries' sentencing discretion. It may also be noted that the former New York definitions of first- and second-degree murder were somewhat unusual. See Wechsler & Michael, 37 Col. L. Rev., at 704 n. 13, 709 n. 26.

10. The practice of jury sentencing arose in this country during the colonial period for cases not involving capital punishment. It has been suggested that this was a "reaction to harsh penalties imposed by judges appointed and controlled by the Crown" and a result of "the early distrust of governmental power." President's Commission on Law Enforcement and Administration of Justice, Task Force Report: The Courts 26 (1967).

Laws 1837–1838, c. 29, but other States followed suit, as did the Federal Government in 1897.[11] Act of Jan. 15, 1987, c. 29, § 1, 29 Stat. 487. Shortly thereafter, in *Winston* v. *United States,* 172 U. S. 303 (1899), this Court dealt with the federal statute for the first time.[12] The Court reversed a murder conviction in which the trial judge instructed the jury that it should not return a recommendation of mercy unless it found the existence of mitigating circumstances. The Court found this instruction to interfere with the scheme of the Act to commit the whole question of capital punishment "to the judgment and the consciences of the jury." *Id.,* at 313.

> "How far considerations of age, sex, ignorance, illness or intoxication, of human passion or weakness, of sympathy or clemency, or the irrevocableness of an executed sentence of death, or an apprehension that explanatory facts may exist which have not been brought to light, or any other consideration whatever, should be allowed weight in deciding the question whether the accused should or should not be capitally punished, is committed by the act of Congress to the sound discretion of the jury, and of the jury alone." *Ibid.*

This Court subsequently had occasion to pass on the correctness of instructions to the jury with respect to recommendations of mercy in *Andres* v. *United States,* 333 U. S. 740 (1948). The Court approved, as consistent with the governing statute, an instruction that:

> "This power [to recommend mercy] is conferred solely upon you and in this connection the Court can not extend or prescribe to you any definite rule defining the exercise of this power, but commits the entire matter of its exercise to your judgment." *Id.,* at 743 n. 4.

The case was reversed, however, on the ground that other instructions on the power to recommend mercy might have been interpreted by the jury as requiring them to return an unqualified

---

11. California and Ohio, the two States involved in these cases, abolished mandatory death penalties in favor of jury discretion in 1874 and 1898. Act of Mar. 28, 1874, c. 508, Cal. Amendatory Acts 1873–1874, p. 457; Ohio Laws 1898, p. 223. Except for four States that entirely abolished capital punishment in the middle of the last century, every American jurisdiction has at some time authorized jury sentencing in capital cases. None of these statutes have provided standards for the choice between death and life imprisonment. See Brief for the United States as Amicus Curiae 128–137.

12. See also *Calton* v. *Utah,* 130 U. S. 83 (1889), in which the Court reversed a conviction under the statutes of Utah Territory in which the jury had not been informed of its right under the territorial code to recommend a sentence of imprisonment for life at hard labor instead of death.

verdict of guilty unless they unanimously agreed that mercy should be extended. The Court determined that the proper construction was to require a unanimous decision to withhold mercy as well, on the ground among others that the latter construction was "more consonant with the general humanitarian purpose of the statute." *Id.*, at 749. The only other significant discussion of standardless jury sentencing in capital cases in our decisions is found in *Witherspoon* v. *Illinois*, 391 U. S. 510 (1968). In reaching its conclusion that persons with conscientious scruples against the death penalty could not be automatically excluded from sentencing juries in capital cases, the Court relied heavily on the fact that such juries "do little more—and must do nothing less—than express the conscience of the community on the ultimate question of life or death." *Id.*, at 519 (footnote omitted). The Court noted that "one of the most important functions any jury can perform in making such a selection is to maintain a link between contemporary community values and the penal system—a link without which the determination of punishment could hardly reflect 'the evolving standards of decency that mark the progress of a maturing society.'" *Id.*, at 519 n. 15. The inner quotation is from the opinion of Mr. Chief Justice Warren for four members of the Court in *Trop* v. *Dulles*, 356 U.S. 86, 101 (1958).

In recent years academic and professional sources have suggested that jury sentencing discretion should be controlled by standards of some sort. The American Law Institute first published such a recommendation in 1959.[13] Several States have enacted new crim-

13. Model Penal Code § 201.6 (Tent. Draft No. 9, 1959). The criteria were revised and approved by the Institute in 1962 and now appear in § 210.6 of the Proposed Official Draft of the Model Penal Code. . . More recently the National Commission on Reform of Federal Criminal Laws published a Study Draft of a New Federal Criminal Code (1970). Section 3605 contained standards virtually identical to those of the Model Penal Code. The statement of the Chairman of the Commission, submitting the Study Draft for public comment, described it as "something more than a staff report and less than a commitment by the Commission or any of its members to every aspect of the Draft." Study Draft xx. The primary differences between the procedural provisions for capital sentencing in the Model Penal Code and those in the Study Draft are that the Code provides that the court and jury "shall" take the criteria into account, while the Study Draft provided that they "may" do so; and the Model Penal Code forbids imposition of the death penalty where no aggravating circumstances are found, while the Study Draft showed this only as an alternative provision. The latter feature is affected by the fact that only a very few murders were to be made capital. See *Id.*, at 307. In its Final Report (1971), the Commission recommended abolition of the death penalty for federal crimes. An alternate version, said to represent a "substantial body of opinion in the Commission," *id.*, comment to provisional § 3601, provided for retention of capital punishment for murder and treason with procedural provisions which did not significantly differ from those in the Study Draft.

inal codes in the intervening 12 years, some adopting features of the Model Penal Code.[14] Other States have modified their laws with respect to murder and the death penalty in other ways.[15] None of these States have followed the Model Penal Code and adopted statutory criteria for imposition of the death penalty. In recent years, challenges to standardless jury sentencing have been presented to many state and federal appellate courts. No court has held the challenge good. See n. 8, *supra.* As petitioners recognize, it requires a strong showing to upset this settled practice of the Nation on constitutional grounds. See *Walz* v. *Tax Commission,* 397 U. S. 664, 678 (1970); *Jackman* v. *Rosenbaum Co.,* 260 U. S. 22, 31 (1922); cf. *Palko* v. *Connecticut,* 302 U. S. 319, 325 (1937).

B

Petitioners seek to avoid the impact of this history by the observation that jury sentencing discretion in capital cases was introduced as a mechanism for dispensing mercy—a means for dealing with the rare case in which the death penalty was thought to be unjustified. Now, they assert, the death penalty is imposed on far fewer than half the defendants found guilty of capital crimes. The state and federal legislatures which provide for jury discretion in capital sentencing have, it is said, implicitly determined that some—indeed, the greater portion—of those guilty of capital crimes should be permitted to live. But having made that determination, petitioners argue, they have stopped short—the legislatures have not only failed to provide a rational basis for distinguishing the one group from the other, cf. *Skinner* v. *Oklahoma,* 316 U.S. 535 (1942), but they have failed even to suggest any basis at all. Whatever the merits of providing such a mechanism to take account of the unforeseeable case calling for mercy, as was the original purpose, petitioners contend the mechanism is constitutionally intolerable as a means of selecting the extraordinary cases calling for the death penalty, which is its present-day function.

In our view, such force as this argument has derives largely from its generality. Those who have come to grips with the hard task of actually attempting to draft means of channeling capital sentencing discretion have confirmed the lesson taught by the history recounted above. To identify before the fact those characteristics of

14. See, *e. g.,* N. Y. Penal Law § 65.00 (1967) (criteria for judges in deciding on probation).

15. *E. g.,* N. M. Stat. Ann. §§ 40A-29-2.1, 40A-29-2.2 (Supp. 1969), reducing the class of capital crimes.

criminal homicides and their perpetrators which call for the death penalty, and to express these characteristics in language which can be fairly understood and applied by the sentencing authority, appear to be tasks which are beyond present human ability.

Thus the British Home Office, which before the recent abolition of capital punishment in that country had the responsibility for selecting the cases from England and Wales which should receive the benefit of the Royal Prerogative of Mercy, observed:

> "The difficulty of defining by any statutory provision the types of murder which ought or ought not to be punished by death may be illustrated by reference to the many diverse considerations to which the Home Secretary has regard in deciding whether to recommend clemency. No simple formula can take account of the innumerable degrees of culpability, and no formula which fails to do so can claim to be just or satisfy public opinion." 1–2 Royal Commission on Capital Punishment, Minutes of Evidence 13 (1949).

The Royal Commission accepted this view, and although it recommended a change in British practice to provide for discretionary power in the jury to find "extenuating circumstances," that term was to be left undefined; "[t]he decision of the jury would be within their unfettered discretion and in no sense governed by the principles of law." Report of the Royal Commission on Capital Punishment, 1949–1953, Cmd. 8932, ¶ 553(b). The Commission went on to say, in substantial confirmation of the views of the Home Office:

> "No formula is possible that would provide a reasonable criterion for the infinite variety of circumstances that may affect the gravity of the crime of murder. Discretionary judgment on the facts of each case is the only way in which they can be equitably distinguished. This conclusion is borne out by American experience: there the experiment of degrees of murder, introduced long ago, has had to be supplemented by giving to the courts a discretion that in effect supersedes it." *Id.,* at ¶ 595.

The draftsmen of the Model Penal Code expressly agreed with the conclusion of the Royal Commission that "the factors which determine whether the sentence of death is the appropriate penalty in particular cases are too complex to be compressed within the limits of a simple formula. . . ." Report ¶ 498, quoted in Model Penal Code, § 201.6, Comment 3, p.71 (Tent. Draft No. 9, 1959). The draftsmen did think, however, "that it is within the realm of possibility to point to the main circumstances of aggravation and of mitigation that should be weighed *and weighed against each other* when they are presented in a concrete case." *Ibid.* The circumstances the draftsmen selected, set out in the Appendix to this opinion, were not intended to be exclusive. The Code provides simply that the sentencing authority should "take into account the aggravating and mitigating circumstances enumerated. . . and any other facts that it deems relevant," and that the court should so instruct when the issue was submitted to the jury. *Id.,* at § 210.6(2) (Proposed Official Draft, 1962).[16] The Final Report of the National Commission on Reform of Federal Criminal Laws (1971) recommended entire abolition of the death penalty in federal cases. In a provisional chapter, prepared for the contingency that Congress might decide to retain the death penalty, the Report contains a set of criteria virtually identical with the aggravating and mitigating circumstances listed by the Model Penal Code. With respect to the use to be made of the criteria, the Report provides that: "[i]n deciding whether a sentence of death should be imposed, the court and the jury, if any, *may* consider the mitigating and aggravating circumstances set forth in the subsections below." *Id.,* at provisional § 3604 (1) (emphasis added).

It is apparent that such criteria do not purport to provide more than the most minimal control over the sentencing authority's exercise of discretion. They do not purport to give an exhaustive list of the relevant considerations or the way in which they may be affected by the presence or absence of other circumstances. They do not even undertake to exclude constitutionally impermissible considerations.[17] And, of course, they provide no protection against the jury determined to decide on whimsy or caprice. In short, they do no more than suggest some subjects for the jury to consider during its deliberations, and they bear witness to the intractable nature of the problem of "standards" which the history of capital punishment has from the beginning reflected. Thus, they indeed caution against this Court's undertaking to establish such standards itself, or to pro-

16. The Model Penal Code provides that the jury should not fix punishment at death unless it found at least one of the aggravating circumstances and no sufficiently substantial mitigating circumstances. Model Penal Code § 210.6(2) (Proposed Official Draft, 1962). As the reporter's comment recognized, there is no fundamental distinction between this procedure and a redefinition of the class of potentially capital murders. Model Penal Code § 201.6, Comment 3, pp. 71–72 (Tent. Draft No. 9, 1959). As we understand these petitioners' contentions, they seek standards for guiding the sentencing authority's discretion, not a greater strictness in the definition of the class of cases in which the discretion exists. If we are mistaken in this, and petitioners contend that Ohio's and California's definitions of first-degree murder are too broad, we consider their position constitutionally untenable.

17. The issue whether a defendant is entitled to an instruction that certain factors such as race are not to be taken into consideration is not before us, as the juries were told not to base their decisions on "prejudice," and no more specific instructions were requested. Cf. *Griffin* v. *California,* 380 U.S. 609, 614–615 and n. 6 (1965).

nounce at large that standards in this realm are constitutionally required.

In light of history, experience, and the present limitations of human knowledge, we find it quite impossible to say that committing to the untrammeled discretion of the jury the power to pronounce life or death in capital cases is offensive to anything in the Constitution.[18] The States are entitled to assume that jurors confronted with the truly awesome responsibility of decreeing death for a fellow human will act with due regard for the consequences of their decision and will consider a variety of factors, many of which will have been suggested by the evidence or by the arguments of defense counsel. For a court to attempt to catalog the appropriate factors in this elusive area could inhibit rather than expand the scope of consideration, for no list of circumstances would ever be really complete. The infinite variety of cases and facets to each case would make general standards either meaningless "boiler-plate" or a statement of the obvious that no jury would need.

18. *Giaccio* v. *Pennsylvania,* 382 U.S. 399 (1966), does not point to a contrary result. In *Giaccio* the Court held invalid on its face a Pennsylvania statute which authorized criminal juries to assess costs against defendants whose conduct, although not amounting to the crime with which they were charged, was nevertheless found to be "reprehensible." The Court concluded that the statute was no more sound than one which simply made it a crime to engage in "reprehensible conduct" and consequently that it was unconstitutionally vague. The Court there stated:

"In so holding we intend to cast no doubt whatever on the constitutionality of the settled practice of many States to leave to juries finding defendants guilty of a crime the power to fix punishment within legally prescribed limits." *Id.,* at 405 n. 8.

Appendix E

FURMAN V. GEORGIA

408 U.S. 238 (1972)
(OPINIONS OF JUSTICES STEWART AND WHITE)
(EXCERPTS)

MR. JUSTICE STEWART, concurring.

The penalty of death differs from all other forms of criminal punishment, not in degree but in kind. It is unique in its total irrevocability. It is unique in its rejection of rehabilitation of the convict as a basic purpose of criminal justice. And it is unique, finally, in its absolute renunciation of all that is embodied in our concept of humanity.

For these and other reasons, at least two of my Brothers have concluded that the infliction of the death penalty is constitutionally impermissible in all circumstances under the Eighth and Fourteenth Amendments. Their case is a strong one. But I find it unnecessary to reach the ultimate question they would decide. See *Ashwander* v. *Tennessee Valley Authority,* 297 U.S. 288, 347, (Brandeis, J., concurring).

The opinions of other Justices today have set out in admirable and thorough detail the origins and judicial history of the Eighth Amendment's guarantee against the infliction of cruel and unusual punishments,[1] and the origin and judicial history of capital punishment.[2] There is thus no need for me to review the historical materials here, and what I have to say can, therefore, be briefly stated.

---

1. See dissenting opinion of THE CHIEF JUSTICE, *post,* at 376–379; concurring opinion of MR. JUSTICE DOUGLAS, *ante,* at 242–244; concurring opinion of MR. JUSTICE BRENNAN, *ante,* at 258–269; concurring opinion of MR. JUSTICE MARSHALL, *post,* at 316–328; dissenting opinion of MR. JUSTICE BLACKMUN, *post,* at 407–409; dissenting opinion of MR. JUSTICE POWELL, *post,* at 421–427.

2. See dissenting opinion of THE CHIEF JUSTICE, *post,* at 380; concurring opinion of MR. JUSTICE BRENNAN, *ante,* at 282–285; concurring opinion of MR. JUSTICE MARSHALL, *post,* at 333–341; dissenting opinion of MR. JUSTICE POWELL, *post,* at 421–424.

Legislatures—state and federal—have sometimes specified that the penalty of death shall be the mandatory punishment for every person convicted of engaging in certain designated criminal conduct. Congress, for example, has provided that anyone convicted of acting as a spy for the enemy in time of war shall be put to death.[3] The Rhode Island Legislature has ordained the death penalty for a life term prisoner who commits murder.[4] Massachusetts has passed a law imposing the death penalty upon anyone convicted of murder in the commission of a forcible rape.[5] An Ohio law imposes the mandatory penalty of death upon the assassin of the President of the United States or the Governor of a State.[6]

If we were reviewing death sentences imposed under these or similar laws, we would be faced with the need to decide whether capital punishment is unconstitutional for all crimes and under all circumstances. We would need to decide whether a legislature—state or federal—could constitutionally determine that certain criminal conduct is so atrocious that society's interest in deterrence and retribution wholly outweighs any considerations of reform or rehabilitation of the perpetrator, and that, despite the inconclusive empirical evidence,[7] only the automatic penalty of death will provide maximum deterrence.

On that score I would say only that I cannot agree that retribution is a constitutionally impermissible ingredient in the imposition of punishment. The instinct for retribution is part of the nature of man, and channeling that instinct in the administration of criminal justice serves an important purpose in promoting the stability of a society governed by law. When people begin to believe that organized society is unwilling or unable to impose upon criminal offenders the punishment they "deserve," then there are sown the seeds of anarchy—of self-help, vigilante justice, and lynch law.

The constitutionality of capital punishment in the abstract is not, however, before us in these cases. For the Georgia and Texas

---

3. 10 U. S. C. § 906.
4. R. I. Gen. Laws Ann. § 11-23-2.
5. Mass. Gen. Laws Ann., c. 265, § 2.
6. Ohio Rev. Code Ann., Tit. 29, §§ 2901.09 and 2901.10.
7. Many statistical studies—comparing crime rates in jurisdictions with and without capital punishment and in jurisdictions before and after abolition of capital punishment—have indicated that there is little, if any, measurable deterrent effect. See H. Bedau, The Death Penalty in America 258–332 (1967 rev. ed.). There remains uncertainty, however, because of the difficulty of identifying and holding constant all other relevant variables. See Comment, The Death Penalty Cases, 56 Calif. L. Rev. 1268, 1275–1292. See also dissenting opinion of THE CHIEF JUSTICE, *post,* at 395; concurring opinion of MR. JUSTICE MARSHALL, *post,* at 346–354.

Legislatures have not provided that the death penalty shall be imposed upon all those who are found guilty of forcible rape.[8] And the Georgia Legislature has not ordained that death shall be the automatic punishment for murder.[9] In a word, neither State has made a legislative determination that forcible rape and murder can be deterred only by imposing the penalty of death upon all who perpetrate those offenses. As MR. JUSTICE WHITE so tellingly puts it, the "legislative will is not frustrated if the penalty is never imposed." *Post,* at 311.

Instead, the death sentences now before us are the product of a legal system that brings them, I believe, within the very core of the Eighth Amendment's guarantee against cruel and unusual punishments, a guarantee applicable against the States through the Fourteenth Amendment. *Robinson* v. *California,* 370 U.S. 660. In the first place, it is clear that these sentences are "cruel" in the sense that they excessively go beyond, not in degree but in kind, the punishments that the state legislatures have determined to be necessary. *Weems* v. *United States,* 217 U.S. 349. In the second place, it is equally clear that these sentences are "unusual" in the sense that the penalty of death is infrequently imposed for murder, and that its imposition for rape is extraordinarily rare.[10] But I do not rest my conclusion upon these two propositions alone.

These death sentences are cruel and unusual in the same way that being struck by lightning is cruel and unusual. For, of all the people convicted of rapes and murders in 1967 and 1968,[11] many just as reprehensible as these, the petitioners are among a capriciously

8. Georgia law, at the time of the conviction and sentencing of the petitioner in No. 69–5030, left the jury a choice between the death penalty, life imprisonment, or "imprisonment and labor in the penitentiary for not less than one year nor more than 20 years." Ga. Code Ann. § 26–1302 (Supp. 1971) (effective prior to July 1, 1969). The current Georgia provision for the punishment of forcible rape continues to leave the same broad sentencing leeway. Ga. Crim. Code § 26–2001 (1971 rev.) (effective July 1, 1969). Texas law, under which the petitioner in No. 69–5031 was sentenced, provides that a "person guilty of rape shall be punished by death or by confinement in the penitentiary for life, or for any term of years not less than five." Texas Penal Code, Art. 1189.

9. Georgia law, under which the petitioner in No. 69–5003, was sentenced, left the jury a choice between the death penalty and life imprisonment. Ga. Code Ann. § 26–1005 (Supp. 1971) (effective prior to July 1, 1969). Current Georgia law provides for similar sentencing leeway. Ga. Crim. Code § 26–1101 (1971 rev.) (effective July 1, 1969).

10. See dissenting opinion of THE CHIEF JUSTICE, *post,* at 386–387, n. 11; concurring opinion of MR. JUSTICE BRENNAN, *ante,* at 291–293.

11. Petitioner Branch was sentenced to death in a Texas court on July 26, 1967. Petitioner Furman was sentenced to death in a Georgia court on September 20, 1968. Petitioner Jackson was sentenced to death in a Georgia court on December 10, 1968.

selected random handful upon whom the sentence of death has in fact been imposed.[12] My concurring Brothers have demonstrated that, if any basis can be discerned for the selection of these few to be sentenced to die, it is the constitutionally impermissible basis of race.[13] See *McLaughlin* v. *Florida,* 379 U.S. 184. But racial discrimination has not been proved,[14] and I put it to one side. I simply conclude that the Eighth and Fourteenth Amendments cannot tolerate the infliction of a sentence of death under legal systems that permit this unique penalty to be so wantonly and so freakishly imposed.

For these reasons I concur in the judgments of the Court.

MR. JUSTICE WHITE, concurring.

In *McGautha* v. *California,* 402 U.S. 183, the Court dealt with claims under the Due Process and Equal Protection Clauses of the Fourteenth Amendment. We expressly declined in that case to consider claims under the constitutional guarantee against cruel and unusual punishments. See 398 U. S. 936 (limited grant of certiorari).

The facial constitutionality of statutes requiring the imposition of the death penalty for first-degree murder, for more narrowly defined categories of murder, or for rape would present quite different issues under the Eighth Amendment than are posed by the cases before us. In joining the Court's judgments, therefore, I do not at all intimate that the death penalty is unconstitutional *per se* or that there is no system of capital punishment that would comport with the Eighth Amendment. That question, ably argued by several of my Brethren, is not presented by these cases and need not be decided.

The narrower question to which I address myself concerns the constitutionality of capital punishment statutes under which (1) the legislature authorizes the imposition of the death penalty for murder or rape; (2) the legislature does not itself mandate the penalty in any particular class or kind of case (that is, legislative will is not frustrated if the penalty is never imposed), but delegates to judges or

---

12. A former United States Attorney General has testified before the Congress that only a "small and capricious selection of offenders have been put to death. Most persons convicted of the same crimes have been imprisoned." Statement by Attorney General Clark in Hearings on S. 1760 before the Subcommittee on Criminal Laws and Procedures of the Senate Committee on the Judiciary, 90th Cong., 2d Sess., 93.

13. See concurring opinion of MR. JUSTICE DOUGLAS, *ante,* at 249–251; concurring opinion of MR. JUSTICE MARSHALL, *post,* at 366 n. 155.

14. Cf. Note, A Study of the California Penalty Jury in First-Degree-Murder Cases, 21 Stan. L. Rev. 1297 (1969); dissenting opinion of THE CHIEF JUSTICE, *post,* at 389–390, n. 12.

juries the decisions as to those cases, if any, in which the penalty will be utilized; and (3) judges and juries have ordered the death penalty with such infrequency that the odds are now very much against imposition and execution of the penalty with respect to any convicted murderer or rapist. It is in this context that we must consider whether the execution of these petitioners would violate the Eighth Amendment.

I begin with what I consider a near truism: that the death penalty could so seldom be imposed that it would cease to be a credible deterrent or measurably to contribute to any other end of punishment in the criminal justice system. It is perhaps true that no matter how infrequently those convicted of rape or murder are executed, the penalty so imposed is not disproportionate to the crime and those executed may deserve exactly what they received. It would also be clear that executed defendants are finally and completely incapacitated from again committing rape or murder or any other crime. But when imposition of the penalty reaches a certain degree of infrequency, it would be very doubtful that any existing general need for retribution would be measurably satisfied. Nor could it be said with confidence that society's need for specific deterrence justifies death for so few when for so many in like circumstances life imprisonment or shorter prison terms are judged sufficient, or that community values are measurably reinforced by authorizing a penalty so rarely invoked.

Most important, a major goal of the criminal law—to deter others by punishing the convicted criminal—would not be substantially served where the penalty is so seldom invoked that it ceases to be the credible threat essential to influence the conduct of others. For present purposes I accept the morality and utility of punishing one person to influence another. I accept also the effectiveness of punishment generally and need not reject the death penalty as a more effective deterrent than a lesser punishment. But common sense and experience tell us that seldom-enforced laws become ineffective measures for controlling human conduct and that the death penalty, unless imposed with sufficient frequency, will make little contribution to deterring those crimes for which it may be exacted.

The imposition and execution of the death penalty are obviously cruel in the dictionary sense. But the penalty has not been considered cruel and unusual punishment in the constitutional sense because it was thought justified by the social ends it was deemed to serve. At the moment that it ceases realistically to further these purposes, however, the emerging question is whether its imposition in such circumstances would violate the Eighth Amendment. It is my view that it would, for its imposition would then be the pointless and needless extinction of life with only marginal contributions to any discernible social or public purposes. A penalty with such negligible returns to the State would be patently excessive and cruel and unusual punishment violative of the Eighth Amendment.

It is also my judgment that this point has been reached with respect to capital punishment as it is presently administered under the statutes involved in these cases. Concededly, it is difficult to prove as a general proposition that capital punishment, however administered, more effectively serves the ends of the criminal law that does imprisonment. But however that may be, I cannot avoid the conclusion that as the statutes before us are now administered, the penalty is so infrequently imposed that the threat of execution is too attenuated to be of substantial service to criminal justice.

I need not restate the facts and figures that appear in the opinions of my Brethren. Nor can I "prove" my conclusion from these data. But, like my Brethren, I must arrive at judgment; and I can do no more than state a conclusion based on 10 years of almost daily exposure to the facts and circumstances of hundreds and hundreds of federal and state criminal cases involving crimes for which death is the authorized penalty. That conclusion, as I have said, is that the death penalty is exacted with great infrequency even for the most atrocious crimes and that there is no meaningful basis for distinguishing the few cases in which it is imposed from the many cases in which it is not. The short of it is that the policy of vesting sentencing authority primarily in juries—a decision largely motivated by the desire to mitigate the harshness of the law and to bring community judgment to bear on the sentence as well as guilt or innocence—has so effectively achieved its aims that capital punishment within the confines of the statutes now before us has for all practical purposes run its course.

Judicial review, by definition, often involves a conflict between judicial and legislative judgment as to what the Constitution means or requires. In this respect, Eighth Amendment cases come to us in no different posture. It seems conceded by all that the Amendment imposes some obligations on the judiciary to judge the constitutionality of punishment and that there are punishments that the Amendment would bar whether legislatively approved or not. Inevitably, then, there will be occasions when we will differ with Congress or state legislatures with respect to the validity of punishment. There will also be cases in which we shall strongly disagree among ourselves. Unfortunately, this is one of them. But as I see it, this case is no different in kind from many others, although it may have wider impact and provoke sharper disagreement.

In this respect, I add only that past and present legislative judgment with respect to the death penalty loses much of its force when viewed in light of the recurring practice of delegating sentencing authority to the jury and the fact that a jury, in its own discretion and without violating its trust or any statutory policy, may refuse to impose the death penalty no matter what the circumstances of the crime. Legislative "policy" is thus necessarily defined not by what is legislatively authorized but by what juries and judges do in exercising the discretion so regularly conferred upon them. In my judgment what was done in these cases violated the Eighth Amendment.

I concur in the judgments of the Court.

Appendix F

GREGG V. GEORGIA

428 U.S. 153 (1976) (JOINT OPINIONS OF JUSTICES STEWART, POWELL, AND STEVENS) (EXCERPT)

III

We address initially the basic contention that the punishment of death for the crime of murder is, under all circumstances, "cruel and unusual" in violation of the Eighth and Fourteenth Amendments of the Constitution. In Part IV of this opinion, we will consider the sentence of death imposed under the Georgia statutes at issue in this case.

The Court on a number of occasions has both assumed and asserted the constitutionality of capital punishment. In several cases that assumption provided a necessary foundation for the decision, as the Court was asked to decide whether a particular method of carrying out a capital sentence would be allowed to stand under the Eighth Amendment.[12] But until *Furman* v. *Georgia,* 408 U.S. 238 (1972), the Court never confronted squarely the fundamental claim that the punishment of death always, regardless of the enormity of the offense or the procedure followed in imposing the sentence, is cruel and unusual punishment in violation of the Constitution. Although this issue was presented and addressed in *Furman,* it was not resolved by the Court. Four Justices would have held that capital punishment is not unconstitutional *per se;*[13] two Justices would have reached the opposite conclusion;[14] and three Justices, while agreeing that the statutes then before the Court were invalid as applied, left open the question whether such

---

12. *Louisiana ex rel. Francis* v. *Resweber,* 329 U.S. 459, 464 (1947); *In re Kemmler,* 136 U.S. 436, 447 (1890); *Wilkerson* v. *Utah,* 99 U.S. 130, 134–135 (1879). See also *McGautha* v. *California,* 402 U.S. 183 (1971); *Witherspoon* v. *Illinois,* 391 U.S. 510 (1968); *Trop* v. *Dulles,* 356 U.S. 86, 100 (1958) (plurality opinion).

13. 408 U.S., at 375 (BURGER, C. J., dissenting); *id.,* at 405 (BLACKMUN, J., dissenting); *id.,* at 414 (POWELL, J., dissenting); *id.,* at 465 (REHNQUIST, J., dissenting).

14. *Id.,* at 257 (BRENNAN, J., concurring); *id.,* at 314 (MARSHALL, J., concurring).

punishment may ever be imposed.[15] We now hold that the punishment of death does not invariably violate the Constitution.

A

The history of the prohibition of "cruel and unusual" punishment already has been reviewed at length.[16] The phrase first appeared in the English Bill of Rights of 1689, which was drafted by Parliament at the accession of William and Mary. See Granucci, "Nor Cruel and Unusual Punishments Inflicted:" The Original Meaning, 57 Calif. L. Rev. 839, 852–853 (1969). The English version appears to have been directed against punishments unauthorized by statute and beyond the jurisdiction of the sentencing court, as well as those disproportionate to the offense involved. *Id.,* at 860. The American draftsmen, who adopted the English phrasing in drafting the Eighth Amendment, were primarily concerned, however, with proscribing "tortures" and other "barbarous" methods of punishment." *Id.,* at 842.[17]

In the earliest cases raising Eighth Amendment claims, the Court focused on particular methods of execution to determine whether they were too cruel to pass constitutional muster. The constitutionality of the sentence of death itself was not at issue, and the criterion used to evaluate the mode of execution was its similarity to "torture" and other "barbarous" methods. See *Wilkerson* v. *Utah,* 99 U.S. 130, 136 (1879) ("[I]t is safe to affirm that punishments of torture. . . and

15. *Id.,* at 240 (Douglas, J., concurring); *id.,* at 306 (STEWART, J., concurring); *id.,* at 310 (WHITE, J., concurring).

Since five Justices wrote separately in support of the judgments in *Furman,* the holding of the Court may be viewed as that position taken by those Members who concurred in the judgments on the narrowest grounds—MR. JUSTICE STEWART and MR. JUSTICE WHITE. See n. 36, *infra.*

16. 408 U.S., at 316–328 (MARSHALL, J., concurring).

17. This conclusion derives primarily from statements made during the debates in the various state conventions called to ratify the Federal Constitution. For example, Virginia delegate Patrick Henry objected vehemently to the lack of a provision banning "cruel and unusual punishments":

"What has distinguished our ancestors?—That they would not admit of tortures, or cruel and barbarous punishment. But Congress may introduce the practice of the civil law, in preference to that of the common law. They may introduce the practice of France, Spain, and Germany—of torturing, to extort a confession of the crime." 3 J. Elliot, Debates 447–448 (1863).

A similar objection was made in the Massachusetts convention:

"They are nowhere restrained from inventing the most cruel and unheard-of punishments and annexing them to crimes; and there is no constitutional check on them, but that *racks* and *gibbets* may be amongst the most mild instruments of their discipline." 2 Elliot, *supra,* at 111.

all others in the same line of unnecessary cruelty, are forbidden by that amendment. . ."); *In re Kemmler,* 136 U.S. 436, 447 (1890) ("Punishments are cruel when they involve torture or a lingering death. . . "). See also *Louisiana ex rel. Francis* v. *Resweber,* 329 U.S. 459, 464 (1947) (second attempt at electrocution found not to violate Eighth Amendment, since failure of initial execution attempt was "an unforeseeable accident" and "[t]here [was] no purpose to inflict unnecessary pain nor any unnecessary pain involved in the proposed execution").

But the Court has not confined the prohibition embodied in the Eighth Amendment to "barbarous" methods that were generally outlawed in the 18th century. Instead, the Amendment has been interpreted in a flexible and dynamic manner. The Court early recognized that "a principle to be vital must be capable of wider application than the mischief which gave it birth." *Weems* v. *United States,* 217 U.S. 349, 373 (1910). Thus the Clause forbidding "cruel and unusual" punishments "is not fastened to the obsolete but may acquire meaning as public opinion becomes enlightened by a humane justice." *Id.,* at 378. See also *Furman* v. *Georgia,* 408 U.S., at 429–430 (POWELL, J., dissenting); *Trop* v. *Dulles,* 356 U.S. 86, 100–101 (1958) (plurality opinion).

In *Weems* the Court addressed the constitutionality of the Philippine punishment of *cadena temporal* for the crime of falsifying an official document. That punishment included imprisonment for at least 12 years and one day, in chains, at hard and painful labor; the loss of many basic civil rights; and subjection to lifetime surveillance. Although the Court acknowledged the possibility that "the cruelty of pain" may be present in the challenged punishment, 217 U.S., at 366, it did not rely on that factor, for it rejected the proposition that the Eighth Amendment reaches only punishments that are "inhuman and barbarous, torture and the like." *Id.,* at 368. Rather, the Court focused on the lack of proportion between the crime and the offense:

> "Such penalties for such offenses amaze those who have formed their conception of the relation of a state to even its offending citizens from the practice of the American commonwealths, and believe that it is a precept of justice that punishment for crime should be graduated and proportioned to offense." *Id.,* at 366–367.[18]

Later, in *Trop* v. *Dulles, supra,* the Court reviewed the constitutionality of the punishment of denationalization imposed upon a soldier who escaped from an Army stockade and became a

18. The Court remarked on the fact that the law under review "has come to us from a government of a different form and genius from ours," but it also noted that the punishments it inflicted "would have those bad attributes even if they were found in a Federal enactment and not taken from an alien source." 217 U.S., at 377.

deserter for one day. Although the concept of proportionality was not the basis of the holding, the plurality observed in dicta that "[f]ines, imprisonment and even execution may be imposed depending upon the enormity of the crime." 356 U.S., at 100.

The substantive limits imposed by the Eighth Amendment on what can be made criminal and punished were discussed in *Robinson* v. *California,* 370 U.S. 660 (1962). The Court found unconstitutional a state statute that made the status of being addicted to a narcotic drug a criminal offense. It held, in effect, that it is "cruel and unusual" to impose any punishment at all for the mere status of addiction. The cruelty in the abstract of the actual sentence imposed was irrelevant: "Even one day in prison would be a cruel and unusual punishment for the 'crime' of having a common cold." *Id.,* at 667. Most recently, in *Furman* v. *Georgia, supra,* three Justices in separate concurring opinions found the Eighth Amendment applicable to procedures employed to select convicted defendants for the sentence of death.

It is clear from the foregoing precedents that the Eighth Amendment has not been regarded as a static concept. As Mr. Chief Justice Warren said, in an oft-quoted phrase, "[t]he Amendment must draw its meaning from the evolving standards of decency that mark the progress of a maturing society." *Trop* v. *Dulles, supra,* at 101. See also *Jackson* v. *Bishop,* 404 F. 2d 571, 579 (CA8 1968). Cf. *Robinson* v. *California, supra,* at 666. Thus, an assessment of contemporary values concerning the infliction of a challenged sanction is relevant to the application of the Eighth Amendment. As we develop below more fully, see *infra,* at 175–176, this assessment does not call for a subjective judgment. It requires, rather, that we look to objective indicia that reflect the public attitude toward a given sanction.

But our cases also make clear that public perceptions of standards of decency with respect to criminal sanctions are not conclusive. A penalty also must accord with "the dignity of man," which is the "basic concept underlying the Eighth Amendment." *Trop* v. *Dulles, supra,* at 100 (plurality opinion). This means, at least, that the punishment not be "excessive." When a form of punishment in the abstract (in this case, whether capital punishment may ever be imposed as a sanction for murder) rather than in the particular (the propriety of death as a penalty to be applied to a specific defendant for a specific crime) is under consideration, the inquiry into "excessiveness" has two aspects. First, the punishment must not involve the unnecessary and wanton infliction of pain. *Furman* v. *Georgia, supra,* at 392–393 (BURGER, C. J., dissenting). See *Wilkerson* v. *Utah,* 99 U.S., at 136; *Weems* v. *United States, supra,* at 381. Second, the punishment must not be grossly out of proportion to the severity of the crime. *Trop* v. *Dulles, supra,* at 100 (plurality opinion) (dictum); *Weems* v. *United States, supra,* at 367.

B

Of course, the requirements of the Eighth Amendment must be applied with an awareness of the limited role to be played by the courts. This does not mean that judges have no role to play, for the Eighth Amendment is a restraint upon the exercise of legislative power.

> "Judicial review, by definition, often involves a conflict between judicial and legislative judgment as to what the Constitution means or requires. In this respect, Eighth Amendment cases come to us in no different posture. It seems conceded by all that the Amendment imposes some obligations on the judiciary to judge the constitutionality of punishment and that there are punishments that the Amendment would bar whether legislatively approved or not." *Furman v. Georgia*, 408 U.S., at 313–314 (WHITE, J., concurring).

See also *id.,* at 433 (POWELL, J., dissenting).[19]

But, while we have an obligation to insure that constitutional bounds are not overreached we may not act as judges as we might as legislators.

> "Courts are not representative bodies. They are not designed to be a good reflex of a democratic society. Their judgment is best informed, and therefore most dependable, within narrow limits. Their essential quality is detachment, founded on independence. History teaches that the independence of the judiciary is jeopardized when courts become embroiled in the passions of the day and assume primary responsibility in choosing between competing political, economic and social pressures." *Dennis* v. *United*

19. Although legislative measures adopted by the people's chosen representatives provide one important means of ascertaining contemporary values, it is evident that legislative judgments alone cannot be determinative of Eighth Amendment standards since that Amendment was intended to safeguard individuals from the abuse of legislative power. See *Weems* v. *United States,* 217 U. S. 349, 317–373 (1910); *Furman* v. *Georgia,* 408 U.S., at 258–269 (BRENNAN, J., concurring). *Robinson* v. *California,* 370 U.S. 660 (1962), illustrates the proposition that penal laws enacted by state legislatures may violate the Eighth Amendment because "in the light of contemporary human knowledge" they "would doubtless be universally thought to be an infliction of cruel and unusual punishment." *Id.,* at 666. At the time of *Robinson* nine States in addition to California had criminal laws that punished addiction similar to the law declared unconstitutional in *Robinson.* See Brief for Appellant in *Robinson* v. *California,* O. T. 1961, No. 554, p. 15.

States, 341 U. S. 494, 525 (1951) (Frankfurter, J., concurring in affirmance of judgment).[20]

Therefore, in assessing a punishment selected by a democratically elected legislature against the constitutional measure, we presume its validity. We may not require the legislature to select the least severe penalty possible so long as the penalty selected is not cruelly inhumane or disproportionate to the crime involved. And a heavy burden rests on those who would attack the judgment of the representatives of the people.

This is true in part because the constitutional test is intertwined with an assessment of contemporary standards and the legislative judgment weighs heavily in ascertaining such standards. "[I]n a democratic society legislatures, not courts, are constituted to respond to the will and consequently the moral values of the people." *Furman* v. *Georgia, supra,* at 383 (BURGER, C. J., dissenting). The deference we owe to the decisions of the state legislatures under our federal system, 408 U.S., at 465–470 (REHNQUIST, J., dissenting), is enhanced where the specification of punishments is concerned, for "these are peculiarly questions of legislative policy." *Gore* v. *United States,* 357 U.S. 386, 393 (1958). Cf. *Robinson* v. *California,* 370 U.S., at 664–665; *Trop* v. *Dulles,* 356 U.S., at 103 (plurality opinion); *In re Kemmler,* 136 U.S., at 447. Caution is necessary lest this Court become, "under the aegis of the Cruel and Unusual Punishment Clause, the ultimate arbiter of the standards of criminal responsibility. . . throughout the country." *Powell* v. *Texas,* 392 U.S. 514, 533 (1968) (plurality opinion). A decision that a given punishment is impermissible under the Eighth Amendment cannot be reversed short of a constitutional amendment. The ability of the people to express their preference through the normal democratic processes, as well as through ballot referenda, is shut off. Revisions cannot be made in the light of further experience. See *Furman* v. *Georgia, supra,* at 461–462 (POWELL, J., dissenting).

C

In the discussion to this point we have sought to identify the principles and considerations that guide a court in addressing an Eighth Amendment claim. We now consider specifically whether the sentence of death for the crime of murder is a *per se* violation of the

20. See also *Furman* v. *Georgia, supra,* at 411 (BLACKMUN, J., dissenting):

"We should not allow our personal preferences as to the wisdom of legislative and congressional action, or our distaste for such action, to guide our judicial decision in cases such as these. The temptations to cross that policy line are very great."

Eighth and Fourteenth Amendments to the Constitution. We note first that history and precedent strongly support a negative answer to this question.

The imposition of the death penalty for the crime of murder has a long history of acceptance both in the United States and in England. The common-law rule imposed a mandatory death sentence on all convicted murderers. *McGautha* v. *California,* 402 U. S. 183, 197–198 (1971). And the penalty continued to be used into the 20th century by most American States, although the breadth of the common-law rule was diminished, initially by narrowing the class of murders to be punished by death and subsequently by widespread adoption of laws expressly granting juries the discretion to recommend mercy. *Id.,* at 199–200. See *Woodson* v. *North Carolina, post,* at 289–292.

It is apparent from the text of the Constitution itself that the existence of capital punishment was accepted by the Framers. At the time the Eighth Amendment was ratified, capital punishment was a common sanction in every State. Indeed, the First Congress of the United States enacted legislation providing death as the penalty for specified crimes. C. 9, 1 Stat. 112 (1790). The Fifth Amendment, adopted at the same time as the Eighth, contemplated the continued existence of the capital sanction by imposing certain limits on the prosecution of capital cases:

> "No person shall be held to answer for a capital, or otherwise infamous crime, unless on a presentment or indictment of a Grand Jury. . .; nor shall any person be subject for the same offense to be twice put in jeopardy of life or limb; . . . nor be deprived of life, liberty, or property, without due process of law. . . ."

And the Fourteenth Amendment, adopted over three-quarters of a century later, similarly contemplates the existence of the capital sanction in providing that no State shall deprive any person of "life, liberty, or property" without due process of law.

For nearly two centuries, this Court, repeatedly and often expressly, has recognized that capital punishment is not invalid *per se.* In *Wilkerson* v. *Utah,* 99 U.S., at 134–135, where the Court found no constitutional violation in inflicting death by public shooting, it said:

> "Cruel and unusual punishments are forbidden by the Constitution, but the authorities referred to are quite sufficient to show that the punishment of shooting as a mode of executing the death penalty for the crime of murder in the first degree is not included in that category, within the meaning of the eighth amendment."

Rejecting the contention that death by electrocution was "cruel and unusual," the Court in *In re Kemmler, supra,* at 447, reiterated:

> "[T]he punishment of death is not cruel, within the meaning of that word as used in the Constitution. It implies there something inhuman and barbarous, something more than the mere extinguishment of life."

Again, in *Louisiana ex rel. Francis* v. *Resweber,* 329 U.S., at 464, the Court remarked: "The cruelty against which the Constitution protects a convicted man is cruelty inherent in the method of punishment, not the necessary suffering involved in any method employed to extinguish life humanely." And in *Trop* v. *Dulles,* 356 U. S., at 99, Mr. Chief Justice Warren, for himself and three other Justices, wrote:

> "Whatever the arguments may be against capital punishment, both on moral grounds and in terms of accomplishing the purposes of punishment. . .the death penalty has been employed throughout our history, and, in a day when it is still widely accepted, it cannot be said to violate the constitutional concept of cruelty."

Four years ago, the petitioners in *Furman* and its companion cases predicated their argument primarily upon the asserted proposition that standards of decency had evolved to the point where capital punishment no longer could be tolerated. The petitioners in those cases said, in effect, that the evolutionary process had come to an end, and that standards of decency required that the Eighth Amendment be construed finally as prohibiting capital punishment for any crime regardless of its depravity and impact on society. This view was accepted by two Justices.[21] Three other Justices were unwilling to go so far; focusing on the procedures by which convicted defendants were selected for the death penalty rather than on the actual punishment inflicted, they joined in the conclusion that the statutes before the Court were constitutionally invalid.[22]

The petitioners in the capital cases before the Court today renew the "standards of decency" argument, but developments during the four years since *Furman* have undercut substantially the assumptions upon which their argument rested. Despite the continuing

21. See concurring opinions of MR. JUSTICE BRENNAN and MR. JUSTICE MARSHALL, 408 U.S., at 257 and 314.

22. See concurring opinions of MR. JUSTICE DOUGLAS, MR. JUSTICE STEWART, and MR. JUSTICE WHITE, *id.,* at 240, 306, and 310.

debate, dating back to the 19th century, over the morality and utility of capital punishment, it is now evident that a large proportion of American society continues to regard it as an appropriate and necessary criminal sanction.

The most marked indication of society's endorsement of the death penalty for murder is the legislative response to *Furman.* The legislatures of at least 35 States[23] have enacted new statutes that provide for the death penalty for at least some crimes that result in the death of another person. And the Congress of the United States, in 1974, enacted a statute providing the death penalty for aircraft piracy that results in death.[24] These recently adopted statutes have attempted to address the concerns expressed by the Court in *Furman* primarily (i) by specifying the factors to be weighed and the procedures to be followed in deciding when to impose a capital sentence, or (ii) by making the death penalty mandatory for specified crimes. But all of the post-*Furman* statutes make clear that capital punishment itself has not been rejected by the elected representatives of the people.

In the only statewide referendum occurring since *Furman* and brought to our attention, the people of California adopted a constitutional amendment that authorized capital punishment, in effect negating a prior ruling by the Supreme Court of California in *People* v. *Anderson,* 6 Cal. 3d 628, 493 P. 2d 880, cert. denied, 406

23. Ala. H. B. 212, §§ 2–4, 6–7 (1975); Ariz. Rev. Stat. Ann. §§ 13-452 to 13-454 (Supp. 1973); Ark. Stat. Ann. § 41-4706 (Supp. 1975); Cal. Penal Code §§ 190.1, 209, 219 (Supp. 1976); Colo. Laws 1974, c. 52, § 4; Conn. Gen. Stat. Rev. §§ 53a-25, 53a-35 (b), 53a-46a, 53a-54b (1975); Del. Code Ann. tit. 11, § 4209 (Supp. 1975); Fla. Stat. Ann. §§ 782.04, 921.141 (Supp. 1975–1976); Ga. Code. Ann. §§ 26-3102, 27-2528, 27-2534.1, 27-2537 (Supp. 1975); Idaho Code § 18-4004 (Supp. 1975); Ill. Ann. Stat. c. 38, §§ 9-1, 1005-5-3, 1005-8-1A (Supp. 1976-1977); Ind. Stat. Ann. § 35-13-4-1 (1975); Ky. Rev. Stat. Ann. § 507.020 (1975); La. Rev. Stat. Ann. § 14:30 (Supp. 1976); Md. Ann. Code, art. 27, § 413 (Supp. 1975); Miss. Code Ann. §§ 97-3-19, 97-3-21, 97-25-55, 99-17-20 (Supp. 1975); Mo. Ann. Stat. § 559.009, 559.005 (Supp. 1976); Mont. Rev. Codes Ann. § 94-5-105 (Spec. Crim. Code Supp. 1976); Neb. Rev. Stat. §§ 28-401, 29-2521 to 29-2523 (1975); Nev. Rev. Stat. § 200.030 (1973); N. H. Rev. Stat. Ann. § 630:1 (1974); N. M. Stat. Ann. § 40A-29-2 (Supp. 1975); N. Y. Penal Law § 60.06 (1975); N. C. Gen. Stat. § 14-17 (Supp. 1975); Ohio Rev. Code Ann. §§ 2929.02–2929.04 (1975); Okla. Stat. Ann. tit. 21, § 701.1-701.3 (Supp. 1975–1976); Pa. Laws 1974, Act. No. 46; R. I. Gen. Laws Ann. § 11-23-2 (Supp. 1975); S. C. Code Ann. § 16-52 (Supp. 1975); Tenn. Code Ann. §§ 39-2402, 39-2406 (1975); Tex. Penal Code Ann. § 19.03(a) (1974); Utah Code Ann. §§ 76-3-206, 76-3-207, 76-5-202 (Supp. 1975); Va. Code Ann. §§ 18.2-10, 18.2-31 (1976); Wash. Rev. Code §§ 9A.32.045, 9A.32.046 (Supp. 1975); Wyo. Stat. Ann. § 6-54 (Supp. 1975).

24. Antihijacking Act of 1974, 49 U. S. C. §§ 1472 (i), (n) (1970 ed., Supp. IV).

U.S. 958 (1972), that the death penalty violated the California Constitution.[25]

The jury also is a significant and reliable objective index of contemporary values because it is so directly involved. See *Furman* v. *Georgia,* 408 U.S., at 439–440 (POWELL, J., dissenting). See generally Powell, Jury Trial of Crimes, 23 Wash. & Lee L. Rev. 1 (1966). The Court has said that "one of the most important functions any jury can perform in making. . . a selection [between life imprisonment and death for a defendant convicted in a capital case] is to maintain a link between contemporary community values and the penal system." *Witherspoon* v. *Illinois,* 391 U. S. 510, 519 n. 15 (1968). It may be true that evolving standards have influenced juries in recent decades to be more discriminating in imposing the sentence of death.[26] But the relative infrequency of jury verdicts imposing the death sentence does not indicate rejection of capital punishment *per se.* Rather, the reluctance of juries in many cases to impose the sentence may well reflect the humane feeling that this most irrevocable of sanctions should be reserved for a small number of extreme cases. See *Furman* v. *Georgia, supra,* at 388 (BURGER, C. J., dissenting). Indeed, the actions of juries in many States since *Furman* are fully compatible with the legislative judgments, reflected in the new statutes, as to the continued utility and necessity of capital punishment in appropriate cases. At the close of 1974 at least 254 persons had been sentenced to death since *Furman,*[27] and by the end of March 1976, more than 460 persons were subject to death sentences.

---

25. In 1968, the people of Massachusetts were asked "Shall the commonwealth. . . retain the death penalty for crime?" A substantial majority of the ballots cast answered "Yes." Of 2,348,005 ballots cast, 1,159,348 voted "Yes," 730,649 voted "No," and 458,008 were blank. See *Commonwealth* v. *O'Neal,* ——— Mass. ———, ———, and n. 1, 339 N. E. 2d 676, 708, and n. 1 (1975) (REARDON, J., dissenting). A December 1972 Gallup poll indicated that 57% of the people favored the death penalty; while a June 1973 Harris survey showed support of 59%. Vidmar & Ellsworth, Public Opinion and the Death Penalty, 26 Stan. L. Rev. 1245, 1249 n. 22 (1974). In a December 1970 referendum, the voters of Illinois also rejected the abolition of capital punishment by 1,218,791 votes to 676,302 votes. Report of the Governor's Study Commission on Capital Punishment 43 (Pa. 1973).

26. The number of prisoners who received death sentences in the years from 1961 to 1972 varied from a high of 140 in 1961 to a low of 75 in 1972, with wide fluctuations in the intervening years: 103 in 1962; 93 in 1963; 106 in 1964; 86 in 1965; 118 in 1966; 85 in 1967; 102 in 1968; 97 in 1969; 127 in 1970; and 104 in 1971. Department of Justice, National Prisoner Statistics Bulletin, Capital Punishment 1971–1972, p. 20 (Dec. 1974). It has been estimated that before *Furman* less than 20% of those convicted of murder were sentenced to death in those States that authorized capital punishment. See *Woodson* v. *North Carolina, post,* at 295–296, n.31.

27. Department of Justice, National Prisoner Statistics Bulletin, Capital Punishment 1974, pp. 1, 26–27 (Nov. 1975).

As we have seen, however, the Eighth Amendment demands more than that a challenged punishment be acceptable to contemporary society. The Court also must ask whether it comports with the basic concept of human dignity at the core of the Amendment. *Trop* v. *Dulles,* 356 U.S., at 100 (plurality opinion). Although we cannot "invalidate a category of penalties because we deem less severe penalties adequate to serve the ends of penology," *Furman* v. *Georgia, supra,* at 451 (Powell, J., dissenting), the sanction imposed cannot be so totally without penological justification that it results in the gratuitous infliction of suffering. Cf. *Wilkerson* v. *Utah,* 99 U.S., at 135–136; *In re Kemmler,* 136 U.S., at 447.

The death penalty is said to serve two principal social purposes: retribution and deterrence of capital crimes by prospective offenders.[28]

In part, capital punishment is an expression of society's moral outrage at particularly offensive conduct.[29] This function may be unappealing to many, but it is essential in an ordered society that asks its citizens to rely on legal processes rather than self-help to vindicate their wrongs.

> "The instinct for retribution is part of the nature of man, and channeling that instinct in the administration of criminal justice serves an important purpose in promoting the stability of a society governed by law. When people begin to believe that organized society is unwilling or unable to impose upon criminal offenders the punishment they 'deserve,' then there are sown the seeds of anarchy—of self-help, vigilante justice, and lynch law." *Furman* v. *Georgia, supra,* at 308 (Stewart, J., concurring).

"Retribution is no longer the dominant objective of the criminal law," *Williams* v. *New York,* 337 U. S. 241, 248 (1949), but neither is it a forbidden objective nor one inconsistent with our respect for the dignity of men.

---

28. Another purpose that has been discussed is the incapacitation of dangerous criminals and the consequent prevention of crimes that they may otherwise commit in the future. See *People* v. *Anderson,* 6 Cal. 3d 628, 651, 493 P. 2d 880, 896, cert. denied, 406 U. S. 958 (1972); *Commonwealth* v. *O'Neal, supra,* at ——, 339 N. E. 2d, at 685–686.

29. See H. Packer, Limits of the Criminal Sanction 43–44 (1968).

Appendix G

McCLESKEY V. KEMP

481 U.S. 279 (1987) (EXCERPTS)

McCleskey's first claim is that the Georgia capital punishment statute violates the Equal Protection Clause of the Fourteenth Amendment.[7] He argues that race has infected the administration of Georgia's statute in two ways: persons who murder whites are more likely to be sentenced to death than persons who murder blacks, and black murderers are more likely to be sentenced to death than white murderers.[8]

As a black defendant who killed a white victim, McCleskey claims that the Baldus study demonstrates that he was discriminated

---

7. Although the District Court rejected the findings of the Baldus study as flawed, the Court of Appeals assumed that the study is valid and reached the constitutional issues. Accordingly, those issues are before us. As did the Court of Appeals, we assume the study is valid statistically without reviewing the factual findings of the District Court. Our assumption that the Baldus study is statistically valid does not include the assumption that the study shows that racial considerations actually enter into any sentencing decisions in Georgia. Even a sophisticated multiple-regression analysis such as the Baldus study can only demonstrate a *risk* that the factor of race entered into some capital sentencing decisions and a necessarily lesser risk that race entered into any particular sentencing decision.

8. Although McCleskey has standing to claim that he suffers discrimination because of his own race, the State argues that he has no standing to contend that he was discriminated against on the basis of his victim's race. While it is true that we are reluctant to recognize "standing to assert the rights of third persons," *Arlington Heights* v. *Metropolitan Housing Dev. Corp.*, 429 U. S. 252, 263 (1977), this does not appear to be the nature of McCleskey's claim. He does not seek to assert some right of his victim, or the rights of black murder victims in general. Rather, McCleskey argues that application of the State's statute has created a classification that is "an irrational exercise of governmental power," Brief for Petitioner 41, because it is not "necessary to the accomplishment of some permissible state objective." *Loving* v. *Virginia,* 388 U.S. 1, 11 (1967). See *McGowan* v. *Maryland,* 366 U.S. 420, 425 (1961) (statutory classification cannot be "wholly irrelevant to the achievement of the State's objective"). It would violate the Equal Protection Clause for a State to base enforcement of its criminal laws on "an unjustifiable standard such as race, religion, or other arbitrary classification." *Oyler* v. *Boles,* 368 U.S. 448, 456 (1962). See *Cleveland Bd. of Ed.* v. *Lafleur,* 414 U. S. 632, 652–653 (1974) (POWELL, J., concurring). Because McCleskey raises such a claim, he has standing.

against because of his race and because of the race of his victim. In its broadest form, McCleskey's claim of discrimination extends to every actor in the Georgia capital sentencing process, from the prosecutor who sought the death penalty and the jury that imposed the sentence, to the State itself that enacted the capital punishment statute and allows it to remain in effect despite its allegedly discriminatory application. We agree with the Court of Appeals, and every other court that has considered such a challenge,[9] that this claim must fail.

A

Our analysis begins with the basic principle that a defendant who alleges an equal protection violation has the burden of proving "the existence of purposeful discrimination." *Whitus* v. *Georgia,* 385 U.S. 545, 550 (1967).[10] A corollary to this principle is that a criminal defendant must prove that the purposeful discrimination "had a discriminatory effect" on him. *Wayte* v. *United States,* 470 U.S. 598, 608 (1985). Thus, to prevail under the Equal Protection Clause, McCleskey must prove that the decisionmakers in *his* case acted with discriminatory purpose. He offers no evidence specific to his own case that would support an inference that racial considerations played a part in his sentence. Instead, he relies solely on the Baldus study.[11] McCleskey argues that the Baldus study compels an inference that his sentence rests on purposeful discrimination. McCleskey's claim that these statistics are sufficient proof of discrimination, without regard to the facts of a particular case, would extend to all capital cases in Georgia, at least where the victim was white and the defendant is black.

9. See, *e.g., Shaw* v. *Martin,* 733 F. 2d 304, 311–314 (CA4), cert. denied, 469 U. S. 873 (1984); *Adams* v. *Wainwright,* 709 F. 2d 1443 (CA11 1983) *(per curiam),* cert. denied, 464 U.S. 1063 (1984); *Smith* v. *Balkcom,* 660 F. 2d 573, 584–585, modified, 671 F. 2d 858, 859–860 (CA5 Unit B 1981) *(per curiam),* cert. denied, 459 U. S. 882 (1982); *Spinkellink* v. *Wainwright,* 578 F. 2d 582, 612–616 (CA5 1978), cert. denied, 440 U. S. 976 (1979).

10. See *Arlington Heights* v. *Metropolitan Housing Dev. Corp., supra,* at 265; *Washington* v. *Davis,* 426 U. S. 229, 240 (1976).

11. McCleskey's expert testified:

"Models that are developed talk about the effect on the average. They do not depict the experience of a single individual. What they say, for example, [is] that on the average, the race of the victim, if it is white, increases on the average the probability...(that) the death sentence would be given.

"Whether in a given case that is the answer, it cannot be determined from statistics." 580 F. Supp., at 372.

The Court has accepted statistics as proof of intent to discriminate in certain limited contexts. First, this Court has accepted statistical disparities as proof of an equal protection violation in the selection of the jury venire in a particular district. Although statistical proof normally must present a "stark" pattern to be accepted as the sole proof of discriminatory intent under the Constitution,[12] *Arlington Heights* v. *Metropolitan Housing Dev. Corp.,* 429 U.S. 252, 266 (1977), "[b]ecause of the nature of the jury-selection task, . . . we have permitted a finding of constitutional violation even when the statistical pattern does not approach [such] extremes." *Id.,* at 266, n. 13.[13] Second, this Court has accepted statistics in the form of multiple-regression analysis to prove statutory violations under Title VII of the Civil Rights Act of 1964. *Bazemore* v. *Friday,* 478 U.S. 385, 400–401 (1986) (opinion of BRENNAN, J., concurring in part).

But the nature of the capital sentencing decision, and the relationship of the statistics to that decision, are fundamentally different from the corresponding elements in the venire-selection or Title VII cases. Most importantly, each particular decision to impose the death penalty is made by a petit jury selected from a properly constituted venire. Each jury is unique in its composition, and the Constitution requires that its decision rest on consideration of innumerable factors that vary according to the characteristics of the individual defendant and the facts of the particular capital offense. See *Hitchcock* v. *Dugger, post,* at 398–399; *Lockett* v. *Ohio,* 438 U.S. 586, 602–605 (1978) (plurality opinion of BURGER, C.J.). Thus, the

12. *Gomillion* v. *Lightfoot,* 364 U.S. 339 (1960), and *Yick Wo* v. *Hopkins,* 118 U.S. 356 (1886), are examples of those rare cases in which a statistical pattern of discriminatory impact demonstrated a constitutional violation. In *Gomillion,* a state legislature violated the Fifteenth Amendment by altering the boundaries of a particular city "from a square to an uncouth twenty-eight-sided figure." 364 U.S., at 340. The alterations excluded 395 of 400 black voters without excluding a single white voter. In *Yick Wo,* an ordinance prohibited operation of 310 laundries that were housed in wooden buildings, but allowed such laundries to resume operations if the operator secured a permit from the government. When laundry operators applied for permits to resume operation, all but one of the white applicants received permits, but none of the over 200 Chinese applicants were successful. In those cases, the Court found the statistical disparities "to warrant and require," *Yick Wo* v. *Hopkins, supra,* at 373, a "conclusion [that was] irresistible, tantamount for all practical purposes to a mathematical demonstration," *Gomillion* v. *Lightfoot, supra,* at 341, that the State acted with a discriminatory purpose.

13. See, *e.g., Castaneda* v. *Partida,* 430 U.S. 482, 495 (1977) (2-to-1 disparity between Mexican-Americans in county population and those summoned for grand jury duty); *Turner* v. *Fouche,* 396 U.S. 346, 359 (1970) (1.6-to-1 disparity between blacks in county population and those on grand jury lists); *Whitus* v. *Georgia,* 385 U.S. 545, 552 (1967) (3-to-1 disparity between eligible blacks in county and blacks on grand jury venire).

application of an inference drawn from the general statistics to a specific decision in a trial and sentencing simply is not comparable to the application of an inference drawn from general statistics to a specific venire- selection or Title VII case. In those cases, the statistics relate to fewer entities,[14] and fewer variables are relevant to the challenged decisions.[15]

Another important difference between the cases in which we have accepted statistics as proof of discriminatory intent and this case is that, in the venire-selection and Title VII contexts, the decisionmaker has an opportunity to explain the statistical disparity. See *Whitus* v. *Georgia,* 385 U. S., at 552; *Texas Dept. of Community Affairs* v. *Burdine,* 450 U. S. 248, 254 (1981); *McDonnell Douglas Corp.* v.

14. In venire-selection cases, the factors that may be considered are limited, usually by state statute. See *Castaneda* v. *Partida, supra,* at 485 ("A grand juror must be a citizen of Texas and of the county, be a qualified voter in the county, be 'of sound mind and good moral character,' be literate, have no prior felony conviction, and be under no pending indictment 'or other legal accusation for theft or of any felony'"); *Turner* v. *Fouche, supra,* at 354 (jury commissioners may exclude any not "upright" and "intelligent" from grand jury service); *Whitus* v. *Georgia, supra,* at 548 (same). These considerations are uniform for all potential jurors, and although some factors may be said to be subjective, they are limited and, to a great degree, objectively verifiable. While employment decisions may involve a number of relevant variables, these variables are to a great extent uniform for all employees because they must all have a reasonable relationship to the employee's qualifications to perform the particular job at issue. Identifiable qualifications for a single job provide a common standard by which to assess each employee. In contrast, a capital sentencing jury may consider *any* factor relevant to the defendant's background, character, and the offense. See *Eddings* v. *Oklahoma,* 455 U.S. 104, 112 (1982). There is no common standard by which to evaluate all defendants who have or have not received the death penalty.

15. We refer here not to the number of entities involved in any particular decision, but to the number of entities whose decisions necessarily are reflected in a statistical display such as the Baldus study. The decisions of a jury commission or of an employer over time are fairly attributable to the commission or the employer. Therefore, an unexplained statistical discrepancy can be said to indicate a consistent policy of the decisionmaker. The Baldus study seeks to deduce a state "policy" by studying the combined effects of the decisions of hundreds of juries that are unique in their composition. It is incomparably more difficult to deduce a consistent policy by studying the decisions of these many unique entities. It is also questionable whether any consistent policy can be derived by studying the decisions of prosecutors. The District Attorney is elected by the voters in a particular county. See Ga. Const., Art. 6, § 8, ¶ 1. Since decisions whether to prosecute and what to charge necessarily are individualized and involve infinite factual variations, coordination among district attorney offices across a State would be relatively meaningless. Thus, any inference from statewide statistics to a prosecutorial "policy" is of doubtful relevance. Moreover, the statistics in Fulton County alone represent the disposition of far fewer cases than the statewide statistics. Even assuming the statistical validity of the Baldus study as a whole, the weight to be given the results gleaned from this small sample is limited.

Green, 411 U.S. 792, 802 (1973). Here, the State has no practical opportunity to rebut the Baldus study. "[C]ontrolling considerations of. . .public policy," *McDonald* v. *Pless,* 238 U.S. 264, 267 (1915), dictate that jurors "cannot be called. . .to testify to the motives and influences that led to their verdict." *Chicago, B. & Q. R. Co.* v. *Babcock,* 204 U.S. 585, 593 (1907). Similarly, the policy considerations behind a prosecutor's traditionally "wide discretion"[16] suggest the impropriety of our requiring prosecutors to defend their decisions to seek death penalties, "often years after they were made."[17] See *Imbler* v. *Pachtman,* 424 U.S. 409, 425–426 (1976).[18] Moreover, absent far stronger proof, it is unnecessary to seek such a rebuttal, because a legitimate and unchallenged explanation for the decision is apparent from the record: McCleskey committed an act for which the United States Constitution and Georgia laws permit imposition of the death penalty.[19]

Finally, McCleskey's statistical proffer must be viewed in the context of his challenge. McCleskey challenges decisions at the heart of the State's criminal justice system. "[O]ne of society's most basic tasks is that of protecting the lives of its citizens and one of the most basic ways in which it achieves the task is through criminal laws against murder." *Gregg* v. *Georgia,* 428 U.S. 153, 226 (1976) (WHITE, J., concurring). Implementation of these laws necessarily requires

16. See *Wayte* v. *United States,* 470 U.S. 598, 607 (1985); *United States* v. *Goodwin,* 457 U. S. 368, 380, n. 11 (1982); *Bordenkircher* v. *Hayes,* 434 U. S. 357, 365 (1978). See also ABA Standards for Criminal Justice 3-3.8, 3-3.9 (2d ed. 1982).

17. Requiring a prosecutor to rebut a study that analyzes the past conduct of scores of prosecutors is quite different from requiring a prosecutor to rebut a contemporaneous challenge to his own acts. See *Batson* v. *Kentucky,* 476 U.S. 79 (1986).

18. Although *Imbler* was decided in the context of damages actions under 42 U.S.C. § 1983 brought against prosecutors, the considerations that led the Court to hold that a prosecutor should not be required to explain his decisions apply in this case as well: "[I]f the prosecutor could be made to answer in court each time. . . a person charged him with wrongdoing, his energy and attention would be diverted from the pressing duty of enforcing the criminal law." 424 U. S., at 425. Our refusal to require that the prosecutor provide an explanation for his decisions in this case is completely consistent with this Court's longstanding precedents that hold that a prosecutor need not explain his decisions unless the criminal defendant presents a prima facie case of unconstitutional conduct with respect to his case. See, *e. g., Batson* v. *Kentucky, supra; Wayte* v. *United States, supra.*

19. In his dissent, JUSTICE BLACKMUN misreads this statement. See *post,* at 348–349. We do not suggest that McCleskey's conviction and sentencing by a jury bears on the prosecutor's motivation. Rather, the fact that the United States Constitution and the laws of Georgia authorized the prosecutor to seek the death penalty under the circumstances of this case *is* a relevant factor to be weighed in determining whether the Baldus study demonstrates a constitutionally significant risk that this decision was motivated by racial considerations.

discretionary judgments. Because discretion is essential to the criminal justice process, we would demand exceptionally clear proof before we would infer that the discretion has been abused. The unique nature of the decisions at issue in this case also counsels against adopting such an inference from the disparities indicated by the Baldus study. Accordingly, we hold that the Baldus study is clearly insufficient to support an inference that any of the decisionmakers in McCleskey's case acted with discriminatory purpose.

B

McCleskey also suggests that the Baldus study proves that the State as a whole has acted with a discriminatory purpose. He appears to argue that the State has violated the Equal Protection Clause by adopting the capital punishment statute and allowing it to remain in force despite its allegedly discriminatory application. But "'[d]iscriminatory purpose'. . . implies more than intent as volition or intent as awareness of consequences. It implies that the decisionmaker, in this case a state legislature, selected or reaffirmed a particular course of action at least in part 'because of,' not merely 'in spite of,' its adverse effects upon an identifiable group." *Personnel Administrator of Massachusetts* v. *Feeney,* 442 U.S. 256, 279 (1979) (footnote and citation omitted). See *Wayte* v. *United States,* 470 U.S., at 608–609. For this claim to prevail, McCleskey would have to prove that the Georgia Legislature enacted or maintained the death penalty statute *because of* an anticipated racially discriminatory effect. In *Gregg* v. *Georgia, supra,* this Court found that the Georgia capital sentencing system could operate in a fair and neutral manner. There was no evidence then, and there is none now, that the Georgia Legislature enacted the capital punishment statute to further a racially discriminatory purpose.[20]

Nor has McCleskey demonstrated that the legislature maintains the capital punishment statute because of the racially disproportionate impact suggested by the Baldus study. As legislatures

20. McCleskey relies on "historical evidence" to support his claim of purposeful dis-crimination by the State. This evidence focuses on Georgia laws in force during and just after the Civil War. Of course, the "historical background of the decision is one evidentiary source" for proof of intentional discrimination. *Arlington Heights* v. Metropolitan Housing Dev. Corp., 429 U.S., at 267. But unless historical evidence is reasonably contemporaneous with the challenged decision, it has little probative value. Cf. *Hunter* v. *Underwood,* 471 U.S. 222, 228–233 (1985) (relying on legislative history to demonstrate discriminatory motivation behind state statute). Although the history of racial discrimination in this country is undeniable, we cannot accept official actions taken long ago as evidence of current intent.

necessarily have wide discretion in the choice of criminal laws and penalties, and as there were legitimate reasons for the Georgia Legislature to adopt and maintain capital punishment, see *Gregg* v. *Georgia, supra,* at 183–187 (joint opinion of STEWART, POWELL, and STEVENS, JJ.), we will not infer a discriminatory purpose on the part of the State of Georgia.[21] Accordingly, we reject McCleskey's equal protection claims.

VI

Accordingly, we affirm the judgment of the Court of Appeals for the Eleventh Circuit.

It is so ordered.

JUSTICE BRENNAN, with whom JUSTICE MARSHALL joins, and with whom JUSTICE BLACKMUN and JUSTICE STEVENS join in all but Part I, dissenting.

II

At some point in this case, Warren McCleskey doubtless asked his lawyer whether a jury was likely to sentence him to die. A candid reply to this question would have been disturbing. First, counsel would have to tell McCleskey that few of the details of the crime or of McCleskey's past criminal conduct were more important than the fact that his victim was white. Petitioner's Supplemental Exhibits (Supp. Exh.) 50. Furthermore, counsel would feel bound to tell McCleskey that defendants charged with killing white victim is Georgia are 4.3 times as likely to be sentenced to death as defendants

21. JUSTICE BLACKMUN suggests that our "reliance on legitimate interests underlying the Georgia Legislature's enactment of its capital punishment statute is. . . inappropriate [because] it has no relevance in a case dealing with a challenge to the Georgia capital sentencing system *as applied* in McCleskey's case." *Post,* at 349 (emphasis in original). As the dissent suggests, this evidence is not particularly probative when assessing the application of Georgia's capital punishment system through the actions of prosecutors and juries, as we did in Part II-A, *supra.* But that is not the challenge that we are addressing here. As indicated above, the question we are addressing is whether the legislature maintains its capital punishment statute because of the racially disproportionate impact suggested by the Baldus study. McCleskey has introduced no evidence to support this claim. It is entirely appropriate to rely on the legislature's legitimate reasons for enacting and maintaining a capital punishment statute to address a challenge to the *legislature's* intent.

charged with killing blacks. Petitioner's Exhibit DB 82. In addition, frankness would compel the disclosure that it was more likely than not that the race of McCleskey's victim would determine whether he received a death sentence: 6 of every 11 defendants convicted of killing a white person would not have received the death penalty if their victims had been black, Supp. Exh. 51, while, among defendants with aggravating and mitigating factors comparable to McCleskey's, 20 of every 34 would not have been sentenced to die if their victims had been black. *Id.*, at 54. Finally, the assessment would not be complete without the information that cases involving black defendants and white victims are more likely to result in a death sentence than cases featuring any other racial combination of defendant and victim. *Ibid.* The story could be told in a variety of ways, but McCleskey could not fail to grasp its essential narrative line: there was a significant chance that race would play a prominent role in determining if he lived or died.

The Court today holds that Warren McCleskey's sentence was constitutionally imposed. It finds no fault in a system in which lawyers must tell their clients that race casts a large shadow on the capital sentencing process. The Court arrives at this conclusion by stating that the Baldus study cannot "*prove* that race enters into any capital sentencing decisions or that race was a factor in McCleskey's particular case." *Ante,* at 308 (emphasis in original). Since, according to Professor Baldus, we cannot say "to a moral certainty" that race influenced a decision, *ante,* at 308, n. 29, we can identify only "a likelihood that a particular factor entered into some decisions," *ante,* at 308, and "a discrepancy that appears to correlate with race." *Ante,* at 312. This "likelihood" and "discrepancy," holds the Court, is insufficient to establish a constitutional violation. The Court reaches this conclusion by placing four factors on the scales opposite McCleskey's evidence: the desire to encourage sentencing discretion, the existence of "statutory safeguards" in the Georgia scheme, the fear of encouraging widespread challenges to other sentencing decisions, and the limits of the judicial role. The Court's evaluation of the significance of petitioner's evidence is fundamentally at odds with our consistent concern for rationality in capital sentencing, and the considerations that the majority invokes to discount that evidence cannot justify ignoring its force. . .

B

The Baldus study indicates that, after taking into account some 230 nonracial factors that might legitimately influence a sentence, the jury *more likely than not* would have spared McCleskey's life had his victim been black. The study distinguishes between those cases in which (1) the jury exercises virtually no discretion because the strength or weakness of aggravating factors usually suggests that only one outcome is appropriate;[2] and (2) cases reflecting an "intermediate" level of aggravation, in which the jury has considerable discretion in choosing a sentence.[3] McCleskey's case falls into the intermediate range. In such cases, death is imposed in 34% of white-victim crimes and 14% of black-victim crimes, a difference of 139% in the rate of imposition of the death penalty. Supp. Exh. 54. In other words, just under 59%—almost 6 in 10—defendants comparable to McCleskey would not have received the death penalty if their victims had been black.[4]

Furthermore, even examination of the sentencing system as a whole, factoring in those cases in which the jury exercises little discretion, indicates the influence of race on capital sentencing. For the Georgia system as a whole, race accounts for a six percentage point difference in the rate at which capital punishment is imposed. Since death is imposed in 11% of all white-victim cases, the rate in comparably aggravated black-victim cases is 5%. The rate of capital sentencing in a white-victim case is thus 120% greater than the rate in a black-victim case. Put another way, over half—55%—of defendants in white-victim crimes in Georgia would not have been sentenced to die if their victims had been black. Of the more than 200 variables potentially relevant to a sentencing decision, race of the victim is a powerful explanation for variation in death sentence

---

2. The first two and the last of the study's eight case categories represent those cases in which the jury typically sees little leeway in deciding on a sentence. Cases in the first two categories are those that feature aggravating factors so minimal that juries imposed no death sentences in the 88 cases with these factors during the period of the study. Supp. Exh. 54. Cases in the eighth category feature aggravating factors so extreme that the jury imposed the death penalty in 88% of the 58 cases with these factors in the same period. *Ibid.*

3. In the five categories characterized as intermediate, the rate at which the death penalty was imposed ranged from 8% to 41%. The overall rate for the 326 cases in these categories was 20%. *Ibid.*

4. The considerable racial disparity in sentencing rates among these cases is consistent with the "liberation hypothesis" of H. Kalven and H. Zeisel in their landmark work, The American Jury (1966). These authors found that, in close cases in which jurors were most often in disagreement, "[t]he closeness of the evidence makes it possible for the jury to respond to sentiment by *liberating it* from the discipline of the evidence." *Id.,* at 165. While "the jury does not often consciously and explicitly yield to sentiment in the teeth of the law. . .it yields to sentiment in the apparent process of resolving doubts as to evidence. The jury, therefore, is able to conduct its revolt from the law within the etiquette of resolving issues of fact." *Ibid.* Thus, it is those cases in which sentencing evidence seems to dictate neither life imprisonment nor the death penalty that impermissible factors such as race play the most prominent role.

rates—as powerful as nonracial aggravating factors such as a prior murder conviction or acting as the principal planner of the homicide.[5]

These adjusted figures are only the most conservative indication of the risk that race will influence the death sentences of defendants in Georgia. Data unadjusted for the mitigating or aggravating effect of other factors show an even more pronounced disparity by race. The capital sentencing rate for all white-victim cases was almost *11 times* greater than the rate for black-victim cases. Supp. Exh. 47. Furthermore, blacks who kill whites are sentenced to death at nearly *22 times* the rate of blacks who kill blacks, and more than *7 times* the rate of whites who kill blacks. *Ibid.* In addition, prosecutors seek the death penalty for 70% of black defendants with white victims, but for only 15% of black defendants with black victims, and only 19% of white defendants with black victims. *Id.,* at 56. Since our decision upholding the Georgia capital sentencing system in *Gregg,* the State has executed seven persons. All of the seven were convicted of killing whites, and six of the seven executed were black.[6] Such execution figures are especially striking in light of the fact that, during the period encompassed by the Baldus study, only 9.2% of Georgia homicides involved black defendants and white victims, while 60.7% involved black victims.

McCleskey's statistics have particular force because most of them are the product of sophisticated multiple-regression analysis. Such analysis is designed precisely to identify patterns in the aggregate, even though we may not be able to reconstitute with certainty any individual decision that goes to make up that pattern. Multiple-regression analysis is particularly well suited to identify the influence of impermissible considerations in sentencing, since it is able to control for permissible factors that may explain an apparent arbitrary pattern.[7] While the decisionmaking process of a body such as a jury may be complex, the Baldus study provides a massive compilation of the details that are most relevant to that decision. As we held in the context of Title VII of the Civil Rights Act of 1964 last Term in *Bazemore* v. *Friday,* 478 U.S. 385 (1986), a multiple-regression analysis need not include every conceivable variable to establish a party's case, as long as it includes those variables that account for the major factors that are likely to influence decisions. In this case, Professor

---

5. The fact that a victim was white accounts for a nine percentage point difference in the rate at which the death penalty is imposed, which is the same difference attribute to a prior murder conviction or the fact that the defendant was the "prime mover" in planning a murder. Supp. Exh. 50.

6. NAACP Legal Defense and Educational Fund, Death Row, U.S.A. 4 (Aug. 1, 1986).

7. See generally Fisher, Multiple Regression in Legal Proceedings, 80 Colum. L. Rev. 701 (1980).

Baldus in fact conducted additional regression analyses in response to criticisms and suggestions by the District Court, all of which confirmed, and some of which even strengthened, the study's original conclusions.

The statistical evidence in this case thus relentlessly documents the risk that McCleskey's sentence was influenced by racial considerations. This evidence shows that there is a better than even chance in Georgia that race will influence the decision to impose the death penalty: a majority of defendants in white-victim crimes would not have been sentenced to die if their victims had been black. In determining whether this risk is acceptable, our judgment must be shaped by the awareness that "[t]he risk of racial prejudice infecting a capital sentencing proceeding is especially serious in light of the complete finality of the death sentence," *Turner* v. *Murray,* 476 U. S. 28, 35 (1986), and that "[i]t is of vital importance to the defendant and to the community that any decision to impose the death sentence be, and appear to be, based on reason rather than caprice or emotion," *Gardner* v. *Florida,* 430 U.S. 349, 358 (1977). In determining the guilt of a defendant, a State must prove its case beyond a reasonable doubt. That is, we refuse to convict if the chance of error is simply less likely than not. Surely, we should not be willing to take a person's life if the chance that his death sentence was irrationally imposed is *more* likely than not. In light of the gravity of the interest at stake, petitioner's statistics on their face are a powerful demonstration of the type of risk that our Eighth Amendment jurisprudence has consistently condemned.

C

Evaluation of McCleskey's evidence cannot rest solely on the numbers themselves. We must also ask whether the conclusion suggested by those numbers is consonant with our understanding of history and human experience. Georgia's legacy of a race-conscious criminal justice system, as well as this Court's own recognition of the persistent danger that racial attitudes may affect criminal proceedings, indicates that McCleskey's claim is not a fanciful product of mere statistical artifice.

For many years, Georgia operated openly and formally precisely the type of dual system the evidence shows is still effectively in place. The criminal law expressly differentiated between crimes committed by and against blacks and whites, distinctions whose lineage traced back to the time of slavery. During the colonial period, black slaves who killed whites in Georgia, regardless of whether in self-defense or in defense of another, were automatically executed. A. Higginbotham, In the Matter of Color: Race in the American Legal Process 256 (1978).[8]

By the time of the Civil War, a dual system of crime and punishment was well established in Georgia. See Ga. Penal Code (1861). The state criminal code contained separate sections for "Slaves and Free Persons of Color," Pt. 4, Tit. 3, Ch. 1, and for all other persons, Pt. 4, Tit. 1, Divs. 1–16. The code provided, for instance, for an automatic death sentence for murder committed by blacks, Pt. 4, Tit. 1, Art. II, § 4704, but declared that anyone else convicted of murder might receive life imprisonment if the conviction were founded solely on circumstantial testimony *or* simply if the jury so recommended. Pt. 4, Tit. 1, Div. 4, § 4220. The code established that the rape of a free white female by a black "shall be" punishable by death. § 4704. However, rape by anyone else of a free white female was punishable by a prison term not less than 2 nor more than 20 years. The rape of *blacks* was punishable "by fine and imprisonment, at the discretion of the court." § 4249. A black convicted of assaulting a free white person with intent to murder could be put to death at the discretion of the court, § 4708, but the same offense committed against a black, slave or free, was classified as a "minor" offense whose punishment lay in the discretion of the court, as long as such punishment did not "extend to life, limb, or health." Art. III, §§ 4714, 4718. Assault with intent to murder by a white person was punishable by a prison term of from 2 to 10 years. Div. 4, § 4258. While sufficient provocation could reduce a charge of murder to manslaughter, the code provided that "[o]bedience and submission being the duty of a slave, much greater provocation is necessary to reduce a homicide of a white person by him to voluntary manslaughter, than is prescribed for white persons." Art. II, § 4711.

In more recent times, some 40 years ago, Gunnar Myrdal's epochal study of American race relations produced findings mirroring McCleskey's evidence:

> "As long as only Negroes are concerned and no whites are disturbed, great leniency will be shown in most cases. . . .

---

8. Death could also be inflicted upon a slave who "grievously wound[ed], maim[ed], or bruis[ed] any white person," who was convicted for the third time of striking a white person, or who attempted to run away out of the province. A. Higginbotham, In the Matter of Color: Race in the American Legal Process 256 (1978). On the other hand, a person who willfully murdered a slave was not punished until the second offense, and then was responsible simply for restitution to the slave owner. Furthermore, conviction for willful murder of a slave was subject to the difficult requirement of the oath of two white witnesses. *Id.,* at 253–254, and n. 190.

> The sentences for even major crimes are ordinarily reduced when the victim is another Negro.
>
> •
>
> "For offenses which involve any actual or potential danger to whites, however, Negroes are punished more severely than whites.
>
> •
>
> "On the other hand, it is quite common for a white criminal to be set free if his crime was against a Negro." G. Myrdal, An American Dilemma 551–553 (1944).

This Court has invalidated portions of the Georgia capital sentencing system three times over the past 15 years. The specter of race discrimination was acknowledged by the Court in striking down the Georgia death penalty statute in *Furman*. JUSTICE DOUGLAS cited studies suggesting imposition of the death penalty in racially discriminatory fashion, and found the standardless statutes before the Court "pregnant with discrimination." 408 U.S., at 257 (concurring opinion). JUSTICE MARSHALL pointed to statistics indicating that "Negroes [have been] executed far more often than whites in proportion to their percentage of the population. Studies indicate that while the higher rate of execution among Negroes is partially due to a higher rate of crime, there is evidence of racial discrimination." *Id.,* at 364 (concurring opinion). Although Justice Stewart declined to conclude that racial discrimination had been plainly proved, he stated that "[m]y concurring Brothers have demonstrated that, if any basis can be discerned for the selection of these few to be sentenced to die, it is the constitutionally impermissible basis of race." *Id.,* at 310 (concurring opinion). In dissent, Chief Justice Burger acknowledged that statistics "suggest, at least as a historical matter, that Negroes have been sentenced to death with greater frequency than whites in several States, particularly for the crime of interracial rape." *Id.,* at 289, n. 12. Finally, also in dissent, JUSTICE POWELL intimated that an Equal Protection Clause argument would be available for a black "who could demonstrate that members of his race were being singled out for more severe punishment than others charged with the same offense." *Id.,* at 449. He noted that although the Eighth Circuit had rejected a claim of discrimination in *Maxwell* v. *Bishop,* 398 F. 2d 138 (1968), vacated and remanded on other grounds, 398 U. S. 262 (1970), the statistical evidence in that case "tend[ed] to show a pronounced disproportion in the number of Negroes receiving death sentences for rape in parts of Arkansas and elsewhere in the South." 408 U. S., at 449. It is clear that the Court regarded the opportunity for the operation of racial prejudice a particularly troublesome aspect of the unbounded discretion afforded by the Georgia sentencing scheme.

Five years later, the Court struck down the imposition of the death penalty in Georgia for the crime of rape. *Coker* v. *Georgia,* 433 U.S. 584 (1977). Although the Court did not explicitly mention race, the decision had to have been informed by the specific observations on rape by both the Chief Justice and JUSTICE POWELL in *Furman.* Furthermore, evidence submitted to the Court indicated that black men who committed rape, particularly of white women, were considerably more likely to be sentenced to death than white rapists. For instance, by 1977 Georgia had executed 62 men for rape since the Federal Government began compiling statistics in 1930. Of these men, 58 were black and 4 were white. See Brief for Petitioner in *Coker* v. *Georgia,* O.T. 1976, No. 75-5444, p. 56; see also Wolfgang & Riedel, Rape, Race, and the Death Penalty in Georgia, 45 Am. J. Orthopsychiatry 658 (1975).

Three years later, the Court in *Godfrey* found one of the State's statutory aggravating factors unconstitutionally vague, since it resulted in "standardless and unchanneled imposition of death sentences in the uncontrolled discretion of a basically uninstructed jury. . . ." 446 U.S., at 429. JUSTICE MARSHALL, concurring in the judgment, noted that "the disgraceful distorting effects of racial discrimination and poverty continue to be painfully visible in the imposition of death sentences." *Id.,* at 439 (footnote omitted).

This historical review of Georgia criminal law is not intended as a bill of indictment calling the State to account for past transgressions. Citation of past practices does not justify the automatic condemnation of current ones. But it would be unrealistic to ignore the influence of history in assessing the plausible implications of McCleskey's evidence. "[A]mericans share a historical experience that has resulted in individuals within the culture ubiquitously attaching a significance to race that is irrational and often outside their awareness." Lawrence, The Id, The Ego, and Equal Protection: Reckoning With Unconscious Racism, 39 Stan. L. Rev. 327 (1987). See generally *id.,* at 328–344 (describing the psychological dynamics of unconscious racial motivation). As we said in *Rose* v. *Mitchell,* 443 U. S. 545, 558–559 (1979):

> "[W]e. . . cannot deny that, 114 years after the close of the War Between the States and nearly 100 years after *Strauder,* racial and other forms of discrimination still remain a fact of life, in the administration of justice as in our society as a whole. Perhaps today that discrimination takes a form more subtle than before. But it is not less real or pernicious."

The ongoing influence of history is acknowledged, as the majority observes, by our "'unceasing efforts' to eradicate racial prejudice from our criminal justice system." *Ante,* at 309 (quoting *Batson* v. *Kentucky,* 476 U. S. 79, 85 (1986)). These efforts, however, signify not the elimination of the problem but its persistence. Our cases reflect a realization of the myriad of opportunities for racial considerations to influence criminal proceedings: in the exercise of peremptory challenges, *Batson* v. *Kentucky, supra;* in the selection of the grand jury, *Vasquez* v. *Hillery,* 474 U. S. 254 (1986); in the selection of the petit jury, *Whitus* v. *Georgia,* 385 U. S. 545 (1967); in the exercise of prosecutorial discretion, *Wayte* v. *United States,* 470 U. S. 598 (1985); in the conduct of argument, *Donnelly* v. *DeChristoforo,* 416 U. S. 637 (1974); and in the conscious or unconscious bias of jurors, *Turner* v. *Murray,* 476 U. S. 28 (1986), *Ristaino* v. *Ross,* 424 U. S. 589 (1976).

The discretion afforded prosecutors and jurors in the Georgia capital sentencing system creates such opportunities. No guidelines govern prosecutorial decisions to seek the death penalty, and Georgia provides juries with no list of aggravating and mitigating factors, nor any standard for balancing them against one another. Once a jury identifies one aggravating factor, it has complete discretion in choosing life or death, and need not articulate its basis for selecting life imprisonment. The Georgia sentencing system therefore provides considerable opportunity for racial considerations, however subtle and unconscious, to influence charging and sentencing decisions.[9]

History and its continuing legacy thus buttress the probative force of McCleskey's statistics. Formal dual criminal laws may no longer be in effect, and intentional discrimination may no longer be

---

9. The Court contends that it is inappropriate to take into account the wide latitude afforded actors in the Georgia capital sentencing system, since "[w]e have held that discretion in a capital punishment system is necessary to satisfy the Constitution," *ante,* at 314, n. 37, and "no suggestion is made as to how greater 'rationality' could be achieved under any type of statute that authorizes capital punishment." *Ibid.* The first point is true, but of course the Court struck down the death penalty in *Furman* v. *Georgia,* 408 U. S. 238 (1972), because the sentencing systems before it provided *too much* discretion. Since *Gregg* v. *Georgia,* 428 U. S. 153 (1976), the Court's death penalty jurisprudence has rested on the premise that it is possible to establish a system of *guided discretion* that will both permit individualized moral evaluation and prevent impermissible considerations from being taken into account. As JUSTICE BLACKMUN has persuasively demonstrated, *post,* at 357–358, Georgia provides *no* systematic guidelines for prosecutors to utilize in determining for which defendants the death penalty should be sought. Furthermore, whether a State has chosen an effective combination of guidance and discretion in its capital sentencing system as a whole cannot be established in the abstract, as the Court insists on doing, but must be determined empirically, as the Baldus study has done.

prominent. Nonetheless, as we acknowledged in *Turner,* "subtle, less consciously held racial attitudes" continue to be of concern, 476 U. S., at 35, and the Georgia system gives such attitudes considerable room to operate. The conclusions drawn from McCleskey's statistical evidence are therefore consistent with the lessons of social experience.

With respect to the Court's criticism that McCleskey has not shown how Georgia could do a better job, *ante,* at 315, n. 37, once it is established that the particular system of guided discretion chosen by a State is not achieving its intended purpose, the burden is on the *State,* not the defendant, to devise a more rational system if it wishes to continue to impose the death penalty.

The majority thus misreads our Eighth Amendment jurisprudence in concluding that McCleskey has not demonstrated a degree of risk sufficient to raise constitutional concern. The determination of the significance of his evidence is at its core an exercise in human moral judgment, not a mechanical statistical analysis. It must first and foremost be informed by awareness of the fact that death is irrevocable, and that as a result "the qualitative difference of death from all other punishments requires a greater degree of scrutiny of the capital sentencing determination." *California* v. *Ramos,* 463 U.S., at 998–999. For this reason, we have demanded a uniquely high degree of rationality in imposing the death penalty. A capital sentencing system in which race more likely than not plays a role does not meet this standard. It is true that every nuance of decision cannot be statistically captured, nor can any individual judgment be plumbed with absolute certainty. Yet the fact that we must always act without the illumination of complete knowledge cannot induce paralysis when we confront what is literally an issue of life and death. Sentencing data, history, and experience all counsel that Georgia has provided insufficient assurance of the heightened rationality we have required in order to take a human life.

Appendix H

PAYNE V. TENNESSEE

111 S.CT. 2597 (1991)

Chief Justice REHNQUIST delivered the opinion of the court.

In this case we reconsider our holdings in *Booth v. Maryland,* 482 U.S. 496, 107 S.Ct. 2529, 96 L.Ed.2d 440 (1987), and *South Carolina v. Gathers,* 490 U.S. 805, 109 S.Ct. 2207, 104 L.Ed.2d 876 (1989), that the Eighth Amendment bars the admission of victim impact evidence during the penalty phase of a capital trial.

Booth and Gathers were based on two premises: that evidence relating to a particular victim or to the harm that a capital defendant causes a victim's family do not in general reflect on the defendant's "blameworthiness," and that only evidence relating to "blameworthiness" is relevant to the capital sentencing decision. However, the assessment of harm caused by the defendant as a result of the crime charged has understandably been an important concern of the criminal law, both in determining the elements of the offense and in determining the appropriate punishment. Thus, two equally blameworthy criminal defendants may be guilty of different offenses solely because their acts cause differing amounts of harm. "If a bank robber aims his gun at a guard, pulls the trigger, and kills his target, he may be put to death. If the gun unexpectedly misfires, he may not. His moral guilt in both cases is identical, but his responsibility in the former is greater." *Booth,* 482 U.S., at 519, 107 S.Ct., at 2541 (SCALIA, J., dissenting). The same is true with respect to two defendants, each of whom participates in a robbery, and each of whom acts with reckless disregard for human life; if the robbery in which the first defendant participated results in the death of a victim, he may be subjected to the death penalty, but if the robbery in which the second defendant participates does not result in the death of a victim, the death penalty may not be imposed. *Tison v. Arizona,* 481 U.S. 137, 148, 107 S.Ct. 1676, 1683, 95 L.Ed.2d 127 (1987).

The principles which have guided criminal sentencing—as opposed to criminal liability—have varied with the times. The book of Exodus prescribes the *Lex talionis,* "An eye for an eye, a tooth for a tooth." Exodus 21:22–23. In England and on the continent of

Europe, as recently as the 18th century crimes which would be regarded as quite minor today were capital offenses. Writing in the 18th century, the Italian criminologist Cesare Beccaria advocated the idea that "the punishment should fit the crime." He said that "[w]e have seen that the true measure of crimes is the injury done to society." J. Farrer, Crimes and Punishments, 199 (London, 1880).

Gradually the list of crimes punishable by death diminished, and legislatures began grading the severity of crimes in accordance with the harm done by the criminal. The sentence for a given offense, rather than being precisely fixed by the legislature, was prescribed in terms of a minimum and a maximum, with the actual sentence to be decided by the judge. With the increasing importance of probation, as opposed to imprisonment, as a part of the penological process, some States such as California developed the "indeterminate sentence," where the time of incarceration was left almost entirely to the penological authorities rather than to the courts. But more recently the pendulum has swung back. The Federal Sentencing Guidelines, which went into effect in 1987, provided for very precise calibration of sentences, depending upon a number of factors. These factors relate both to the subjective guilt of the defendant and to the harm caused by his acts.

[3] Wherever judges in recent years have had discretion to impose sentence, the consideration of the harm caused by the crime has been an important factor in the exercise of that discretion:

> "The first significance of harm in Anglo–American jurisprudence is, then, as a prerequisite to the criminal sanction. The second significance of harm—one no less important to judges—is as a measure of the seriousness of the offense and therefore as a standard for determining the severity of the sentence that will be meted out." S. Wheeler, K. Mann, and A. Sarat, Sitting in Judgment: The Sentencing of White-Collar Criminals 56 (1988).

Whatever the prevailing sentencing philosophy, the sentencing authority has always been free to consider a wide range of relevant material. *Williams v. New York,* 337 U.S. 241, 69 S.Ct. 1079, 93 L.Ed. 1337 (1949). In the federal system, we observed that "a judge may appropriately conduct an inquiry broad in scope, largely unlimited as to the kind of information he may consider, or the source from which it may come." *United States v. Tucker,* 404 U.S. 443, 446, 92 S.Ct. 589, 591, 30 L.Ed.2d 592 (1972). Even in the context of capital sentencing, prior to *Booth* the joint opinion of Justices Stewart, Powell, and STEVENS in *Gregg v. Georgia,* 428 U.S. 153, 203–204, 96 S.Ct. 2909, 2939, 49 L.Ed.2d 859 (1976), had rejected petitioner's attack on the Georgia statute because of the "wide scope of evidence and argument allowed at presentence hearings." The joint opinion stated:

> "We think that the Georgia court wisely has chosen not to impose unnecessary restrictions on the evidence that can be offered at such a hearing and to approve open and far-ranging argument. . . .So long as the evidence introduced and the arguments made at the presentence hearing do not prejudice a defendant, it is preferable not to impose restrictions.
>
> We think it desirable for the jury to have as much information before it as possible when it makes the sentencing decision."

The Maryland statute involved in *Booth* required that the presentence report in all felony cases include a "victim impact statement" which would describe the effect of the crime on the victim and his family. *Booth, supra,* 482 U.S., at 498, 107 S.Ct., at 2530–2531. Congress and most of the States have, in recent years, enacted similar legislation to enable the sentencing authority to consider information about the harm caused by the crime committed by the defendant. The evidence involved in the present case was not admitted pursuant to any such enactment, but its purpose and effect was much the same as if it had been. While the admission of this particular kind of evidence—designed to portray for the sentencing authority the actual harm caused by a particular crime—is of recent origin, this fact hardly renders it unconstitutional. *Williams v. Florida,* 399 U.S. 78, 90 S.Ct. 1893, 26 L.Ed.2d 446 (1970) (upholding the constitutionality of a notice-of-alibi statute, of a kind enacted by at least 15 states dating from 1927); *United States v. DiFrancesco,* 449 U.S. 117, 142, 101 S.Ct. 426, 440, 66 L.Ed.2d 328 (1980) (upholding against a double jeopardy challenge an Act of Congress representing "a considered legislative attempt to attack a specific problem in our criminal justice system, that is, the tendency on the part of some trial judges 'to mete out light sentences in cases involving organized crime management personnel' ").

"We have held that a State cannot preclude the sentencer from considering 'any relevant mitigating evidence' that the defendant proffers in support of a sentence less than death." *Eddings v. Oklahoma,* 455 U.S. 104, 114, 102 S.Ct. 869, 877, 71 L.Ed.2d 1 (1982). See also *Skipper v. South Carolina,* 476 U.S. 1, 106 S.Ct. 1669, 90 L.Ed.2d 1 (1986). Thus we have, as the Court observed in *Booth,* required that the capital defendant be treated as a "'uniquely individual human bein[g],'" 482 U.S., at 504, 107 S.Ct., at 2534 (quoting *Woodson v. North Carolina,* 428 U.S., at 304, 96 S.Ct. at 2991). But it was never held or even suggested in any of our cases preceding

Booth that the defendant, entitled as he was to individualized consideration, was to receive that consideration wholly apart from the crime which he had committed. The language quoted from *Woodson* in the *Booth* opinion was not intended to describe a class of evidence that *could not* be received, but a class of evidence which *must* be received. Any doubt on the matter is dispelled by comparing the language in *Woodson* with the language from *Gregg v. Georgia,* quoted above, which was handed down the same day as *Woodson.* This misreading of precedent in *Booth* has, we think, unfairly weighted the scales in a capital trial; while virtually no limits are placed on the relevant mitigating evidence a capital defendant may introduce concerning his own circumstances, the State is barred from either offering "a glimpse of the life" which a defendant "chose to extinguish," *Mills v. Maryland,* 486 U.S. 367, 397, 108 S.Ct. 1860, 1876, 100 L.Ed.2d 384 (1988) (REHNQUIST, C.J., dissenting), or demonstrating the loss to the victim's family and to society which have resulted from the defendant's homicide.

Booth reasoned that victim impact evidence must be excluded because it would be difficult, if not impossible, for the defendant to rebut such evidence without shifting the focus of the sentencing hearing away from the defendant, thus creating a "'mini-trial' on the victim's character." *Booth, supra,* 482 U.S., at 506–507, 107 S.Ct. at 2534–2535. In many cases the evidence relating to the victim is already before the jury at least in part because of its relevance at the guilt phase of the trial. But even as to additional evidence admitted at the sentencing phase, the mere fact that for tactical reasons it might not be prudent for the defense to rebut victim impact evidence makes the case no different than others in which a party is faced with this sort of a dilemma. As we explained in rejecting the contention that expert testimony on future dangerousness should be excluded from capital trials, "the rules of evidence generally extant at the federal and state levels anticipate that relevant, unprivileged evidence should be admitted and its weight left to the factfinder, who would have the benefit of cross examination and contrary evidence by the opposing party." *Barefoot v. Estelle,* 463 U.S. 880, 898, 103 S.Ct. 3383, 3397, 77 L.Ed.2d 1090 (1983).

Payne echoes the concern voiced in *Booth's* case that the admission of victim impact evidence permits a jury to find that defendants whose victims were assets to their community are more deserving of punishment than those whose victims are perceived to be less worthy. *Booth, supra,* 482 U.S., at 506, n. 8, 107 S.Ct., at 2534 n. 8. As a general matter, however, victim impact evidence is not offered to encourage comparative judgments of this kind—for instance, that the killer of a hardworking, devoted parent deserves the death penalty, but that the murderer of a reprobate does not. It is designed to show instead *each* victim's "uniqueness as an individual human being," whatever the jury might think the loss to the community resulting from his death might be. The facts of *Gathers* are an excellent illustration of this: the evidence showed that the victim was an out of work, mentally handicapped individual, perhaps not, in the eyes of most, a significant contributor to society, but nonetheless a murdered human being.

Under our constitutional system, the primary responsibility for defining crimes against state law, fixing punishments for the commission of these crimes, and establishing procedures for criminal trials rests with the States. The state laws respecting crimes, punishments, and criminal procedure are of course subject to the overriding provisions of the United States Constitution. Where the State imposes the death penalty for a particular crime, we have held that the Eighth Amendment imposes special limitations upon that process.

> "First, there is a required threshold below which the death penalty cannot be imposed. In this context, the State must establish rational criteria that narrow the decisionmaker's judgment as to whether the circumstances of a particular defendant's case meet the threshold. Moreover, a societal consensus that the death penalty is disproportionate to a particular offense prevents a State from imposing the death penalty for that offense. Second, States cannot limit the sentencer's consideration of any relevant circumstance that could cause it to decline to impose the penalty. In this respect, the State cannot challenge the sentencer's discretion, but must allow it to consider any relevant information offered by the defendant." *McCleskey v. Kemp,* 481 U.S. 279, 305–306, 107 S.Ct. 1756, 1774–1775, 95 L.Ed.2d 262 (1987).

But as we noted in *California v. Ramos,* 463 U.S. 992, 1001, 103 S.Ct. 3446, 3453, 77 L.Ed.2d 1171 (1983), "[b]eyond these limitations. . . the Court has deferred to the State's choice of substantive factors relevant to the penalty determination."

"Within the constitutional limitations defined by our cases, the States enjoy their traditional latitude to prescribe the method by which those who commit murder should be punished." *Blystone v. Pennsylvania,* 494 U.S. 299, 309, 110 S.Ct. 1078, ———, 108 L.Ed.2d 255 (1990). The States remain free, in capital cases, as well as others, to devise new procedures and new remedies to meet felt needs. Victim impact evidence is simply another form or method of informing the sentencing authority about the specific harm caused by the crime in question, evidence of a general type long considered by sentencing authorities. We think the *Booth* Court was wrong in stating that this kind of evidence leads to the arbitrary imposition of the death penalty. In the majority of cases, and in this case, victim impact evidence serves entirely legitimate purposes. In the event that evidence is introduced that is so unduly prejudicial that it renders the trial fundamentally unfair, the Due Process Clause of the Fourteenth Amendment provides a mechanism for relief. See *Darden v. Wainwright,* 477 U.S. 168, 179–183, 106 S.Ct. 2464, 2470–2472, 91 L.Ed.2d 144 (1986). Courts have always taken into consideration the harm done by the defendant in imposing sentence, and the evidence adduced in this case was illustrative of the harm caused by Payne's double murder.

We are now of the view that a State may properly conclude that for the jury to assess meaningfully the defendant's moral culpability and blameworthiness, it should have before it at the sentencing phase evidence of the specific harm caused by the defendant. "[T]he State has a legitimate interest in counteracting the mitigating evidence which the defendant is entitled to put in, by reminding the sentencer that just as the murder should be considered as an individual, so too the victim is an individual whose death represents a unique loss to society and in particular to his family." *Booth,* 482 U.S., at 517, 107 S.Ct. at 2540 (WHITE, J., dissenting) (citation omitted). By turning the victim into a "faceless stranger at the penalty phase of a capital trial," *Gathers,* 490 U.S., at 821, 109 S.Ct. at 2216 (O'CONNOR, J., dissenting), *Booth* deprives the State of the full moral force of its evidence and may prevent the jury from having before it all the information necessary to determine the proper punishment for a first-degree murder.

The present case is an example of the potential for such unfairness. The capital sentencing jury heard testimony from Payne's girlfriend that they met at church, that he was affectionate, caring, kind to her children, that he was not an abuser of drugs or alcohol, and that it was inconsistent with his character to have committed the murders. Payne's parents testified that he was a good son, and a clinical psychologist testified that Payne was an extremely polite prisoner and suffered from a low IQ. None of this testimony was related to the circumstances of Payne's brutal crimes. In contrast, the only evidence of the impact of Payne's offenses during the sentencing phase was Nicholas' grandmother's description—in response to a single question—that the child misses his mother and baby sister. Payne argues that the Eighth Amendment commands that the jury's death sentence must be set aside because the jury heard this testimony. But the testimony illustrated quite poignantly some of the harm that Payne's killing had caused; there is nothing unfair about allowing the jury to bear in mind that harm at the same time as it considers the mitigating evidence introduced by the defendant. The Supreme Court of Tennessee in this case obviously felt the unfairness of the rule pronounced by *Booth* when it said "[i]t is an affront to the civilized members of the human race to say that at sentencing in a capital case, a parade of witnesses may praise the background, character and good deeds of Defendant (as was done in this case), without limitation as to relevancy, but nothing may be said that bears upon the character of, or the harm imposed, upon the victims." 791 S.W.2d, at 19.

In *Gathers,* as indicated above, we extended the holding of *Booth* barring victim impact evidence to the prosecutor's argument to the jury. Human nature being what it is, capable lawyers trying cases to juries try to convey to the jurors that the people involved in the underlying events are, or were, living human beings, with something to be gained or lost from the jury's verdict. Under the aegis of the Eighth Amendment, we have given the broadest latitude to the defendant to introduce relevant mitigating evidence reflecting on his individual personality, and the defendant's attorney may argue that evidence to the jury. Petitioner's attorney in this case did just that. For the reasons discussed above, we now reject the view—expressed in *Gathers*—that a State may not permit the prosecutor to similarly argue to the jury the human cost of the crime of which the defendant stands convicted. We reaffirm the view expressed by Justice Cardozo in *Snyder v. Massachusetts,* 291 U.S. 97, 122, 54 S.Ct. 330, 338, 78 L.Ed. 674 (1934): "justice, though due to the accused, is due to the accuser also. The concept of fairness must not be strained till it is narrowed to a filament. We are to keep the balance true."

We thus hold that if the State chooses to permit the admission of victim impact evidence and prosecutorial argument on that subject, the Eighth Amendment erects no *per se* bar. A State may legitimately conclude that evidence about the victim and about the impact of the murder on the victim's family is relevant to the jury's decision as to whether or not the death penalty should be imposed. There is no reason to treat such evidence differently than other relevant evidence is treated.

Justice MARSHALL, with whom Justice BLACKMUN joins, dissenting.

Power, not reason, is the new currency of this Court's decisionmaking. Four Terms ago, a five-Justice majority of this Court held that "victim impact" evidence of the type at issue in this case could not constitutionally be introduced during the penalty phase of a capital trial. *Booth v. Maryland,* 482 U.S. 496, 107 S.Ct. 2529, 96 L.Ed.2d 440 (1987). By another 5–4 vote, a majority of this Court rebuffed an attack upon this ruling just two Terms ago. *South Carolina v. Gathers,* 490 U.S. 805, 109 S.Ct. 2207, 104 L.Ed.2d 876 (1989). Nevertheless, having expressly invited respondent to renew the attack, 498 U.S. ———, 111 S.Ct. 1031, 112 L.Ed.2d 1032 (1991), today's majority overrules *Booth* and *Gathers* and credits the dissenting views expressed in those cases. Neither the law nor the facts supporting *Booth* and *Gathers* underwent any change in the last four years. Only the personnel of this Court did.

I

Speaking for the Court as then constituted, Justice Powell and Justice Brennan set out the rationale for excluding victim-impact evidence from the sentencing proceedings in a capital case. See *Booth v. Maryland, supra,* 482 U.S., at 504–509, 107 S.Ct., at 2533–2536; *South Carolina v. Gathers, supra,* 490 U.S., at 810–811, 109 S.Ct., at 2210–2211. As the majorities in *Booth* and *Gathers* recognized, the core principle of this Court's capital jurisprudence is that the sentence of death must reflect an "'*individualized* determination'" of the defendant's "'personal responsibility and moral guilt'" and must be based upon factors that channel the jury's discretion "'so as to minimize the risk of wholly arbitrary and capricious action.'" *Booth v. Maryland, supra,* 482 U.S., at 502, 107 S.Ct., at 2532, quoting *Zant v. Stephens,* 462 U.S. 862, 879, 103 S.Ct. 2733, 2744, 77 L.Ed.2d 235 (1983); *Enmund v. Florida,* 458 U.S. 782, 801, 102 S.Ct. 3368, 73 L.Ed.2d 1140 (1982), and *Gregg v. Georgia,* 428 U.S. 153, 189, 96 S.Ct. 2909, 2932–2933, 49 L.Ed.2d 859 (1976) (joint opinion of Stewart, Powell, and STEVENS, JJ.); accord, *South Carolina v. Gathers, supra,* 490 U.S., at 810, 109 S.Ct., at 2210. The State's introduction of victim-impact evidence, Justice Powell and Justice Brennan explained, violates this fundamental principle. Where, as is ordinarily the case, the defendant was unaware of the personal circumstances of his victim, admitting evidence of the victim's character and the impact of the murder upon the victim's family predicates the sentencing determination on "factors. . . wholly unrelated to the blameworthiness of [the] particular defendant." *Booth v. Maryland, supra,* 482 U.S., at 504, 107 S.Ct., at 2534; *South Carolina v. Gathers, supra,* 490 U.S., 810, 109 S.Ct., at 2210. And even where the defendant *was* in a position to foresee the likely impact of his conduct, admission of victim-impact evidence creates an unacceptable risk of sentencing arbitrariness. As Justice Powell explained in *Booth,* the probative value of such evidence is always outweighed by its prejudicial effect because of its inherent capacity to draw the jury's attention away from the character of the defendant and the circumstances of the crime to such illicit considerations as the eloquence with which family members express their grief and the status of the victim in the community. See *Booth v. Maryland, supra,* 482 U.S., at 505–507, and n. 8, 107 S.Ct., at 2534–2535, and n. 8; *South Carolina v. Gathers, supra,* 490 U.S., at 810–811, 109 S.Ct., at 2210–2211. I continue to find these considerations wholly persuasive, and I see no purpose in trying to improve upon Justice Powell's and Justice Brennan's exposition of them.

There is nothing new in the majority's discussion of the supposed deficiencies in *Booth* and *Gathers.* Every one of the arguments made by the majority can be found in the dissenting opinions filed in those two cases, and, as I show in the margin, each argument was convincingly answered by Justice Powell and Justice Brennan.[1]

---

1. The majority's primary argument is that punishment in criminal law is frequently based on an "assessment of [the] harm caused by the defendant as a result of the crime charged." *Ante,* at 2605. See also *Booth v. Maryland,* 482 U.S. 496, 516, 107 S.Ct. 2529, 2539–2540, 96 L.Ed.2d 440 (1987) (WHITE, J., dissenting); *id.,* at 519–520, 107 S.Ct., at 2541–2542 (SCALIA, J., dissenting); *South Carolina v. Gathers,* 490 U.S. 805, 818–819, 109 S.Ct. 2207, 2214–2215, 104 L.Ed.2d 876 (1989) (O'CONNOR, J., dissenting). Nothing in *Booth* or *Gathers,* however, conflicts with this unremarkable observation. These cases stand merely for the proposition that the State may not put on evidence of *one* particular species of harm—namely, that associated with the victim's personal characteristics independent of the circumstances of the offense—in the course of *a capital murder proceeding.* See *Booth v. Maryland, supra,* 482 U.S., at 507, n. 10, 107 S.Ct., at 2535, n. 10 (emphasizing that decision does not bar reliance on victim-impact evidence in capital sentencing so long as such evidence "relate[s] directly to the circumstances of the crime"); *id.,* at 509, n. 12, 107 S.Ct., at 2536, n. 12 (emphasizing that decision does not bar reliance on victim-impact evidence in sentencing for noncapital crimes). It may be the case that such a rule departs from the latitude of sentencers in criminal law generally "[to] tak[e] into consideration the harm done by the defendant." *Ante,* at 2608. But as the *Booth* Court pointed out, because this Court's capital sentencing jurisprudence is founded on the premise that "death is a 'punishment different from all other sanctions,'" it is completely unavailing to attempt to infer from sentencing considerations in noncapital settings the proper treatment of any particular sentencing issue in a capital case. 482 U.S., at 509, n. 12, 107 S.Ct., at 2536, n. 12, quoting *Woodson v. North Carolina,* 428 U.S. 280, 303–304, 305, 96 S.Ct. 2978, 2990–2991, 2991–2992, 49 L.Ed.2d 944 (1976) (opinion of Stewart, Powell, and STEVENS, JJ.).

The majority also discounts Justice Powell's concern with the inherently prejudicial quality of victim-impact evidence. "[T]he mere fact that for tactical reasons it might not be prudent for the defense to rebut victim impact evidence," the majority protests, "makes the case no different than others in which a party is faced with this sort of a dilemma." *Ante,* at 2607. See also *Booth v. Maryland, supra,* 482 U.S., at 518, 107 S.Ct.,

But contrary to the impression that one might receive from reading the majority's lengthy rehearsing of the issues addressed in *Booth* and *Gathers,* the outcome of this case does not turn simply on who—the *Booth* and *Gathers* majorities or the *Booth* and *Gathers* dissenters—had the better of the argument. Justice Powell and Justice Brennan's position carried the day in those cases and became the law of the land. The real question, then, is whether today's majority has come forward with the type of extraordinary showing that this Court has historically demanded before overruling one of its precedents. In my view, the majority clearly has not made any such showing. Indeed, the striking feature of the majority's opinion is its radical assertion that it need not even try.

---

at 2540–2541 (WHITE, J., dissenting). Unsurprisingly, this tautology is completely unresponsive to Justice Powell's argument. The *Booth* Court established a rule excluding introduction of victim-impact evidence not merely because it is difficult to rebut—a feature of victim-impact evidence that may be "no different" from that of many varieties of relevant, legitimate evidence—but because the effect of this evidence in the sentencing proceeding is *unfairly prejudicial:* "The prospect of a 'mini- trial' on the victim's character is more than simply unappealing; it could well distract the sentencing jury from its constitutionally required task—determining whether the death penalty is appropriate in light of the background and record of the accused and the particular circumstances of the crime." 482 U.S., at 507, 107 S.Ct., at 2535. The law is replete with *per se* prohibitions of types of evidence the probative effect of which is generally outweighed by its unfair prejudice. See, *e.g.,* Fed. Rules Evid. 404, 407–412. There is nothing anomalous in the notion that the Eighth Amendment would similarly exclude evidence that has an undue capacity to undermine the regime of individualized sentencing that our capital jurisprudence demands.

Finally, the majority contends that the exclusion of victim-impact evidence "deprives the State of the full moral force of its evidence and may prevent the jury from having before it all the information necessary to determine the proper punishment for a first- degree murder." *Ante,* at 2608. The majority's recycled contention, see *Booth, supra,* at 517, 107 S.Ct. at 2540 (WHITE, J., dissenting); *id.,* at 520, 107 S.Ct., at 2542 (SCALIA, J., dissenting); *Gathers, supra,* 490 U.S., at 817–818, 109 S.Ct., at 2214–2215 (O'CONNOR, J., dissenting), begs the question. Before it is possible to conclude that the exclusion of victim-impact evidence prevents the State from making its case or the jury from considering relevant evidence, it is necessary to determine whether victim-impact evidence is consistent with the substantive standards that define the scope of permissible sentencing determinations under the Eighth Amendment. The majority offers no persuasive answer to Justice Powell and Justice Brennan's conclusion that victim-impact evidence is frequently *irrelevant* to any permissible sentencing consideration and that such evidence risks exerting *illegitimate* "moral force" by directing the jury's attention on illicit considerations such as the victim's standing in the community.

Bibliography

The literature on the death penalty, most of it by opponents of capital punishment, is enormous. Franklin Zimring and Gordon Hawkins, *Capital Punishment and the American Agenda* (Cambridge: Cambridge University Press, 1986), provides an overview of the debates from what the authors acknowledge to be a partisan abolitionist perspective. For advocates' presentations of the cases for and against the death penalty, see Ernest van den Haag and John Conrad, *The Death Penalty: A Debate* (New York: Plenum Press, 1983); Walter Berns, *For Capital Punishment: Crime and the Morality of the Death Penalty* (New York: Basic Books, 1979). Other surveys are William J. Bowers, with Glenn L. Pierce and John F. McDevitt, *Legal Homicide: Death as Punishment in America, 1864–1982* (Boston: Northeastern University Press, 1984); Hugo Adam Bedau, ed., *The Death Penalty in America* (3d. ed., New York: Oxford University Press, 1982); and Hugo Adam Bedau, *Death Is Different: Studies in the Morality, Law, and Politics of Capital Punishment* (Boston: Northeastern University Press, 1987). Michael Radelet, ed., *Facing the Death Penalty: Essays on a Cruel and Unusual Punishment,* (Philadelphia: Temple University Press, 1989), presents essays by death penalty opponents about the experience of working with prisoners sentenced to death.

The basic study of the Eighth Amendment's background is Anthony Granucci, "'Nor Cruel and Unusual Punishments Inflicted': The Original Meaning," *California Law Review 57* (1969): 839. An alternative interpretation of the history is forcefully but in most scholars' judgment ineffectively offered by Raoul Berger, *Death Penalties: The Supreme Court's Obstacle Course* (Cambridge: Harvard University Press, 1982). (For a critique of Berger's argument, see Stephen Gillers, Book Review, *Yale Law Journal 92* [1983]: 731.) Philip English Mackey, ed., *Voices Against Death: American Opposition to Capital Punishment, 1787–1975* (New York: Burt Franklin, 1976), collects statements by abolitionists and has a useful historical introduction.

Michael Meltsner, *Cruel and Unusual: The Supreme Court and Capital Punishment* (New York: Random House, 1973), provides an inside look at the Inc. Fund's strategy and its perspective on the cases up to *Furman*. Barrett Prettyman, Jr., *Death and the Supreme Court* (New York: Harcourt, Brace & World, 1961), describes six death penalty cases from the pre-*Furman* era, showing how the Court responded to nondeath related claims when life was at stake.

Pollsters and social scientists regularly compile information about public attitudes toward the death penalty. A recent overview, on which I have relied, is James Alan Fox, Michael L. Radelet, and Julie L. Bonsteel, "Death Penalty Opinion in the Post-*Furman* Years," *New York University Review of Law & Social Change* 18 (1990–91): 499. The basic study of Justice Marshall's hypothesis is Austin Sarat and Neil Vidmar, "Public Opinion, the Death Penalty, and the Eighth Amendment: Testing the Marshall Hypothesis," *Wisconsin Law Review* 1976 (1976): 171.

Thorsten Sellin, *The Penalty of Death* (Beverly Hills, Calif.: Sage, 1980), collects essays by a sociologist who did some of the pioneering studies of deterrence and the death penalty. Studies of racial discrimination in capital sentencing, supporting the Baldus study discussed in the *McCleskey* case, are Samuel Gross and Robert Mauro, *Death and Discrimination: Racial Disparities in Capital Sentencing* (Boston: Northeastern University Press, 1989); Barry Nakell and Kenneth Hardy, *The Arbitrariness of the Death Penalty* (Philadelphia: Temple University Press, 1987). A forceful critique of the *McCleskey* decision, stressing the discrimination against African-American victims, is Randall Kennedy, "*McCleskey v. Kemp:* Race, Capital Punishment, and the Supreme Court," *Harvard Law Review* 101 (1988): 1388.

The law of habeas corpus is changing rapidly, and legal commentary soon goes out of date. A critical survey of recent developments and proposals is Vivian Berger, "Justice Delayed or Justice Denied?—A Comment on Recent Proposals to Reform Death Penalty Habeas Corpus," *Columbia Law Review* 90 (1990): 1665.

Index

A

Abusive petitions in habeas corpus cases, 91, 92–93
Adams, Randall, 130
Adamson v. California (1947), 11
Aggravating circumstances, 56, 58, 60, 61, 62, 64, 67, 118
Aikens v. California (1972), 46–47
American Civil Liberties Union, 97, 98
American Law Institute, 42
Amsterdam, Anthony, 29
  argument in *Maxwell* case, 37
  brief in *Boykin* case, 45
  in *Witherspoon* case, 33–34
Anderson v. California (1972), 47
Anti-Federalists, 15
  demand for Bill of Rights, 13
Antisympathy instruction in death penalty cases, 86–87
Appeals courts, role in death penalty cases, 66–68
Armstrong, Scott, 56, 57
Aryan Brotherhood, 113–14

B

Baldus, David, 81–85
Barclay v. Florida (1983), 69–70
Barrett, Nicole, 96
Barron v. Baltimore (1833), 10–11
Beccaria, Cesare di, 17, 19–20, 132
Bedau, Hugo Adam, 133
Berger, Vivian, 124–26
Berns, Walter, 5
Betts v. Brady (1942), 23
Bifurcated trials, 40–44
  defined, 32
  discussions in *Maxwell* case, 37–38
Bill of Rights, English, 12–13
Bird, Rose, 107
Black, Hugo, on incorporation doctrine, 11
  in Willie Francis case, 25–26
  opinion in *Maxwell* case, 171–72
  opinion in *McGautha* case, 44
  opinion in *Witherspoon* case, 34
Blackmun, Harry, as appeals judge in *Maxwell* case, 37
  in *Gregg* case, 61
  in *Mills* case, 65–66
  in *Shuman* case, 59
  in *Spaziano* case, 68–69
  opinion in *Furman* case, 52

views on death penalty, 41
Blystone v. Pennsylvania (1990), 59–60, 71–72
Bolles, Donald, 122
Booth v. Maryland (1987), 86
Boykin v. Alabama (1969), 45–46
Branch v. Texas (1972), 46
Brantley, Clarence, 130
Brennan, William J., in *Blystone* case, 60
comments on *Rudolph* case, 27
in *Brown* case, 87
in *Furman* case, 48–49
in *Gregg* case, 63
in *McCleskey* case, 85, 208–17
in *McGautha* case, 43–44
in *Spaziano* case, 68
in *Tison* case, 76
on original intent of Eighth Amendment, 14
views in *Maxwell* case, 39
views on 1976 death penalty cases, 57
vote in *Rudolph* case, 28
Brown v. Mississippi (1936), 23–24
Burger, Warren, in *Furman* case, 52–53
in *Gilmore* case, 98
in *Lockett* case, 72
views on death penalty, 39
views on impact of *Furman* decision, 55
Burt, Robert, 57, 121
Burton, Harold, in Willie Francis case, 25–26

C

Cadena temporal, 15
Caldwell v. Mississippi (1985), 66
California Supreme Court, 31, 47
California v. Brown (1987), 86–87
California v. Ramos (1983), 3
Canada, abolition of death penalty in, 132
Cardozo, Benjamin, 21
Carswell, G. Harrold, 41
"Cause and prejudice," 92–93
Chessman, Caryl, 27
China, death penalty in, 132
Class actions, 31, 109, 110
Clemency, executive, 26, 134
Coker v. Georgia (1977), 73–74, 75, 77, 78
Coleman v. Thompson (1991), 105
Coleman, Roger Keith, 104–06, 112, 131
Coppola, Frank, 112
Counsel, assistance of, 23, 92, 124–27
Crampton v. Ohio (1971), 40–44
Cruel and unusual punishments clause. *See* Eighth Amendment

D

Dawson v. Delaware (1992), 113–14
Deans, Marie, 103
Death row conditions, 122
Death penalty, cost compared to imprisonment, 2
 crimes subject to, 20–21
 deliberations in 1976 cases, 57–58
 difficulties for defense counsel of, 125–26
 early abolitions of, 22
 effects on other doctrines, 22–23
 in international perspective, 131–32
 mandatory, 21, 56, 58–60
 and miscarriages of justice, 22
 moratorium on executions, 30–31
 movement to abolish, 93–94, 120–32
 race discrimination in administration of, 28, 30, 31
 rape, for 27–28
 responses to criticisms of modern system of, 128–29
 reversal rates of, 121
Death-qualified juries, 116
 constitutionality of, 33–35
 defined, 32
Dershowitz, Alan, 27
Deterrence, and death penalty, 5–10
 as justification for death penalty, 59, 62
 studies of, 6–9
Douglas, William O., draft opinion in *Maxwell* case, 38–39, 163–71
 in *Furman* case, 51
 in *McGautha* case, 43–44
 retirement of, 55
 vote in *Rudolph* case, 28
Drug "kingpin" statutes, 74

E

Ehrlich, Isaac, critics of, 7–9
 and studies of death penalty's deterrence, 7–9
Eighth Amendment, interpretation of, 16
 original intent of, 12–14, 15
 text of, 10
Electric chair, constitutionality of, 14
Enlightenment, effects on theory of capital punishment, 17, 19–22
Enmund v. Florida (1982), 74–75, 77, 78
Escape, possibility of, 3
Evans, Wilbert Lee, 103
Executions, of innocent defendants, 130–31
 number of, 1, 22
 public, 21
 rates, 121–22
Executioner's Song, The (Mailer), 95, 98

F

Felony murder cases, 74–77
Fifth Amendment, text of, 10
Ford v. Wainwright (1986), 78
Fortas, Abe, resignation of, 39
 views in *Maxwell* case, 38–39, 172–73
Francis, Willie, 24–26
Frankfurter, Felix, in Willie Francis case, 25–26
Furman v. Georgia (1972), 46–54, 55, 56, 71, 74, 184–90

G

Gas chamber, as cruel and unusual punishment, 109, 110–11, 124
Giarratano, Joseph, 101–04, 112
Gideon v. Wainwright (1963), 23
Gilmore, Bessie, 97–98
Gilmore, Gary, 1, 88, 95–98, 112
Gilmore v. Utah (1976), 97–98
Glorious Revolution of 1688, 13, 15
Godfrey v. Georgia (1980), 70–71
Goldberg, Arthur, on constitutionality of death penalty, 27–28
 memorandum to Court on constitutionality of death penalty, 149–62
Gomez v. District Court (1992), 110
Gray v. Lucas (1983), 124
Great Britain, abolition of death penalty in, 132
Greenberg, Jack, 28–29, 99
Gregg v. Georgia (1976), 60–64, 71, 191–201
Gross, Samuel, 85
Guided discretion death penalty statutes, 58, 60–64

H

Habeas corpus, 36, 88–93
 and "abuse of the writ," 91, 92–93
 and actual innocence, 93, 118
 and delay, 90–91
 and exhaustion of state remedies, 90
 and new rules, 90–92, 114–15
 and successive petitions, 91, 92–93
Harlan, John Marshall, in *McGautha* case, 41–43
 views in *Maxwell* case, 38, 173–74
Harris, Robert Alton, 106–11, 124
Hawkins, Gordon, 132
Haynsworth, Clement, 41
Henley, J. Smith, 36

Howard, Jacob, 11
Hughes, Charles Evans, 24

I

In re Kemmler (1890), 14, 22
Inc. Fund. *See* NAACP Legal Defense Fund
Incapacitation, as purpose of punishment, 2–3
Incorporation doctrine, 10–12
International perspectives on death penalty, 79, 131–32

J

Jackson v. Georgia (1972), 46
Jackson, Robert, 22
James II of England, 13
Jeffreys, Lord Chief Justice, 13
Jenner, Albert, 33
Judges, role in imposing death penalty, 68–70
Judicial override of jury recommendations, 68–70
Judy, Steven, 112
Jurek v. Texas (1976), 64
Juries, instructions to, 66
  role in death penalty cases, 65–66, 80

K

Kennedy, Anthony, 123
  appointment to Supreme Court, 55, 86
  in *Giarratano* case, 103
  in *Medina* case, 117
Kilpatrick, James J., 103
Koestler, Arthur, 35

L

LDF. *See* NAACP Legal Defense Fund
Lempert, Richard, 9, 134
Lewis v. Adamson (1990), 123
Lockett v.Ohio (1978), 72
Louisiana ex rel. Francis v. Resweber (1947), 24–26

M

Mailer, Norman, 95, 98
Marshall, Thurgood, in *Barclay* case, 69–70
  and LDF, 28
  in *Ford* case, 78, 138
  in *Furman* case, 49–51
  in *Gilmore* case, 97
  in *Gregg* case, 63
  in *Payne* case, 87–88, 224–28
  in *Spaziano* case, 68
  in *Spenkelink* case, 100
  in *Washington* case, 127
  views on public opinion re death penalty, 120
  views on death penalty, 132–33
Mauro, Robert, 85
Maxwell, William, 35, 136

Maxwell v. Bishop (1970), 35–40, 163–74
Maynard v. Cartwright (1988), 67
McCleskey v. Kemp (1987), 81–85, 128, 202–17
McCleskey v. Zant (1991), 92–93
McGautha v. California (1971), 40–44, 62, 175–83
McKenna, Joseph, 15
Medina v. California (1992), 116–17
Mental retardation, as mitigating circumstance, 77, 79
Mills v. Maryland (1988), 65–66
Mitigating circumstances, 56, 58, 60, 64, 65–66, 67, 70, 72–73
Morgan v. Illinois (1992), 116
Murder, degrees of, 21
Murray v. Giarratano (1989), 102–03

N

NAACP Legal Defense Fund (LDF), actions in death penalty cases, 33–34, 35, 36, 45
  strategy against death penalty, 28–32
Noonan, John, 108–09

O

Oates, Titus, 12–13
O'Connor, Sandra Day, 123
  appointment to Supreme Court, 55
  in *Brown* case, 87
  in *Coleman* case, 105
  in *Penry* case, 79
  in *Riggins* case, 115
  in *Thompson* case, 77–78
  in *Tison* case, 76–77
O'Neil v. Vermont (1892), 135
Original intent, and Eighth Amendment, 12–13
  in general, 12

P

Palko v. Connecticut (1937), 11
Parole, relation to death penalty of, 3, 120
Patel, Marilyn Hall, 109
Payne v. Tennessee (1991), 86, 87–88, 218–28
Penry v. Lynaugh (1989), 79
Powell v. Alabama (1932), 22–23
Powell, Lewis F., in *Booth* case, 86
  in *Ford* case, 138
  in *Furman* case, 53–54
  in *Gregg* case, 61–63
  in *McCleskey* case, 84–85
  in *Spenkelink* case, 100
  views on 1976 death penalty cases, 56–57
Pregerson, Harry, 111

Proportionality, and death penalty, 5, 13, 15, 16, 31, 45
Prosecutors, arguments in death penalty cases, 66, 71–72, 87
Public opinion on death penalty, 1, 18, 33, 45, 50, 55, 61, 63, 79, 119–20, 132–33
Pulley v. Harris (1984), 107–08
Purposes of punishment, 2–10, 11–12, 16, 27, 49–50, 53

R

Race discrimination in administration of death penalty, 50, 53, 79–85, 124, 129–30
Rape, death penalty for, 27–28, 29, 35–40, 53–54, 73–74
Reagan, Ronald, Supreme Court appointments by, 55
Reed, Stanley, in Willie Francis case, 25
Rehabilitation, 2
Rehnquist, William H., in *Blystone* case, 60
in *Dawson* case, 114
in *Furman* case, 53
in *Giarratano* case, 103
in *Payne* case, 86, 218–24
in *Sawyer* case, 118
in *Spenkelink* case, 100–01
in *Witt* case, 35
Retribution, as justification for death penalty, 3–5, 59, 62, 63, 88, 134
Retroactivity of decisions, 91–92
Ricketts v. Adamson (1987), 122–23
Riggins v. Nevada (1992), 115
Roberts v. Louisiana (1976), 58–59
Robinson v. California (1962), 11–12
Rockefeller, Laurence, 136
Rosenberg, Julius and Ethel, 27
Rudolph v. Alabama (1963), 27–28
Rush, Benjamin, 20

S

Salem witch trials, 19
Sawyer v. Whitley (1992), 117–18, 122, 128
Scalia, Antonin, appointment to Supreme Court, 55
in *Stanford* case, 78
in *Walton* case, 88
views on death penalty statutes, 118–19
Schwarzschild, Henry, 98
Scottsboro cases, 22–23
Sellin, Thorsten, 3
Simon, Tobias, 31
Sochor v. Florida (1992), 115–16

Souter, David, appointment to Supreme Court, 55
South Africa, death penalty in, 132
South Carolina v. Gathers (1989), 86
Spaziano v. Florida (1984), 68–69
Special circumstances, 70
Spenkelink, John, 98–101, 130
Standards for administering death penalty, 32, 37–38, 40–44, 62
Standing to challenge death penalty, 97–98
Stanford v. Kentucky (1989), 78
Statistical evidence in death penalty cases, 37, 80–85
Stevens, John Paul, appointment to Supreme Court, 55
  in *Blystone* case, 60
  in *Gregg* case, 61–63
  in *Harris* case, 110–11, 124
  in *Sawyer* case, 118
  in *Spaziano* case, 68–69
  in *Thompson* case, 77
Stewart, Potter, on addressing constitutionality of death penalty, 45
  draft opinion in *Maxwell* case, 38
  in *Furman* case, 51, 184–87
  in *Godfrey* case, 71
  in *Gregg* case, 61–63
  in *Witherspoon* case, 34
  retirement of, 55
Strickland v. Washington (1984), 126–27
Stringer v. Black (1992), 114–15
Successive petitions in habeas corpus cases, 91, 92–93
Sumner v. Shuman (1987), 59, 70, 75
Supreme Court, changing composition of, 55–56, 119
Sutherland, George, 23

T

Thomas, Clarence, appointment to Supreme Court, 55
Thompson v. Oklahoma (1988), 77–78
Tison v. Arizona, 75–77
Treason, death penalty for, 74
"Troika," in 1976 death penalty cases, 57–64, 191–201
Trop v. Dulles (1958), 16, 48
Tuttle, Elbert, 100
Twining v. New Jersey (1908), 11

V

Vasquez v. Harris (1992), 111
Victim-impact evidence, 85–88

Vigurie, Richard, 103

W

Wainwright v. Witt (1985), 34–35
Walton v. Arizona (1990), 88
Warren, Earl, 16, 17
  retirement of, 38
  views in *Maxwell* case, 39
Weems v. United States (1910), 14–16, 48, 142–48
Weisberg, Robert, 72, 125, 133
White, Byron, in *Coker* case, 73–74
  in *Enmund* case, 75
  in *Furman* case, 51–52, 187–90
  in *Gilmore* case, 97
  in *Gregg* case, 61
  in *Harris* case, 107–08
  in *Maxwell* case, 36–37
  in *Morgan* case, 116
  views on mandatory death penalty, 57
Whitmore v. Arkansas (1990), 88
Wilder, Douglas, 103–04
Witherspoon v. Illinois (1968), 33–34, 35, 37, 116
Wolfgang, Marvin, 36–37
Woodson v. North Carolina (1976), 58
Woodward, Bob, 56, 57
Wright, J. Skelly, 25

Y

Youth, as mitigating circumstance, 77–78

Z

Zimring, Franklin, 132